THE INVENTION
OF THE UNITED STATES
SENATE

JOHNS HOPKINS UNIVERSITY PRESS

INTERPRETING AMERICAN POLITICS
Michael Nelson, Series Editor

THE INVENTION
OF THE UNITED STATES
SENATE

Daniel Wirls and Stephen Wirls

The Johns Hopkins University Press
Baltimore and London

© 2004 The Johns Hopkins University Press
All rights reserved. Published 2004
Printed in the United States of America on acid-free paper
9 8 7 6 5 4 3 2 1

The Johns Hopkins University Press
2715 North Charles Street
Baltimore, Maryland 21218-4363
www.press.jhu.edu

Library of Congress Cataloging-in-Publication Data

Wirls, Daniel, 1960–
    The invention of the United States Senate / Daniel Wirls and Stephen Wirls.
        p. cm. — (Interpreting American politics)
    Includes bibliographical references and index.
    ISBN 0-8018-7438-6 (hardcover : alk. paper)
    ISBN 0-8018-7439-4 (pbk. : alk. paper)
        1. United States. Congress. Senate—History. — I. Wirls, Stephen, 1954–
II. Title. III. Series.
    JK1161.W57 2003
    328.73′071—dc21
    2003006241

A catalog record for this book is available from the British Library.

Contents

Series Editor's Foreword

In a story made famous by David Halberstam in his book *The Best and the Brightest*, Lyndon B. Johnson rushes to the Capitol after attending his first cabinet meeting as John F. Kennedy's vice president. Johnson could not wait to tell Speaker of the House Sam Rayburn about all of the president's brilliant advisers, including Arthur Schlesinger and McGeorge Bundy from Harvard and Dean Rusk from the Rockefeller Foundation. "Well, Lyndon, you may be right and they may be every bit as intelligent as you say," Rayburn replied, "but I'd feel a whole lot better if just one of them had run for sheriff."

As familiar as Rayburn's testimony to the value of scholars seasoning their ideas in the political arena has become, the American experience includes an even deeper tradition of doing so. Clinton Rossiter observed in his book *1787: The Grand Convention* that the delegates to the Constitutional Convention embodied the nexus between philosophical thought and political action which nearly all modern scholars and politicians lack—the scholars because they are too busy thinking to act and the politicians because they are too busy acting to think. The nexus Rossiter described was not just between scholarship and politics as careers but also between the qualities that these careers foster when they converge. Political reason is one such quality, but it is "tested reason—reason applied within the limits of history." A higher form of political experience is another: "digested experience—experience appraised with the aid of critical intelligence."

To a one, the framers of the Constitution were deeply familiar with political history and philosophy. To a one, they also were experienced politicians, four-fifths of whom had served in the Congress formed when the United States declared its independence from Great Britain in 1776. The delegates' character as "scholar-politicians" animated their approach to the design of a new constitution. As scholars, they strove to design the best government that they could imagine. As politicians, they strove to design a government that they could persuade the wide range of states— small, large, commercial, agricultural, slave, and free—to ratify.

Sometimes the imperatives of practical politics prevailed over higher concerns. Southern states, for example, would not ratify a constitution that did not count their slaves for purposes of representation in the House of Representatives, and northern states would not ratify a constitution that did. The result: a split-the-difference political compromise that counted each slave as three-fifths of a person.

On some other issues, the political interests of states and regions were so unclear that the convention could function almost as a conclave of scholars. For nearly four months, the delegates debated the proper design of the executive with little regard to how their constituents in, say, Connecticut or South Carolina would react—there was no way of telling. The public, they presumed, would accept any well-designed executive that the convention proposed as long as it wasn't a king. The challenge then became to design the best executive that their collective wisdom could conceive.

As Daniel Wirls and Stephen Wirls show in this wonderfully readable book, when it came to designing the Senate the delegates were required to draw on everything they knew as scholars and all that they had experienced as politicians. To be sure, many delegates had strong ideas about the ideal design of a senate based on their study of classical (e.g., Polybius) and contemporary (e.g., Montesquieu) writings on the subject. But the delegates also represented state governments that demanded a place in any new constitutional scheme, and many of them represented small states that insisted on an equal place.

In the many and various ways that Wirls and Wirls describe, the scholar-politicians at the Constitutional Convention created the Senate in hopes that it would be both institutionally sound and politically appealing. Assessing not just how well the delegates did so but also how their design has fared since 1787 is the authors' well-realized ambition in this book.

Michael Nelson

Acknowledgments

This book arose from an argument in the dining room of the Wawona Lodge amid the awesome serenity of Yosemite National Park, where we should have been thinking about things other than government and politics, let alone the Senate. One of us criticized the Senate as an undemocratic constitutional atavism while the other defended bicameralism in general and the Senate in particular as essential to moderate and free government. One of us was commencing work on the nature and consequences of bicameralism; the other had spent considerable time on the theoretical roots of American constitutional thought and practice. Each returned home with the nagging suspicion that he did not have supporting evidence commensurate with the certainty of his declarations. Subsequent discussions gave rise to plans for a study of the origins, development, and contemporary behavior of the Senate, which were gradually pared down to the study before you as we realized that there was more to the story of the Senate's birth than we had anticipated. Consequently, we did not resolve the initial dispute, but we have developed considerable appreciation for one another's arguments as they have evolved over the years of this project.

Numerous people and institutions helped us along the way. Peter Ahrendsdorf, Ross Baker, Robert Bartlett, David Brady, John Dizekes, John Ferejohn, Sam Kernell, Michael Nelson, Walter Nicogorski, Bruce I. Oppenheimer, Thomas Pangle, David Robertson, Elaine Swift, Jennifer Nicoll Victor, and Elizabeth Wirls read and commented on various parts of this work at different stages of its development. Anonymous reviewers provided vital input, and we thank Michael Nelson, Henry Tom, and the staff of the Johns Hopkins University Press for helping us bring this to fruition. We were fortunate to have Julia Ridley Smith as our copyeditor. All of these contributions improved the final results and surely spared us some embarrassments, though we are of course responsible for any remaining flaws. We thank Annie Oliveto, Karen Berntsen, Laurie Hauf, Brian Edwards, Holly Piscopo, Brian Douglas—all University of California, Santa Cruz students—for their excellent research assistance. Daniel would like to thank the American Political Science Association for his ability to participate in the Congressional Fellowship program. Although his year in Congress (1993–94) did not contribute directly to this study, it was invaluable for understanding contemporary bicameralism and the Senate as a way to reflect on the difference between original intent and modern practice. The offices of Senator Christopher Dodd and former representative Lee Hamilton provided wonderful experiences, and Daniel learned a lot about Congress in general from Larry Evans and Walter Oleszek with whom he roamed the halls as they worked on the issue of congressional reform.

Portions of this research were presented at the annual meetings of the American Political Science Association (2000 and 2002), the Western Political Science Association (2000), the Southern Political Science Association (1994 and 1999), and the Northeastern Political Science Association (1997). Daniel would like to thank Sam Kernell in particular for providing two timely and stimulating opportunities to present his work at University of California, San Diego, first as part of the UCSD American Political Institutions Colloquium Series and later for a conference on James Madison's political science. The Library of Congress has done scholars an invaluable service by making available vital documents and records on-line especially through the project, "A Century of Lawmaking for a New Nation." Electronic access to the *House Journal, Senate Journal, Senate Executive Journal,* and other documents made basic research and systematic analysis easy and even fun. The Office of the Senate Historian provided rapid responses to several inquiries. The libraries of the University of California and Rhodes College were, of course, essential. Leaves from both institutions were indispensable and greatly appreciated.

We dedicate this book to our families—Elizabeth, Cyrus, and John; Alice, Steven, and Ruth. Their loving presence in our lives made the work easier and, more importantly, kept it in perspective.

THE INVENTION
OF THE UNITED STATES
SENATE

ONE

The Republican Institution

This House is a sanctuary; a citadel of law, of order, and of liberty; and it is here—it is here, in this exalted refuge; here, if anywhere, will resistance be made to the storms of political phrensy and the silent arts of corruption; and if the Constitution be destined ever to perish by the sacrilegious hands of the demagogue or the usurper, which God avert, its expiring agonies will be witnessed on this floor.

FROM AARON BURR'S FAREWELL ADDRESS TO THE SENATE,
MARCH 2, 1805.

Happily, the U.S. Constitution has not suffered "expiring agonies," and the Senate has been spared this decisive trial of character. Burr's exaltation of the Senate is, nonetheless, representative of the noble and grandiose sentiments this upper house tends to evoke. Its name alone lent the Senate the venerable aspect of an ancient republican lineage, which the pedestrian House of Representatives, the newfangled presidency, and the untested Supreme Court could never match. Seated in the Roman senate were republican heroes: Brutus, Publius, Cincinnatus, Scipio, Cato. These models of virtue graced an assembly reputed for its courage, wisdom, integrity, and stability, qualities that had led Rome to greatness and protected its glory from foreign threats and popular imprudence. American patriots proudly appropriated these names in the long debates over the Revolution and the Constitution. Burr was hardly the last to be inspired by this ancestry, to offer a paean to the wise and sober guardian of the republic. The Senate has regularly presented itself as something other than an ordinary legislative body, and senators have adorned themselves in pretensions to match.

Yet in the history of both republics, there is a considerable distance separating image and reality. Indeed, Burr's example invites some nosing around for hypocrisy, for the poseur beneath the toga. Eight months earlier, Vice President Burr had fled to avoid arrest for killing Alexander Hamilton, and when he addressed the Senate, he was already involved in treasonous activities that would result in a politically tainted trial and acquittal. Yet Burr's sentiment was not without an authoritative foundation. James Madison, despite his disappointment in the Constitutional

Convention's upper house, declared the Senate to be nothing less than "the great anchor of the Government."[1]

Throughout the eighteenth century a particular variety of republicanism was taking shape in America. Distinguished from civic republicanism by principles of individualism, this new "liberal republicanism" was poised between the traditional standard of mixed government and an age of democracy. This new order needed to balance popular sovereignty with individual rights and both of these with governmental power, authority, and deliberation. Democratic accountability was to be tempered by institutional designs that put some distance between popular demands and political decisions. Elaborate institutional arrangements gave the public ultimate control over the government while allowing the governing institutions leeway to resist and refine the public's will. Power was to be vested only in institutions designed to prevent its concentration and abuse. "In framing a government," Madison noted, "the great difficulty lies in this: you must first enable the government to control the governed; and in the next place oblige it to control itself."[2]

In more concrete terms, the proper mixture of separation, checks, and balances would limit the dangers of governmental power, and various types of representation would temper majority rule. Early American political development added another layer to this balancing act: the tension between the parts and the whole, between states and nation, in a compound republic. Republican constitutionalism had to accommodate the practical and inescapable reality of the American confederation. One way or another, the new republic had to resolve or balance the tensions between the separated powers and balanced powers, between participation and decision, between majority rule and wise deliberation, and between sovereign states and national government.

At the fulcrum of these balances is one institution, the Senate. The framers turned repeatedly to the Senate to resolve a variety of critical constitutional dilemmas. Consequently, unlike the House, this legislative body shares powers with the executive, including appointment to the judiciary; it is intended to check and refine the democratic House with stability and wisdom; it is the institutional embodiment of federalism. No other institution is saddled with such elaborate purposes and responsibilities.

This rich mixture of purposes and powers continues to make the Senate unique among political institutions. As the equal partner in one of the most independent and robust legislatures, it is the most powerful upper house in the world. The majority of the world's legislatures are unicameral, and most bicameral legislatures have upper houses that are less powerful or less consequential in comparison to the lower house. Whereas many other countries have reduced their upper houses or senates to symbolic importance, confined their authority within a strictly federal function, or in a few cases even eliminated them, the U.S. Senate combines a formidable array of institutional characteristics and powers that make it distinctive and autonomous. The higher age and citizenship requirements for members, and the longer and staggered terms, all contribute, more or less, to differences in character. Similarly, state equality in the Senate contrasts sharply with the proportional representation of the House. The distinctions produced by elections are reinforced by the institutional elements. The House and Senate are granted nearly equal powers; in fact, the Senate has a few exclusive powers, including the approval of treaties and appointments, which give it a singular status among upper houses. Furthermore, unlike many upper houses, the modern Senate has enjoyed at least equal (un)popularity and (dis)respect among the people.[3]

How the United States came to have such an institution is the subject of this study. Though much has been written on various aspects of Senate history, no previous work has attempted to examine and link the three central components of the Senate's creation: the precedents in theory and practice leading up to the Constitutional Convention, the work of the Constitutional Convention on the composition and powers of the Senate, and the initial institutionalization of the Senate from ratification through the early years of Congress. Our account provides a comprehensive analysis and argument by exploring the options available to the American framers, the rationales behind those options, how the framers sorted through them, and the consequences of their choices. How was an institution with ancient foundations adapted to the modern architecture of liberal-republican constitutions, and how did this new conception fare in the deliberations of American framers and the initial workings of the government they designed?

The existing literature on the creation of the Senate falls short on one dimension or another and has left in its wake a series of partial truths about the creation of the Senate. While few scholars might subscribe to an unadulterated version of any of these, there has been a tendency to deal in epigrammatic summaries of the Senate's birth:

[T]his masterpiece of the Constitution-makers was in fact a happy accident.[4]

The United States Senate came into existence as a result of a political deal.[5]

[T]he framers created a Senate that was nothing short of an American House of Lords.[6]

Political theory and practical politics produced the U.S. Senate.[7]

Such epigrams usually emerge from more subtle and complex arguments about the Senate's creation but nevertheless reflect the partial nature of most accounts as much as any genuine scholarly disagreements. To begin with, general works on the Senate, Senate history, or bicameralism give relatively short shrift to origins.[8] Most of these provide little more than pro forma reviews of the standard facts and elements. Moreover, in the political science literature on bicameralism, the Senate is not infrequently explained by functionalist arguments.[9] First among these is that the Senate and House are *mutual* checks upon the legislative process and mitigate the likelihood of its producing decisions that are hasty or ill-considered. Second, as a representation of states, the Senate is the institutional embodiment of federalism in the national government and, as such, a defender of a type of minority interest.

Functional consequences, however, do not necessarily equal original intent and may not explain how an institution came to be. An emphasis on these functional explanations for, or justifications of, the Senate overlooks or distorts what we will argue were the republican purposes that motivated many of the framers to create a Senate in the first place. While these functional consequences are evident in the Senate's framing, design, and contemporary practice, they hardly cover the range of options and intentions. These explanations do not begin with the more intricate problems posed by liberal republican principles and politics. Indeed, they pass over one of the purposes for a senate that is most commonly cited in the writings and debates surrounding the founding—the senate as a provision for more thorough practical wisdom in legislative matters. They miss, therefore, the more interesting and delicate problems of reconciling the various purposes and of designing a form that achieved the ends they sought. This is not to say that the largely mechanical check on the House and federalism were not important components of the Senate's creation. They were, of course. Yet checked power, as such, was not considered the equivalent of, or even a substitute for, wise and just government, and some framers, James Madison in particular, envisioned a senate whose fundamental purpose was antithetical to a representation of states. In general, many framers sought a more stable house of superior practical knowledge that would, in the main, contribute *positive* improvements to the substance of law and provide a general stewardship over public policy. Indeed, the Senate, in theory and design, was given an important, if not exclusive, role in handling some special tasks and executive powers that could not be trusted to the legislature as a whole or to the president alone. The functional explanations cannot account for these executive responsibilities either logically or historically.

If the general accounts are inadequate or tend toward functionalist explanations for the Senate, the historical scholarship directly related to the Senate's origins is fragmented. The many accounts of the Constitutional Convention are one important but partial source as are the works on the intellectual origins of American politics and constitutions; yet even where they recognize the importance of the Senate, they do not address the origins or implications carefully.[10] Work on state legislatures and upper houses in revolutionary America is strong on the evolution of upper houses in state constitutions prior to the convention but weaker on theoretical influences and the national Senate.[11] Elaine K. Swift's *The Making of an American Senate,* one of the most complete modern treatments, makes an argument about the origins of the Senate, but the bulk of the book is an account of the initial evolution of the Senate from the first Congress onward or, as she calls it, the process of reconstitutive change.[12]

Even within the more detailed historical literature on the Constitutional Convention, there is considerable disagreement, at least implicitly, about what mattered most in the framers' deliberations and decisions regarding the construction of the Senate, as a variety of principles and philosophical commitments mixed with material and political interests.[13] In recent years, scholarship on the convention has centered on more subtle, if not more correct, arguments about the interplay of interest and ideology—that principle and interest mixed freely at the convention and that the distinction is often a difficult if not false one.[14] If the convention was not simply a meeting of great and disinterested minds, it certainly was not a predetermined clash of interests in which ideas were tossed about as thinly disguised rationalizations. James Madison, however mindful of or biased by being a Virginian, was not simply advancing principles in service of his state or regional interests. We think the same can be said of most of the other delegates, albeit to a lesser extent with some.

They came to Philadelphia carrying an assortment of philosophical ideals, experiences, and political commitments, and the delegates, including Madison, learned as the weeks and months progressed. The analytic difficulties associated with attempts to understand the convention's decisions are multiplied because the principles and interests at stake were being defined as the convention proceeded. As far as principles were concerned, the debate about republicanism on a continental scale was wholly novel, and even Madison seemed to be adapting to new formulations. Likewise, though many of the interests at stake were familiar to the delegates coming into the convention, there were several categories of interests from which to choose, and the convention did much to shape and reshape delegates' perceptions of which interests might matter the most. The problems of social choice presented by the convention were formidable indeed, and nothing shows that better than the debates and decisions about the composition of the Senate. Our argument joins this more integrative way of looking at the politics of the convention by showing the ways in which principles about a properly constructed Senate interacted with political interests and power politics in the multidimensional struggle to construct the Senate *before, during, and after* the convention.

Only by giving roughly equal treatment to and integrating each phase of the Senate's invention does the institution, we think, come into proper focus. By giving short shrift to the mix of theory and practice that preceded the convention, most accounts oversimplify the variety in theory and practice and yet miss the larger idea, which we see as a nascent liberal-republican synthesis about the form and purpose of a senate. Too much emphasis on institutional precedents can make the Senate seem like the inevitable outcome of a well-traveled pathway of American bicameralism and the ever-present model of the British Parliament. Accounts that focus on the Constitutional Convention often have dwelt on the practical politics and deal making surrounding the Senate, at the expense of adequate attention to the substance of the deliberations. A focus on the politics of the Constitutional Convention can make the Senate appear to be largely the product of self-interested actors cutting political deals: the Senate as little more than the outcome of a struggle between large and small states. Finally, there has been a general lack of attention to how the Senate was institutionalized early on in terms of its constitutional standing—how the Senate saw its place in the new system and how its constitutional ambiguities were resolved. As will be evident, we put some emphasis on political ideas or the framers' views of good government, but without neglecting interests and institutions.

A comprehensive history of the Senate's origins also contributes to a current and lively interest within the discipline of political science in the role of institutions in political life.[15] Institutionalism of various stripes has tended to concentrate on the effect of existing institutions on political choice and policy. Institutions are treated as an independent and exogenous variable used to explain stability, comparative variations, or change in policy regimes. But what about the creation of institutions, such as at the moment of constitutional choice? What does it mean to look at a formal political institution as a dependent variable? All of institutional theory, historical and otherwise, has been better at explaining the evolution of existing institutions, or the effect of institutions on behavior or outcomes, than it has been at explaining the origins of specific governmental institutions.[16]

If the new institutionalism has done more to describe the effects of institutions than to explain their origins, then an account that seeks to redress imbalances, misreadings, and gaps in the story of an important institution—a case study—provides a service. We show the multiplicity and interrelatedness of factors that created the Senate: historical precedents, various elements of republican and liberal constitutional theory, genuine deliberation, and the pulling and hauling of interest-based politics. Thus do such notions as historical constraints, intellectual-normative commitments, political learning, and rational-actor gaming all come together, in no particular ranking, to produce an institution that is more than one thing, that embodies elements of all these forces.

We also think that a careful look at the invention and evolution of the Senate's purposes and design bridges history to the real world of politics. Bicameralism and the Senate are means to particular political goals. Making the story of the Senate more accurate and complete leads us through the debates over the principles, practical problems, and alternatives faced by the framers and their theoretical precursors. What were (and are) the political and constitutional purposes of a senate or, at least, this senate, in a liberal and republican constitution? Does its form, in fact, effect those aims? The convention and the ensuing ratification debates were an extraordinarily deliberate and methodical consideration of the relationship between various institutional arrangements, motives, behaviors, and results. This deliberate matching of design and constitutional purpose can provide some standards for an evaluation and suggest even some options for reform. We are not claiming that the founders' standards and choices must be ours. Some certainly still are, however, and they have consequences that affect the character of the Senate, the quality of our politics and policies, and the possibilities for reform. In studying the founders' debates and actions, we also hope to contribute to the development of standards for understanding and evaluating the place and purpose of the modern Senate.

The argument begins with two chapters that take the reader from the ancient ideas of a senate to the theory and practice of those ideas in revolutionary America on the eve of the Constitutional Convention. We show how the idea of a senate evolved from ancient republicanism to modern liberal constitutionalism and emphasize the attempts to reconcile and adapt a remodeled republican senate, as an essential provision for prudence in government, to the liberal constitutional principle of equal and separated powers. Though hardly alone in his attempts to think through the place and purpose of a senate, James Madison emerges as the most thoughtful and thorough proponent of a senate as the essential provision for prudence in government.

In the spring of 1787 Madison brought the idea of a national senate to Philadelphia, where his vision was tested against the myriad forces and competing claims that shaped the Constitutional Convention and the senate it produced. Chapter 4 uses the records of the Constitutional Convention to reexamine the relationship between the construction of the Senate and the resolution of the representational question—proportional representation in the House and equal representation in the Senate— commonly referred to as the Great Compromise. We demonstrate the significant ways in which the widespread agreement on the need for a properly constructed senate in a stronger national system helped to shape and produce the compromise, rather than the other way around. A senate was crucial to the new system, regardless of any political compromises. The shared ideals that helped shape the representational compromise demonstrate that the majority of delegates sought to create a truly republican Senate rather than either a citadel for states' rights or an American House of Lords. The subsequent decisions on the Senate's composition and powers, discussed in chapter 5, made it far less than a House of Lords but something more than an ordinary legislative institution. In particular, the Senate was placed at the crossroads of the system of separated institutions sharing power. The Senate was to check the House, share in the executive power of appointments and treaties, and have a potentially decisive role in the composition of the Supreme Court. The politics of the convention added another special purpose—the Senate would be the institutional embodiment of federalism and state power in the national government. In this way, the Senate became the crucible for resolving several of the thorniest problems of American constitutionalism.

The process of ratification, the focus of chapter 6, revealed harshly contrasting opinions about the Senate, and the national debate produced the initial attempts by both proponents and opponents of the Constitution to define the Senate. While the Senate lay at the center of the anti-Federalists' fears of the institutional powers of the proposed government, Federalists, some of whom did not like the prospect of equal representation, were able to use the Senate to their advantage in these debates. A careful look at the early years of the Senate, in chapter 7, shows how neither the hopes of the founders nor the fears of the Constitution's critics were realized in the practice of the early upper chamber. By the end of Washington's two terms as president, important precedents were set in the Senate's relationship to the House and the presidency, mostly at the expense of the Senate's potential power and influence. During the same period, the advent of national politics on a partisan basis further circumscribed the Senate's role as a republican institution.

We conclude, in chapter 8, by summarizing key aspects of the Senate's evolution to show the irony of a Senate that became neither the embodiment of wisdom and stability nor the vigorous defender of federalism. We are not inclined to contrast today's supposedly lesser lights with virtuous orators of some Golden Age. We tend to think that the motives and capabilities of politicians have remained relatively constant; it is the institutional and broader political contexts within which they operate that have changed. The modern Senate is both unchanging and greatly changed. It is a democratized institution, characterized by entrenched institutional rules that bestow significant advantages upon individuals and minority interests, and by the equal representation of vastly unequal states. With these characteristics in mind, we consider the contemporary debate about the Senate in an era when governmental capabilities and public faith are severely strained. While our aim is neither to praise nor to bury the U.S. Senate, we believe the contrast between the invention of the Senate and the evolution to its contemporary status should prompt a reconsideration of the Senate's place and purpose in our government as we confront the problems and promise of a new century.

TWO

Sources and Models
Mixed, Republican, and Liberal

Why, during the founding era in the United States, were certain types of senates proposed and tried? After a decade of experience and constitutional experimentation, why had no one form gained authoritative status? Part of the answer can be found in the principles on which American framers drew. The senates that were proposed and debated in this era were informed by three intersecting sets of constitutional principles: mixed constitutionalism, which was the standard remedy for the dangerous antagonism between social classes; republicanism, which argued for popular participation in a government devoted to common goods; and liberalism, which directed government toward the protection of the rights of individuals. Because these principles were, in part, contradictory, they generated not only a variety of model senates but also some of the quandaries that complicated the search for a fitting form.

This review of sources concentrates on two developments in modern constitutional thought. One is the methodical demotion of the senate, in functions and influence, to accommodate a separation of powers, the new basis of a constitution of liberty. This project, evident in the liberalism of John Locke and Baron de Montesquieu, required a thorough reevaluation of prudence, the distinctively senatorial virtue. The other development, evident in the republican constitutions of James Harrington and David Hume, heads in a significantly different direction. On the foundation of a modernized prudence, Harrington and Hume elevate the senate to the central and dominant position in their constitutions of liberty. Both strands of modern constitutionalism are evident in the founding era. Almost unanimously, American framers embraced the liberal principle of separated powers, and searching for a strictly republican senate, many of them also borrowed from Harrington and Hume. Yet these two strands are, in various ways, incompatible. How they were adapted and reconciled is discussed in chapter 3. The tensions between these two strands are examined here.

Because the demotion of the senate in the modern republic is, in some ways, a reaction to fatal flaws in the aristocratic senate of the old standard, the mixed constitution, it is appropriate to start with Rome. The Roman example orients liberalism's reconsideration of virtue and, particularly, prudence; Rome's principal provision for this paramount political virtue was its senate. The Roman constitution, moreover, figures prominently in contemporary scholarship on the origins of the Senate. Rome is used as an example of the "virtuous republic," which has informed important studies of eighteenth-century American political thought,[1] and scholars have used the inclusion of senates as crucial evidence that American framers intended to establish mixed constitutions.[2]

It is, however, a long road from Rome to the United States. The *Federalist* invokes the Roman constitution as "instructive" proof of the need for a senate to "blend stability with liberty." In the same passage, however, Publius warns that the ancient republics are "as unfit for the imitation, as they are repugnant to the genius of America."[3] Where could American framers look for an example of a prudent senate that fit the circumstances of their time and place?

THE MIXED CONSTITUTION

Mixed constitution is not a precise notion. All constitutions given the label *mixed* involve the separation of disharmonious classes into different institutions of government. These parameters encompass a broad range of constitutions. Cicero's ideal Roman constitution, for example, is a means of controlling democratic passions and securing the ruling influence of virtuous aristocrats. Polybius emphasizes the mixing of rival classes for the sake of checking their ambitions. A democratic variation mixes the honest interests of the many, as the ends of government, with the wisdom of the few, as the necessary means. Another variation uses the antagonism between classes as merely a practical means for checking power and securing a separation of powers. Each of these variations is discussed below as a form of mixed constitution, but rather than trying to shore up *mixed* as a coherent category or paradigm, we will concentrate on the widely divergent ideas that produce the variations.

Cicero's Virtuous Regime and Senate

The constitution in Cicero's idealization of the Roman republic is defined by the rule of virtue and, specifically, prudence, the virtue of correct deliberation and decision in practical matters. Aristotle calls prudence the "ruling part" of a political order and the "legislative science" because it concerns the best means of achieving the most good in practice. One essential element of prudence, therefore, is extensive practical knowledge about the means appropriate to a just or constructive end, and this knowledge is generally gained through extensive experience in public affairs.[4] The other essential element is moderation, or rational control of passions and desires. Without this self-mastery, private inclinations would distort judgment and use practical knowledge to pursue ends that are neither general nor just. Finally, Cicero argues that a natural sociability, which fosters a sense of duty to serve others, will help direct those with practical knowledge to serve the public good.[5]

The "mind and reason of the prudent man" is the "standard" of justice, and the prudent would be able and disposed to take the comprehensive and just view of any public matter. Only what is wise in this sense is properly law; if prudence does not rule, the constitution of government is a practical and moral failure. Consequently, only those wise in this way should be legislators. The body of prudent legislators, the senate, should therefore be seen as "the leader of public policy." The senate's deliberation must be removed from the unwise "inconstancy" of the general citizenry so that it can "conduct the government by its wisdom."[6]

The fundamental political conflict is, then, between the passionate and imprudent, on the one hand, and the rational, moderate, and wise, on the other. The constitutional resolution of this conflict cannot be some mixing of these two parts into a truer whole; how would sound political judgment be improved by adulteration?[7] The democratic principle of liberty is reduced, more or less, to an irrational desire not to be ruled, and the best constitution, Cicero argues, artfully accommodates this passion. The tribunes, the representatives of the plebeians, are defended as being less dangerous than the people themselves and as moderating the consuls, more or less the executive arm of the constitution. The main justification, though, is that the tribunate provides an outlet for the democratic desire for liberty without impeding the senate's rule.

The senate's influence must be comprehensive. In particular, the prudent few must be able to influence popular opinion in the elections of magistrates—those officers who put the law into effect—not only because these elections greatly affect the ruling of the state but also because they determine future senators. In general, the "senatorial order" must be a "model" of virtue for the rest of the citizenry, and in this responsibility, Cicero notes, is "everything"; the character of the best citizens determines the character of the rest and, therefore, the well-being, nobility, and truth of the whole.[8]

Institutions and Checks in Polybius's Mixed Constitution

Polybius's account of the best practicable constitution is more likely to call to mind elements of American constitutionalism. The heart of his mixed order is not the right and benevolent rule of virtue but rather an array of institutions and powers that channel and check the antagonistic parts. Institutional arrangements, moreover, are used to shape political behavior and define the parts to be mixed. Like Cicero, however, Polybius seeks to sustain the senate's prudent management of political life, at least at critical moments, against the politically imprudent impulses of the general population.[9]

Polybius is somewhat cagey about the senate's status. He introduces it as an apparently equal part of a mixed constitution, which is designed to overcome the instability inherent in the simple constitutions: kingship, aristocracy, and democracy. Each of these good constitutions tends to degenerate into its counterpart, as monarchy into tyranny, and each bad constitution tends to provoke a revolutionary response that establishes a good constitution of a different form, as tyranny into aristocracy. The new government's goodness, its careful attention to public order and justice, is sustained for the while by fearful memories of disorder and tyranny, but as security and prosperity blur these memories, the public spirit of the new rulers decays. Polybius extracts from this cycle what seems to be a natural principle of preservation (the virtues forged by adversity and fear) and a natural principle of decay (the selfish impulses that emerge in good times).[10] The mixed constitution uses these principles to achieve a more stable order.

The mix of monarchy (consuls), aristocracy (senators), democracy (tribunes) is not, however, intended to produce some sort of harmony of principles and dispositions. The properly mixed constitution can instead satisfy the pride of each part. It was impossible, Polybius observes, "for even a native to pronounce with certainty whether the constitution was aristocratic, democratic, or monarchical," and each part could believe that its institution defined the constitution as a whole. In fact, each institution was given significant power, including a capacity to check and degrade the authority of the other parts. Each part, therefore, had cause to fear for its power and honors, and this institutionalized fear inhibited corrupt ambition and desires. It also elicited virtuous behavior as the best means of fending off intrusions.[11]

Polybius's senators are not, however, simply virtuous and fully fit to rule; the senate's goodness, particularly its prudence, is in part the product of threats from the other institutions. Up to a point, then, Polybius's constitution of checks rests on a premise that many American framers could embrace: political orders must accommodate our ineradicable selfishness. These checks are particularly necessary in peaceful and prosperous times, when the citizens are "insolent and overbearing." Any institution that "aims at supremacy and tends to become too predominant" can be intimidated and checked by the other institutions.[12] This sort of check requires only that all constitutional officers have a primary interest in preserving the status and authority of their offices, and Polybius does not seem particularly concerned about securing virtuous rule.

Yet Polybius does not assume that the government under this constitution can function well without a ruler or commander of sorts, and his constitution is not simply a balance between equal parts. The well mixed constitution must also place political skill and good judgment in control.[13] Although the senate is the obvious candidate for this commanding position, the distribution of powers in Rome's constitution did not seem to favor the authority of the senate.[14] The consuls and the people had direct control over some very important decisions. The senate's powers, on the other hand, were generally indirect. These indirect powers, however, afford the senate a comprehensive influence, and Polybius's muted descriptions seem to mimic the tactful manner in which the senate's powers ought to be used.[15]

In general, the senate's ability to "counteract" the other institutions and to secure their "cooperation" came from its significant influence on private interests and passions. For example, the senate could decide whether to continue a consul in office after his term had expired as well as whether, and how, to honor consuls for their accomplishments as military commanders. It controlled, in other words, the means of satisfying the ambitious consul's craving for public honor and enduring fame.[16]

This sort of relationship is more evident in Polybius's account of how the senate could resist the apparently fearsome authority of the people to impair and remove the senate's authority and privileges. Against these direct checks, the senate wielded potent indirect influence over the people. Its command of the treasury and public spending gave it control over "a vast number of contracts" and public employment in general. What is "even more important," the fact that senators were the judges in major civil trials made the people afraid to offend them. Altogether, the senate's manipulation of interests, hopes, and fears led the people and their representatives to be "submissive," to seek the senate's favor and avoid its displeasure.[17]

Polybius's endorsement of the senate's broad influence suggests that even in times of peace and prosperity the government may need a deliberate manager and that the senate, at least when threatened by other institutions, will curb its selfishness enough to fill that role. In these good times, however, the correctly mixed constitution is principally a balanced antagonism between imminently corrupt parties. Emergencies, on the other hand, require prudent leadership, and because dire threats "compel" citizens to work "in concord," such leadership is possible. But neither the popular representatives nor individual consuls could produce the steady and prudent political judgments necessary to manage a crisis, and Polybius's example, which will "make manifest . . . the perfection and strength" of the Roman constitution, centers on the indispensable rule of a prudent senate. When facing terrible choices, this body was peculiarly "steadfast and high-minded."[18] Only the senate was able to master natural passions and immediate interests, adhere to remote and larger goods, and see how those goods could be attained.

In general, Polybius's mixed constitution lowers the bar; the rule of reason and virtue is not the aim of the regime, and senators need not be exemplars of rational self-mastery. Consequently, it also reduces the inequality in power and status between the aristocratic and democratic parts. Only in emergencies could the senate rule directly. Even so, maintaining a balance that sustains senatorial influence against democratic resistance requires complicated institutional arrangements, some sleight of hand, and, as Cicero and Polybius argue, the cowing effects of superstitious religion.[19]

A tempting response to these convoluted remedies would be to dismiss the problem; the mixed constitution could be discarded once those with aristocratic pretensions abandoned, or were forced to abandon, any claim to distinctive political status and privileges. Yet the principal argument in favor of an elite, prudent senate is difficult to circumvent. The case for the rule of prudence begins with the rather commonsensical argument that politics is a complicated business and the well-being of the citizenry depends upon wise political decisions, a proposition American framers accepted implicitly. How then can a political order prosper without giving special status and influence to steady and wise political judgment? Once it is admitted, though, that some few will be significantly wiser than the rest in political matters, we have returned to the problem of securing to those few a disproportionate influence within the government. Must any constitution providing for prudence in government, therefore, be mixed—and mixed with an aristocratic bias?

LIBERALISM AND THE DEMOTION OF THE SENATE

In stark contrast to Polybius's and Cicero's mixed constitutions, which require a virtuous senate to manage the government, liberal constitutionalism comes close to undermining all arguments for a senate. The fundamental principles of seventeenth- and eighteenth-century liberalism—the denial of any natural right of a person or class of persons to rule the rest, and the liberty of individuals to rule their own lives in pursuit of happiness as they understand it—were direct assaults on aristocratic pretensions. This new, individualistic, and ultimately democratic republicanism dispensed with virtue as a purpose of political life and deliberately reduced the need for political prudence and particularly legislative prudence. The separation of powers denied to each institution the authority to direct the others. The new order, in sum, methodically demoted the senate, and in the constitutionalism of liberalism's foremost proponent, it all but disappears.

The Optional Senate in Locke's Democratic Constitution

John Locke's *Second Treatise of Government,* a source book for eighteenth-century understanding of liberal principles of government, says little about specific senates and still less about senates and bicameralism in general. This omission is explained, at least in part, by the radically reduced responsibilities of his sort of liberal government. His constitution certainly eschews virtue as an objective of political life, and the limited responsibilities of liberal government—the protection of life, liberty, and property—reduce the demands upon practical political judgment. The powers needed for these limited responsibilities can be adequately regulated by democratic responsibility and a separation of powers that does not rely on a mixture of antagonistic classes. An upper legislative house, let alone a prudent senate, is not an essential element of his constitutionalism.

Locke's main purpose in the *Second Treatise* is to establish the right definition of political power through an examination of the origin of civil society and legitimate government.[20] In our natural state, he argues, all persons are equal insofar as no one person or class of persons has a natural right to rule another in his life and, ultimately, in his liberty and property. Just political power is established therefore only by the consent of each of the governed, and the security of individuals, defined by their equal rights to "life, liberty and estates," is the proper and exclusive end of government. Justice, in general, is a simple and relatively indisputable matter because it is essentially the same for each person: the preservation of rights that are natural and are possessed without the intervention of another human being.[21]

The most important consequence of this argument is that all oligarchic/aristocratic claims to distinctive status and privileges are excluded from political consideration and relegated to the private sphere. The properly aristocratic claim that superior virtue justifies higher political status is undermined, at least in part, by the fact that virtue is not the purpose of political life. Government has almost no legitimate role in the delicate and complicated matters of moral life and the health of the soul.[22] Each individual is free to discover and pursue his peculiar happiness in his own way, and the aspiring aristocrat has no basis for asserting his virtues and happiness as models for the rest of the citizenry. The government's job is mainly to police individuals as they come into contact with the life, liberty, and property of others. Those vices that are under the legitimate rule of the government would be regulated by law and punishment rather than by example and instruction.[23]

By denying aristocrats any peculiar claim on authority, Locke undermines many arguments for a mixed constitution. This form is no longer required either by justice or by the general purposes of liberal government. It might also be argued that a mixed government is less necessary as a means of regulating class conflict; one contender, the oligarchic/aristocratic party, is denied any moral cover for its ambitions, and political life is less attractive to aristocratic pretensions. Even claims of superior prudence as a necessary means of good government are weakened by the reduced demands on political wisdom and judgment. Domestic policies concerning property, trade, and taxation, for example, can be managed, in large part, by rules, administrators, and courts. The challenges of defense and foreign policy are reduced in number and complexity as honor, martial courage, and national glory are replaced by commerce, general prosperity, and national security as the principal motives and aims of international relations.[24]

Locke does not prescribe a specific institutional arrangement to replace the mixed constitution, but he does give the liberal constitution a general form. Legitimate government is fundamentally republican insofar as our natural political equality requires the consent of each to be governed, and our consent makes government a representation of society's legitimate interest in its liberty.[25] Reasoning about the means of securing this liberty leads to the general principle of form: the separation of the legislative power, which establishes general rules, from the executive power, which enforces them. The distinction between these powers is evident in our natural state, but the *institutional* separation of the executive and legislature is a requirement of prudence. Liberty is secure only when general laws rule, and the law will rule only when these powers are separated.[26] In the absence of this separation, individuals would be subjected to the rule of person(s), that is, to a government of biased and irregular willfulness. When the powers are separated, legislators' actions are moderated because they cannot exempt themselves from the enforcement of unjust or imprudent laws, and the executive power can be confined to the enforcement of established laws. This separation, moreover, allows for appeals to the legislature over unjust actions of the executive and to the executive over unjust actions of the legislature.[27] In general, this separation of abstract powers replaces the balance between democrats and aristocrats as the basic constitutional architecture.[28]

The specific institutional structure of the individual powers is left, on the whole, to the practical judgment of each political society. Locke prescribes no specific form for the legislature. It could be shared by a number of institutions, but the suitability of these variations depends upon particular circumstances.[29] In any case, the bicameral form is not essential to a free constitution. Although Locke is particularly attentive to checks that control the use of power, an upper house is not a necessary check, and he does not seem to be particularly concerned that the membership of the legislative body, in part or as a whole, be distinguished for its practical wisdom.

This lack of evident concern over prudence in the legislature is highlighted by Locke's attention to prudence in the executive branch. The executive responsibility, strictly understood, allows the executive no will or judgment independent of the law. Two specific powers, however, allow the executive to act outside of the law, and only in these cases does Locke discuss prudence. One of those, the "federative" power, embraces foreign policy and war powers. Policies in this area are "much less capable to be directed by antecedent, standing, positive laws" and "must necessarily be left to the prudence of those, who have this power committed to them, to be managed by the best of their skill, for the advantage of the commonwealth." The executive exercising this power would be answerable to the legislature, and this check would regulate the executive's judgment. Locke does not, however, suggest any institutional provisions to secure wise and skilled executives.[30]

The other exception to the rule of law, the other occasion for executive prudence, is the prerogative power. The prerogative power is necessary, Locke argues, because laws and legislative judgment are inherently defective. Because legislatures cannot have perfect foresight and existing laws cannot account fully for particular and changing circumstances, strict enforcement of a law could at times be harmful to individual rights and the general welfare. For the government to secure the ends for which it was established, the executive must have the prerogative to act outside of, or even against, the law.[31]

The granting of this broad discretion assumes some degree of prudence; only the executive's ready and accurate perception of, and responses to, emergencies could improve upon the strict rule of law and justify this authority. As with the federative power, though, Locke does not prescribe provisions to enhance either the virtue itself or its independence in determining both the ends and the means of policy. Instead, he minimizes the constitution's dependence upon virtue by surrounding the executive's prerogative with checks. One is legislative. Because the prerogative operates within the realm normally regulated by the law, the legislature may add or amend laws, thereby eliminating, for the moment at least, any justification for acting outside of the law.

If his prerogative is challenged by the legislature, however, the executive can turn to the general citizenry for support, and the average citizen,

Locke notes, tends not to be particularly scrupulous about the law when his interests are served otherwise. Yet reliance upon public opinion is also a check. The executive's latitude of action, the potential satisfaction of his ambitions, depends upon the degree to which his actions please the public. In other words, the counsel of practical wisdom is forced to calculate and adapt to public reactions. Rather than being freed to guide policy toward common goods, prudence is, to a great degree, subordinated to the popular understanding of those goods.[32]

Prudence is removed as a central concern in the constitution of the legislature, confined in the extraordinary powers of the executive, and then tethered to public opinion. This manner of regulating the prerogative power exemplifies Locke's general constitutional strategy: the replacement of aristocratic virtues with interinstitutional and democratic checks.[33] Specifically, an upper legislative house is neither necessary nor even recommended as either a provision for prudence or a check. Decisions by this government will, presumably, be safe for general liberty. Yet they may also be imprudent. Perhaps that is Locke's bargain: provisions for safe government on a firm foundation at the cost of provisions for wise government. In any case, he offers little guidance as to where and how this sort of liberal republican constitution might accommodate legislative prudence—particularly through a senate whose authority rests on its distinctive good judgment and whose good effects require independence from society's will.

Bicameralism in Montesquieu's Constitution of Liberty

Montesquieu's *Spirit of the Laws*, a common authority for American framers particularly on the separation of powers, follows Locke in arguing that the rule of law is a necessary condition for individual liberty and that the separation of powers is a necessary condition for the rule of law.[34] Montesquieu argues explicitly that reducing the importance and status of virtue, particularly prudence, is necessary to achieve these results. Nonetheless, his liberal constitution utilizes a form of mixed government and specifically a bicameral legislature with an upper house whose membership is drawn exclusively from a privileged class. This mixture is, however, a deliberate departure from the Roman model. It is designed neither to establish a ruling senate nor to enhance the influence of political prudence. Montesquieu's upper house is used instead to control the legislative power of the representative lower house. His mixed form is, in other words, a means of putting into practice the separation of powers, which was adopted to replace the old and inherently defective mixed form.

The explanation and defense of a constitution of liberty based on the separation of powers come in the second phase of Montesquieu's argument.[35] The first phase includes an examination of the basic forms of government. Of particular interest is his dissection of the ancient model of republicanism, which evolves into a critique of virtue as the foundation of republican government. This argument deserves some attention not only because it leads into his critical examination of senates, prudence, and the mixed form, but also because it is a *critique* of what some scholars have argued was a broadly embraced civic virtue paradigm in early American political thought.[36]

Montesquieu argues that the two basic types of republics require the ruling part to be endowed with extraordinary virtues. The democratic republic needs a citizenry that is passionately devoted to the laws and the general good. This self-abnegating discipline unites all in a common purpose and, thereby, overcomes ruinous tendencies of ordinary selfishness: the division of the citizenry into contending factions, and the enfeeblement of government as those citizens hesitate to enforce the law against themselves.[37] In the aristocratic republic, the rulers must practice a rigorous "moderation," a thorough self-control over their potentially tyrannical ambition and arrogance.[38]

Practical considerations, however, make these two types almost indistinguishable in form, and at the core of their common form is a senate. The aristocratic republic ought to be more inclusive and broaden its citizenship, but when there are "many nobles," the constitution must have a senate "to rule on the affairs that the body of nobles cannot decide." This senate then becomes the aristocracy, with the whole body of nobles acting as the democracy. Similarly, popular sovereignty in a democratic republic may be complete, but the incompetence of the general citizenry for certain governmental tasks argues for giving greater influence to the more prudent few. A senate is particularly necessary to correct for the people's lack of diligence in public projects and celerity in emergencies.[39]

In theory, the balance between aristocrats and democrats, which sustains the senate's influence, is maintained by the virtuous moderation of each class's desire to rule alone. Democrats defer to offices filled by the more able, and aristocrats are content with a greater share only of political offices.[40] In fact, Montesquieu argues, the virtues necessary to sustain these republics will regularly fail to master the generally selfish and acquisitive nature of human beings. The aristocrats, in particular, will fail to acquire and sustain the moderation necessary to subordinate themselves to the law. In general, the ancient republic was unstable and, ultimately, despotic. Aristocratic republics could be sustained only by fear, either of foreign threats or, in times of peace and prosperity, of an internal institution "to make the nobles tremble."[41]

This need for "violent springs" to compensate for virtue's failure was the main defect of these republics and the old mixed form. Discovering a constitutional form that more readily accommodates the soft and selfish nature of human beings is the task of the second general phase of the argument.[42] To get there, however, Montesquieu must find a way to dispense with the senate as the prudent manager of the government. Indeed, his defense of an alternative principle, the separation of powers, sets the stage for a direct critique of the Roman mixed constitution and its aristocratic senate.

From the perspective afforded by the principle of separation of powers, the Roman republic was a constitution of *shared* powers; the people and the nobles each had some executive and some legislative powers. This blending of powers kept the constitution in a state of flux as the two parties struggled for full control. The constitution was stable only under the pressure of dire external threats, when all could see that public business required "heroic courage . . . and consummate wisdom," and the senate could exercise its comprehensive influence. More regular constitutional stability, however, requires a formal, sure, and complete separation of powers, and that separation requires the elimination of any need for the directing influence of an aristocratic senate. The reduction of the senate's power and influence would be possible only if the regime could be turned toward objects less demanding than glorious conquest, and the government made less attractive to contentious pride.[43]

Setting the stage for this change is Montesquieu's distinctive account of liberty, which is neither derived from fundamental principles, as in Locke, nor related, as in the ancient republics, to the disputable question of who should control the government. Montesquieu's liberty is a feeling of security, a "tranquillity of spirit," that is possible only when citizens do not fear each other.[44] It is not, and need not be, a deliberate aim of government and policy, and therefore it does not invite contests over who or what group could best secure it. Rather, it is the principal *effect* of a moderate government of separated and checked powers, no one of which need intend, or superintend, this general effect. In the absence of any principled purpose, this constitution of liberty provides no foothold for aristocratic claims to govern the whole. By appealing to rudimentary concerns for private security, it directs aspirations away from governing, which had been the republican actualization of liberty.

This more "natural" liberty, Montesquieu admits, suffers the ill effects of ordinary selfishness, which ancient republics needed a rigorous virtue to overcome. In particular, it generates a society of clashing private interests, a "thousand considerations" to which "the public good is sacrificed." Yet in Montesquieu's new republic, with its checked powers and limited range of public goods, this effect is less dangerous. The diversity of private interests may even become a means of moderating political life and the use of coercion. In general, the predictably materialistic pursuits of private life tend to soften prejudices and foster a more "gentle" and peaceful way of life.[45]

In any case, the principal cause of personal insecurity, the principal threat to liberty, is political power wielded by the unpredictable and arbitrary will of persons. Liberty as a feeling of security is possible only when political coercion is surely confined within the strict rule of settled laws that define for the citizens what is and is not permitted. Only then can an individual confidently chart a safe course of action. The rule of law and liberty are possible, Montesquieu argues, only when the executive, legislative, and judicial powers are strictly separated and checked. Each branch is allowed only a limited and checked capacity to reach into the private affairs of citizens.

In some ways, Montesquieu's separation is more strict than Locke's. Although the executive, for example, retains war and foreign policy powers, it is stripped of the prerogative, thereby eliminating the contest over supremacy that is at the core of Locke's separation.[46] The executive must have a veto in order to defend itself, but the executive is not a branch of the legislature and is given "no share in the public debates." Even the domestic power of coercive enforcement is divided into punishing and judging, with the latter removed and placed in the hands of an independent mediating judiciary. Judges, and therefore executives, are required to follow the letter of the law. The legislature, discussed in detail below, is confined to making laws and is subject to the veto. Because it has no control over the executive and the judiciary, its members must worry over how their laws will pinch them.[47]

This strict separation is possible, however, only if the government does not require an overall manager or prudent guide. A significant part of the solution to that problem is expressed in the large portions of the book devoted to what should be the principal concerns of liberal policy: commerce and taxation.[48] With all partisan aspirations checked, politicians are left with the quotidian aims of private security and prosperity. As Montesquieu makes clear, these concerns require not exemplars of high mindedness or heroic courage but rather legislators and administrators with practical knowledge in economics and finance. Without the need for extraordinary virtues, the constitution does not need to blend powers to the end of elevating and maintaining one aristocratic institution over and against democratic resistance.

Indeed, Montesquieu's account of the legislative power begins on the democratic side of the ledger. The principal consideration in forming the legislature of a "free state" is that free persons ought to govern themselves, and "the people as a body," therefore, "should have legislative power."[49] This legislative power is, however, qualified—first, by necessity. Only in a very small republic can the people actually assemble as a body, so the legislative power of the people must be exercised indirectly through representatives. As it turns out, though, representation also compensates for a lack of prudence in the general public: "The people should not enter the government except to choose their representatives; this is quite within their reach. For if there are few people who know the precise degree of a man's ability, yet every one is able to know, in general, if the one he chooses sees more clearly than most of the others." This is Montesquieu's main, and quite modest, provision for practical wisdom in the legislature. It should be recalled that in the ancient republic the defect of prudence called for an aristocratic senate. Representation in Montesquieu's modern republic certainly distinguishes between the many and the few, but it aims at securing not the few best but rather the more competent. On the one hand, representation democratizes legislative prudence. On the other hand, it removes these more competent legislators to some degree from the passions of the public. If left relatively free to "discuss public business," it seems, this body will be adequate to its legislative responsibilities.[50]

Montesquieu argues, nonetheless, for a bicameral legislature. The need for a second legislative house emerges not from a shortfall in prudence but from two imbalances that require an additional check. One is the democratic bias of the representative assembly, which will disturb the security of those, found in every state, "who are distinguished by birth, wealth, or honors." If these relatively few citizens are "mixed among the people" in a single representative house, their voices and peculiar interests will tend to have little weight in legislative deliberations. Then even a regime of law could not make them feel secure because the laws passed by the representative legislature would tend to threaten their privileges and property. Because liberty would to them feel like "enslavement," Montesquieu fears that this elite class, which is important to the health of the nation, would "have no interest in defending" the constitution and might even lean toward a revolutionary change. This threat can be reduced by a second and independent house of "nobles" with the right to "check the enterprises of the people, as the people have the right to check theirs."[51]

This modest beginning is not, however, the start of something bigger. In accord with the strict separation of powers, Montesquieu's upper house is given neither the executive powers nor the judicial powers that were essential to the influence of the Roman senate. Even its legislative powers are confined to a veto, as opposed to the representative house's powers to initiate, amend, and, ultimately, "enact." This upper house is, in sum, removed from direct participation in legislative deliberation.[52]

The absence of a privileged elite, however, does not make an upper house superfluous. The second imbalance to be corrected by an upper house is the relative weakness of the executive and judicial powers in relation to the legislative power, particularly in a regime of law. In controlling the law and appropriations, the legislature has leverage it could use to control the other powers, which are subordinate to the law. A representative assembly, moreover, has a uniquely democratic legitimacy, and it can attract public support more readily than the executive.[53] In the absence of further adjustments, the legislative power threatens the entire structure of separated powers. Locke corrects this imbalance by bolstering the naturally weaker executive power with the prerogative power. Montesquieu "tempers" the legislature by dividing its power between two antagonistic houses. Indeed, he argues, in the absence of a sufficiently elite class, a constitution of separated powers would have to create one, that is, a formally defined, "hereditary" class with a distinct and permanent unifying interest "in preserving its prerogatives." Without this motive and complication of interests, the bicameral order would not provide a sufficient check on the legislative power.[54]

This two-house legislature is a means of frustrating dangerous ambitions. It is designed neither to moderate the "separate views and interests" nor to establish the ruling influence of a steady and wise institution. Prudence is left to find its own way through the more essential provisions for liberty—separation, checks, and balances—that will fetter more than enable the use of political powers. In sum: "The form of these three powers [executive, lower house, upper house] should be rest or inaction. But as they are constrained to move by the necessary motion of things, they will be forced to move in concert."[55] As they are chained to each other, each with a different impulse, the institutions—the executive, lower house, and upper house—will find it difficult to move at all, and Montesquieu prefers the safety of this gridlock to the risks of more energetic government.[56] When necessity requires action, these chained institutions will move together, but without any one of them particularly fit or able to lead.

A NEW SENATE: LIBERAL, REPUBLICAN, AND PRUDENT

That American framers drew heavily from Montesquieu is indisputable. The *Federalist*, for example, cites him as an "oracle," and the admonition that "ambition must be made to counteract ambition" goes a long way toward embracing institutional antagonism as the principal means of preserving a separation of powers.[57] The irregular and usurping behavior of state legislatures in the 1780s afforded direct experience with the threat to a separation of powers posed by the legislative power, and at least some part of the solution seemed to be, as in Montesquieu's vision, a sharper difference in character between the upper and lower houses. As we will see, American framers struggled to translate the core of Montesquieu's bicameralism directly into American circumstances. In the absence of a formally privileged elite or nobility, and under political principles that would preclude the deliberate formation of one, how could an upper house be motivated to check vigorously the legislative and democratic powers?

The problem of framing an effective upper house was complicated also by a competing constitutional and bicameral principle. Montesquieu was content to rely on "necessity" to force the antagonistic institutions into agreement, and his criticisms of the Roman model seem to rule out an upper house justified by its superior prudence. American framers, on the other hand, sought forms of government that would enhance and refine the *deliberate* pursuit of common interests, and at the heart of many of their plans were upper houses distinguished principally by stability and practical knowledge. These efforts drew on the model republics of James Harrington and David Hume.[58] Contrary to Montesquieu's arguments, Harrington and Hume reinstate prudence as a constitutive principle and make their prudent senates the managers of the government as a whole.

The Republican Senate in Harrington's *Oceana*

James Harrington's *Commonwealth of Oceana* was, at least in parts, an inviting model for American framers.[59] This constitutional plan is more purely republican in the sense that it bears none of the vestiges of the feudal monarchy, such as heredity and prerogative, which Locke and Montesquieu incorporated into their constitutions. Like American society, the society of Harrington's imagined commonwealth is free of sharp class distinctions based on either political privilege or economic inequalities great enough to support the political dominion of a few. This relative equality permits a constitution of liberty that does not require elaborate regulation and manipulation of antagonistic classes in order to secure political stability, rule of law, and justice. Government can be based more readily, directly, and completely on the "authority" of prudence, on cooperation and deliberation to the end of promoting common interests.

More specifically, Harrington was free to design an upper house without the complicating need for hard checks on either democracy or the legislative power. The principle of his senate is political wisdom or prudence, and it can be so constituted without competing functions and characteristics. The broad influence of this prudent senate, however, entails two elements that Montesquieu argued were fatal to the Roman mixed constitution: violations of a strict separation of powers and, Harrington's social equality notwithstanding, an aristocratic claim of something like a natural right to rule. Had Harrington in fact discovered a way to establish prudent management in a stable constitution of liberty?

Although Harrington's senate shares little with its Roman counterpart, he does ground his political order on an agrarian law, similar to Rome's, which would regulate the distribution of land ownership.[60] The purpose of this law is to establish and maintain a "balance in lands" that would support a republican constitution. Specifically, the law would prevent any concentration of landed wealth that would allow one (absolute monarchy) or a few families (mixed monarchy) to dominate the rest, either through their ability to field their own armed forces or through their control over economic necessities. A fully enforced agrarian law, as Rome's was not, would soften class antagonism and constrain all citizens to live under the law as "common reason" for the good of the whole.[61]

By closing the avenue of economic and political "dominion," this enforced economic balance directs the ambitious to seek political influence through the "goods of the mind" and, particularly, "prudence," qualities that are the proper basis of "authority." Harrington's aim was not to redirect the energies of an existing aristocratic class. It was rather to erase the old line of class division and draw a new one according to a "natural" distinction between many of the ordinary qualities of mind and the "natural aristocracy," those more fully endowed with these "goods of the mind."[62] Indeed, Harrington's institutional order is designed to fill the highest offices, the senate in particular, with natural aristocrats.

The quality most needed in government is prudence, and this practical wisdom requires natural endowments as well as knowledge and skills acquired through study and experience in public affairs. Consequently, Harrington draws his senate from the natural aristocrats who are members of the "gentry," the upper economic stratum. He certainly does not assume that all of the gentry are natural aristocrats; elevation to the senate and other high national offices entails an elaborate series of increasingly refined elections. He argues instead that only those whose wealth affords them leisure for study and participation in public affairs will be able to cultivate their natural endowments to the degree required by the responsibilities of high public office.[63]

To some degree, therefore, Harrington's republican constitution is a mix between aristocratic and democratic parts. Harrington's natural aristocracy is, however, quite unlike Montesquieu's interested nobility. Insofar as its special claim on political office and influence is based on virtue of some sort, it recalls the Roman model. Yet Harrington's few and their virtues are a very long way from the Roman patricians and their virtues. At the root of this difference are the ends or objects of government. The ends pursued in Harrington's commonwealth are refinements, generalizations, of the ordinary and private interests of the general citizenry, what the

Federalist calls "the permanent and aggregate interests of the community."[64] The general citizenry and the lower house ultimately define the interest of the whole, which is the proper aim of laws and policy.

The natural aristocracy, in other words, does not represent a higher good or an exemplary way of life, nor is its claim on authority based on the peculiar substance of its views. The virtue of Harrington's senators, their prudence, is instead a practical means to ends rooted in private interest. Rather than mixing two competing definitions of the good, Harrington's constitution combines one institution rooted in the interests of the whole with another institution that is needed to perfect the discernment of those interests and of the best means of attaining them.[65]

Harrington's elevation of a virtuous senate, therefore, begins with a demotion of virtue.[66] His standard is not people reasoning beyond themselves to a greater good but rather people reasoning correctly from their private advantages to the dependence of those advantages on the good or interest of the whole. The interest of the whole itself is little more than private interest generalized by a practical understanding of this dependence.[67] The challenge is getting people to reason in this way and to apply it in practice. Although Harrington acknowledges a benevolence in human beings, a "disposition to relieve the present distresses of nature in common," and even "a sense of the national interest" in the few best, these sentiments are not, in general, strong enough to "shake off that [selfish] inclination which is more peculiar unto [human nature] and take up that which regards the common good or interest." Harrington does not rely on the self-mastery or high-mindedness of a virtuous few to correct for selfishness. Instead, he devises institutional orders that will "constrain" individuals to act in the public good.[68]

His institutional arrangement is not, however, an array of checks that merely confines officers within the powers of their particular branch. Nor does it secure the public good only indirectly, by channeling undiluted selfishness, like ambition, to pursue in effect the interest of the whole. Harrington's constitution certainly has checks, but those checks establish circumstances, constraints, that also engage good motives in the pursuit of wise and just policy. Both this understanding of human selfishness and this use of institutional arrangements to foster forthright deliberation about common interests are shared by many American framers.

The core of Harrington's institutional order is a bicameral legislature that embodies his peculiar separation of two fundamentally *legislative* powers. This separation is between the basic elements of deliberation: the "dividing" power, which proposes a course of action, and the "choosing" power, which has the final say in accepting or rejecting that course. He illustrates this distinctive separation of powers through the example of how to arrange fairly the sharing of one piece of cake. Both parties, it is assumed, are selfish, and the most reliable method for achieving an equitable result is that one party divides and the other chooses. The divider is checked by the chooser. He cannot gain any exclusive advantage from the division of public goods because the chooser will respond to any unequal division by gratefully accepting the larger piece. The divider is thereby constrained to check his own selfish tendencies.[69]

There are, of course, serious problems with this analogy. It does not account for the more specific and difficult political problems of just distributions of burdens and benefits. A strictly equal division is not always fair or prudent, and arriving at a just and wise policy can be complicated. At some point, therefore, the chooser will need to be persuaded to pick the just and wise division. In fact, Harrington does not follow his own analogy, which would allow the dividing function to be assigned to either party. Instead, he assigns that demanding responsibility exclusively to his prudent senate. Senators must be "counselors to the people," and Harrington assumes that they will able to demonstrate the wisdom of their judgments.[70]

It is tempting to find a simple and clearly mixed constitution in the match between the two legislative institutions and the two classes—the natural aristocracy and, in a sense, the natural democracy. Harrington's institutional arrangements, however, temper to the point of eliminating any strong class character. To begin with, only the senate is filled exclusively from one class. There is a property threshold for eligibility to the senate, and it is higher than the threshold for citizenship, yet not everyone who meets the property qualification is considered fit for senatorial service. Eligibility is far from an entitlement. Elevation to a seat in the senate is the result of an elaborate series of nominations and elections, which are designed to favor those of proven political merit and to discourage cabals and factions. Even those fully fit for this office are not entitled to a seat. Senators serve for a relatively short term of three years, and they are required to sit out one term before serving again. These features are designed to prevent interested attachments to the office and the development of a character or spirit independent of the senate's duties. The intended result is a prudent senate unsullied by any class interest. The lower house has an even weaker class basis; people of all strata of the citizenry can and will sit there.[71]

The elaborate process of election is worth sketching because some of the features find their way into various American constitutional plans. Only those who are not immediately dependent upon others for their livelihood, and are old enough (thirty years or more) to be settled and experienced in life, can vote, and only those with sufficient wealth to afford them the leisure to cultivate the mind and study public affairs are eligible for the senate.[72] Each stage, from the election of deputies to their election of senators, progressively refines the choice. At each stage, moreover, the choice is confined to a list of nominees, selected by one or a few nominators. This feature serves two purposes. One is to frustrate the corruption and factions that accompany electioneering. The other is to refine the choices by focusing public responsibility for the quality of the candidates on one or a few individuals. The choice from among these nominees is by election rather than by lot because a deliberate choice will tend to favor those with more experience and better judgment.

The eligible citizens of each parish meet to elect "deputies," who serve a one year term. Parish deputies are then organized into larger "tribes," and each tribe of deputies elects two senators as well as members of the lower house.[73] In other words, both the lower and the upper house are indirectly elected. Harrington doubts that the general citizenry will be sufficiently good judges either of the personal qualities of potential candidates or of the fit between personal qualities and the specific responsibilities of the office. Nonetheless, the general tendency of elections will be to elevate people who are more experienced and discerning than the ordinary citizen. Therefore, the deputies, those elected in the first round, can be expected to be more refined and accurate judges of fitness for office. This arrangement also removes the government from the direct influence of popular will. Although the general electorate has ultimate control over office and government, its immediate passions and interests are filtered out in order to establish the influence of prudence.

Other institutional features designed to further refine the senate should seem familiar. A three year term will work to "perfect" the wisdom of senators through experience in the affairs of the office and the nation. To give more weight to that experience and to assure "steadiness and perpetuity" in deliberation, the rotation of members is gradual. Only one third of the senators complete their terms in any one year, leaving always a large majority of experienced senators in place. To further enhance the senate's prudence and deliberation, legislative proposals would originate in smaller "councils," elected by and from the senate, that would function like legislative committees. The four councils, each responsible for one general area of policy, would draft the legislative proposals to be debated by the senate. The senate, with 300 members, would debate and decide whether and how to proceed on a proposal.[74]

At this stage, the senate should be free to "debate," "discern," and "propose" the best means of attaining the general interest. These deliberations ought, therefore, to be kept apart from the passions of the citizenry and their more immediate representatives. Yet no measure can be enacted without the approval of those representatives in the lower house. The "excellency" of the senators and the refinement of their deliberations notwithstanding, a senate that "chooses" as well as "divides" will become "factious." Narrow personal interests will come to the fore as parts seek particular advantages for themselves, and the senate as a whole would be used to serve the interests of a few. The lower house's exclusive power to approve or reject, Harrington argues, will suppress faction and tend to unite senators in a common purpose; to maintain its reputation, authority, and influence, the senate must be able to persuade the lower house that its proposals are designed to serve "the interest of the commonwealth."[75] Harrington does *not* assume that all senators will agree, as a consequence, on a course of action; he prescribes an elaborate procedure for choosing between alternative proposals. Nor does he assume that the proposals of a diligent and upright senate will always be accepted by the lower house. His aim is rather to refine the debate within the senate and to raise the probability that conversation between the two houses will be cooperative and mutually beneficial.

This power to accept or reject legislative proposals is the principal power of the lower house, and the general purpose of this power is to bind deliberation and policy to the interests of the whole. To serve that function well, the lower house must reflect the interest of the whole nation; it must be "so constituted as can never contract any other interest than that of the whole people." Consequently, this house must be comprised of a relatively broad spectrum of citizens, and it must have a relatively large membership (Harrington's is over a thousand). Yet the broader range of membership makes it less learned and skilled in public affairs, and the large size makes it less able to deliberate methodically and soberly. Thus, the characteristics that make it adequately representative also argue for strict limits on its *constructive* powers. Because it is not competent to compose wise and systematic laws, Harrington's lower house cannot initiate legislative proposals, and it cannot amend them. To avoid factious divisions within this house, which would distract the membership from its representative responsibilities, it is forbidden even to debate the matters put before it. It can accept proposals, reject them, or return them for reconsideration.[76]

Although Harrington's constitution is fundamentally democratic, the powers of the most democratic branch are very restricted. Even if the senate were successfully tethered to the interest of the whole, a common interest or good is so general as to leave to the prudence and persuasion of the senate the vast range of subordinate ends that make up most of public policy. This strict division between a dividing senate and a choosing assembly nearly pushes Harrington's exact design off the spectrum of options within the more democratic American theory and practice. Nonetheless, his fundamental principle of separation between the interests of the whole and the practical wisdom to pursue those ends is affirmed in the *Federalist:* "A Good government implies two things; first, fidelity to the object of government, which is the happiness of the people; secondly, a knowledge of the means by which it can be best attained."[77] Like Harrington, Publius uses this distinction to distinguish the functions of the two legislative houses.

Complicating the adaptation of Harrington's constitution and prudent senate was a competing principle and concern: the separation of powers, particularly between the legislature and the executive. Harrington argues for a formal separation of powers and distinguishes the powers, at least in principle. Yet all national executive offices were to be filled from and by the senate, and the result would be something like a parliamentary ministry without a prime minister. The various officers would be more or less directly responsible to the senate, and they would have no check on the legislature, in part or as a whole.[78] Harrington's principal separation is within the legislature, and perhaps his confidence in the moderating effects of this feature made him less concerned than Montesquieu was about legislative interference with, and corruption of, the other powers. Some early American state constitutions exhibited a similar confidence, affirming the principle of separation while giving the power of appointing executives to the legislature. The problems arising from these forms, and the difficulties in adapting a prudent senate to a stricter separation of powers and more reliable checks and balances, will be discussed in the next chapter.

Hume's Revisions of Harrington's Prudent Republic

Two characteristics that would complicate the adaptation of Harrington's republic to America were its weak democratic character and its agrarian foundation. In revising Harrington's constitution, David Hume's "Idea of a Perfect Commonwealth" addresses these problems and, in some ways, enhances the compatibility of a prudent senate and liberal democratic principles.[79]

Although Hume embraces Harrington's constitution, calling it "the only valuable model of a commonwealth, that has yet been offered to the public," its keystone, the agrarian law, is too easily evaded to be a stable foundation. Consequently, Hume removes it from the constitution, without any evident worry about instability in social and political life. He assumes that this sort of constitution is compatible with a dynamic commercial republic, which he recommends elsewhere and which many American framers promoted. He does, however, exhibit a greater distrust of the senate, and he pairs the elimination of the agrarian law with a significant increase in the powers of the lower house, establishing a more equal, checked, and balanced relationship between the lower and the upper houses.[80]

Hume bases his bicameralism, and his constitution generally, on a similar principle of separation between representative and prudent "councils." The "greater" in size represents the people and is designed to keep the senate "honest," that is, attentive to the liberty and interests of society as a whole. The "lesser" in size is a senate, without which the people "would want wisdom." Harrington's government, however, has "no balance" because "the whole legislature may be said to rest in the senate." Because all proposals must come from the senate, the people have no means of initiating "grievances," particularly against existing "abuses," laws, and policies. Harrington's weak representative house is an inadequate "security for liberty." The representatives should retain the final power of enactment, but as a check against the oppressive ambition of the few senators and as an outlet for the complaints of the general citizenry, they must also have the power to propose. Hume admits that an adequately representative assembly would be too large and chaotic for sober deliberation. Representatives should, therefore, assemble "in their respective counties" rather than en masse, and decisions would be made by the majority of county assemblies.[81]

The senate's modest legislative authority comes principally from its right to be the first to debate any proposed law. A proposal approved by it must be sent, with its rationale, to the representatives for a final decision. The senate, moreover, has no final say over proposals. A proposal that is defeated or refused by the senate may, on the request of ten senators or five counties, be sent to the representatives for a decision. At this point, the senate may do no more than articulate its reasons for opposing it. Lacking either a veto or any exclusive legislative authority, the senate's authority must depend upon its superior wisdom in political matters, and that wisdom can have an effect only through persuasion.

Hume's senate is also smaller than Harrington's. It could be as small as thirty and, to maintain its deliberative character, it should not be larger than one hundred. To get prudent senators, Hume recommends a variation on Harrington's progressively refining elections. There ought to be a modest property or income threshold for voting, and all of those elected must meet this requirement. The representatives are popularly elected, and then they elect the senators. As we shall see, this specific form of election was adopted in various American constitutions and proposals, including the Virginia Plan. The "reason of these orders," Hume explains, is that the "lower sort of people" can judge well only between candidates who are "not very distant from them in rank." They should not, therefore, be trusted to fill higher offices requiring refined skills and qualities. The representatives chosen directly by the people, on the other hand, will tend to be "men of fortune and education," making them more fit judges in elections of senators.[82]

To enhance the prudence of his senate, Hume eliminates the requirement that senators sit out a term before they can be eligible again for election. Mandatory rotation, he argues, throws out individuals without regard to their "abilities." Yet Harrington considered the rotation an important remedy for self-interest and faction in the senate, a problem Hume addresses by recommending closer accountability through annual elections. Without rotation, senators of proven merit could be and, Hume seems to assume, would be reelected. He also limits the senate's influence over society by reducing the number of offices it can fill by appointment.[83]

As part of the legislature, Hume's senate is less powerful and more thoroughly checked than Harrington's. Although it is more compatible with the democratic leaning of American founders, Hume's senate is even less compatible with the principle of separation of powers. Although weaker legislatively, Hume's senate has not only the power to appoint executive officials but also the "whole executive power of the commonwealth," which includes all authority over war and diplomacy. Shades of both powers are present in the Constitutional Convention debates and in the Senate's powers in appointments and treaties. Hume argues that particularly war and foreign affairs require a "refined policy" that only the senate can provide. Under a monarchical executive, he suggests, policy is hostage to the accidental character and skills of a single person. A prudent assembly like his senate is a more reliable provision for steadiness and wisdom.[84]

THE NEW REPUBLICAN SENATE, PRUDENCE, AND THE SEPARATION OF POWERS

Harrington and Hume place the senate back in the center of the republican constitution, as a provision for the stability and practical knowledge that even limited and liberal government may require. Their republican constitutions rest not on the sharp separation of powers recommended by Locke and especially Montesquieu, but rather on a bicameral mix of complementary principles. They are more concerned with filtering out unwise people and views than with checking, and these two models blend powers more to refine deliberation and policy than to provide hard checks. Indeed, a combination of significant legislative and executive powers affords their senates broad influence within the government, and they do not worry over the conflicts between many and few that led Montesquieu to reject the Roman mixture of powers.

As such, the Harrington and Hume models chart a middle ground between what have been presented as exclusive and diametrically opposed alternatives in American constitutionalism: either mixed, with a "Lordslike" senate, or highly and strictly democratic; either the populace is virtuous and united, or it is self-interested and factious.[85] Harrington and Hume argue for neither one nor the other half of each dichotomy. The senates in these democratic constitutions are far removed from any particular constituency, and yet they are not even remotely Lords-like. Harrington and Hume do not rely on virtuous mastery of personal interest in all, or any part, of the citizenry, nor do they resign themselves to merely managing the clash of interests in and out of the government. Instead, they put a premium on subduing faction and class interests so that their senates can be fit for deliberate and prudent pursuit of common interests.

To various American framers, this alternative was attractive. In the main, however, these framers were also votaries of the separation of powers as the essential architecture of any constitution of liberty. If we follow the separation of powers back into Locke's constitution, we find no particular model of a senate. In Montesquieu, we find a model that was incompatible with American society and its principle of political equality. In sum, the development of liberal republican constitutionalism left American framers with no clear and settled model for a liberal republican senate. The acknowledged authorities offered conflicting principles, aims, and forms.

The founding era was indeed marked by great disputes as well as by experiments in thought and practice, ranging from a single and sovereign representative legislature to senators for life as members of a strictly separated bicameral legislature. We should not conclude, however, that American senates were therefore indigenously American. Some of the issues, such as property rights and federalism, were new or newly relevant, and direct experience with various forms certainly influenced the debate and later experiments. Yet many of those engaged in the debates and experiments of the founding era were also, directly or indirectly, aware of the models discussed above. Many of the struggles were about the best way to translate these models into American circumstances.

THREE

American Senates in Theory and Practice, 1776–1787

In the conclusion of his careful study of upper houses in early America, Jackson Turner Main notes that although these institutions were more like the Roman senate than the British House of Lords, they were, in fact, neither. American senates were the product, he argues, not of a generally accepted model but rather of somewhat fumbling experiments within the diverse circumstances of individual states and the nation as a whole.[1] Powerful evidence for this contention is the national senate, which seems to have emerged awkwardly from a stew of principles, models, circumstances, and narrow interests.

This observation, however, tends to obscure another part of the story. It is one thing to argue that fallible reason, limited knowledge, and interested partiality make contention and compromise the unavoidable companions of deliberation, even in the framing of institutions of government. It is entirely another to conclude that compromise is the only way the parts could be shaped into a whole. Any observer of legislatures in action understands that a patchwork law necessary to muster a majority was not the only conceivable result; there were wiser and more coherent alternatives that informed and disinterested minds would have affirmed. Very often, moreover, the presence of these alternatives in the legislative debate helped shape the final result.

Did Americans find their way through the competing concerns, principles, and models discussed in chapter 2 and develop a coherent liberal republican senate compatible with both a separation of powers and a principle of political equality? Could that senate also be used to enhance the prudence of the government?

Exactly such a model was outlined by John Adams in his widely circulated *Thoughts on Government,* a vigorous defense of the bicameral form. Indeed, he tries to reconcile Harrington's prudent senate and Montesquieu's strict separation of powers. His model suggests how the complex of practical, moral, and institutional considerations could be assembled into what would necessarily be a new sort of senate. Although it set something of a standard for American senates, it was just a sketch, and the complexity of the problem invited repeated criticism and revision. These variations on Adams's model expose the tenacious difficulties, first of delineating the functions appropriate to a liberal republican senate and then of devising a form that would achieve those aims in practice.

This chapter concludes with a study of James Madison's thoughts on government during the years leading up to the Constitutional Convention. At the heart of his efforts to craft a remedy for the political problems in postrevolutionary America was a model of a prudent national senate. Although the convention's compromises produced a senate that deviated widely from Madison's design, his thoughts on the matter deserve careful consideration. In general, the abstract model shows how the components of his senate cohere, how one element was contingent upon others. This will help explain why Madison tenaciously resisted the compromises, the changes that would, in his view, undermine the upper house's crucial functions. The coherent standards of purpose and form in Madison's model, therefore, also afford us some critical distance from the finished product of the convention's labors.

Before turning to these models of a liberal republican senate, we examine other models in American theory and practice. Of particular interest is the unicameral legislature, against which Adams was arguing. This form has been presented as representing a fundamental alternative in American constitutionalism.[2] As it turns out, the differences are more in appearance than reality. The examples discussed below seem to rely on something akin to civic virtue, but that feature is compatible with the bicameral form. Otherwise, at least in practice, the unicameral and bicameral forms share a moral commitment to liberal individualism, a constitutional commitment to the separation of powers, and an institutionalized attention to prudence in government. We also examine the senates in postrevolutionary state constitutions. Beyond establishing the broad acceptance of bicameralism, however, the state constitutions provide little positive guidance on the form of a senate; the most prominent lessons for later framers were drawn from their failures.

UNICAMERALISM: A FUNDAMENTAL ALTERNATIVE?

Simple Democracy in *Common Sense*

Although Thomas Paine's *Common Sense* affirms the broad and fundamental right of individuals to govern their private lives and enjoy their
property, it argues that government over that society does not require
extensive internal checks and balances. More specifically, it was a prominent dissent from the general principle that liberty required a division of
the legislature into two houses.

Paine's heterodox position is based on what he sees as the constructive
effects of our natural sentiments and interests. Guided by a rudimentary
prudence, individuals will see that their interests are best served through
cooperation with others, and the resulting society, a spontaneous order of
"reciprocal blessings," will organize most human interaction without enforced rules. The coercive restraint of government is necessary only at
the margins, when our normally reliable "conscience" and prudent self-
interest fail to respect the liberty of others and abide by the laws of social
morality. The generally benign quality of human dispositions, moreover,
allows the citizenry to be trusted with direct control over government and
policy. Democratic control will, in turn, prevent those in office from
creating invidious "distinctions" between citizens and otherwise intruding
on liberty.[3]

To facilitate this popular check, the government must be simple in
form. His account of checks and balances in the British constitution treats
the separation of powers not as an essential provision for liberty but rather
as an artifact of the fundamentally defective mixed form. The constitution
of liberty in *Common Sense* is, instead, a single and supreme legislative
assembly. This body should be representative *only* when, and only because, the population is too large for the citizenry itself to assemble conve-
niently. Representatives, therefore, should not act as a check on the citizenry; these delegates should replicate the popular will. To tether them
closely to the will of society, Paine recommends frequent elections and
regular rotation in office. Because popular will can be trusted and because
there is no distinct upper class to represent, a second legislative house
would be superfluous.[4]

Unicameralism and Separation of Powers in the Pennsylvania Constitution

The postrevolutionary constitution that fits Paine's model most closely was the 1776 constitution of Pennsylvania. It was thoroughly liberal, basing government on the consent of the people and devoting it to the protection of individual rights, and it emerged from an explicit rejection of a mixed form of government. The result featured a strictly democratic, unicameral legislature, and the manner in which the legislature and the executive were structured and empowered reflected great trust in the judgment of the citizenry. Even the main provision against rash or imprudent legislation relied upon the maturity of popular judgment; all bills were to be made available for public scrutiny and could not be put to a final vote until the next legislative session.[5]

This account, however, underestimates the importance of another principle. In the Pennsylvania constitution, the three powers and those exercising them were separated almost perfectly, at least on paper. Similarly, the first article of Georgia's more or less unicameral constitution was devoted to an affirmation that the powers of the government "shall be separate and distinct, so that neither exercise the powers properly belonging to the other."[6] Indeed, as M. J. C. Vile argues convincingly, a separation of powers was *the* "basis of the institutional structure of government" in the state constitutions. Separation was generally understood, following Locke and Montesquieu, to be the crucial distinction between a free constitution and despotism. Paine's simple democracy was, in other words, quite exceptional.[7]

Agreement on the principle of separation did not generate agreement on the best ways of maintaining a separation in practice, and the postrevolutionary state constitutions used a variety of means. Most of them, however, shunned interbranch checks, such as an executive veto. Such checks were tainted by association, from experiences with royal government under the colonial charters. In particular, the all-too-close relationship between the royal governors and the upper houses (or councils) suggested that any blending of powers was antithetical to effective separation.[8] Checks involving a blending of powers, moreover, could be considered the peculiar desiderata of a mixed constitution, in which the need to achieve a balance between antagonistic classes and claims of sovereignty must override the separation of abstract powers of government. If so, only outside of a mixed constitution could a true and durable separation of powers be established. With one exception, those states with bicameral legislatures had highly democratic upper houses, the powers of which were strictly legislative. In other words, most of the bicameral state constitutions had more in common with the Pennsylvania constitution than they did with the more clearly mixed models of Montesquieu and Harrington.[9]

Democracy, Prudence, and the Shadow of Mixed Government

Pennsylvania certainly took these tendencies to their extreme in assuming that a separation could be achieved without either an upper legislative house or checks requiring a blending of powers.[10] To maintain the separation, this constitution relied heavily on the judgment of the citizenry. But not entirely. Although free from any mixed forms, this most democratic of state constitutions was not exactly free from the considerations behind those forms. In particular, it manifested doubts about popular judgment and made special provisions for prudence.

Two features of the Pennsylvania constitution suggest that the people were not considered sufficiently competent to manage political power and the constitutional structure. A Council of Censors was designed apparently to compensate for a lack of attentiveness and perspicacity in the citizenry. Every seven years, this council would be popularly elected to sit for one year. It was authorized to conduct what was, in effect, a comprehensive constitutional audit. In order that "the freedom of the commonwealth be preserved inviolate forever," the council was to look for, among other matters, abuses of power and violations of the separation of powers. Remedies for the more specific abuses were direct (censures and ordering of impeachments), but most were indirect (recommendations for repeal of unconstitutional laws and calls for conventions to amend defective parts of the constitution). This extrabranch check served to refine democratic oversight by publicizing abuses of power and constitutional defects the populace might have failed to discern or appreciate.[11]

The constitution also employed a telling distinction between citizens. Section 7 of the frame of government asserted that offices should be filled only by those "most noted for wisdom and virtue."[12] This provision rested on two premises: that some citizens have greater endowments of wisdom and virtue than others and that good government requires officers with these endowments. This sort of distinction is often interpreted as an indicator of a mixed form of government.[13] Yet the same distinction was made in the constitution that is regularly presented as the democratic alternative. Pennsylvania obviously did not establish a separate legislative house to embody these qualities. Nonetheless, representatives were to be something more than merely a conduit of public will. They were, in some way, to refine it. At the very least, the representative branch was to be filled by that class of citizen distinguished by its superior knowledge of the means best suited to the ends willed by the majority.

Whether these modest enhancements of prudence put the Pennsylvania constitution in the category of mixed government is somewhat beside the point. No such provisions can be free from some sort of class distinction and its aristocratic implications. Consequently, as with the separation of powers, Pennsylvania's provisions for prudence argue against viewing unicameral and bicameral legislatures as marking fundamental constitutional alternatives. The various means of enhancing political judgment employed in postrevolutionary state constitutions fall instead along a spectrum; they mark differences of degrees, not of types. Any attempt to draw a sharp ideological or even typological line of distinction will tend to obscure or distort the complicated moral and practical considerations that produced those differences.

This argument does not deny that there was in the founding era an important quarrel between those who were more trusting and those who were less trusting of democratic control over a free government. It suggests instead that this dispute did not entail a parallel division over either considerations of prudence or the basic structure of the legislature. Thomas Jefferson succinctly articulates the case for trust in popular control: "It is the manners and spirit of a people which preserve a republic in vigour. A degeneracy in these is a canker which soon eats to the heart of its laws and constitution." Yet in the same work, Jefferson distinguishes between the political "wisdom" of a few and the "integrity" of the general populace. He argues as well that Virginia ought to sharpen the distinction between its upper and lower houses.[14]

BICAMERALISM IN EARLY STATE CONSTITUTIONS

Eleven postrevolutionary state constitutions had bicameral legislatures. This is somewhat surprising, given the prerevolutionary conflicts between the popular lower houses and the elite councils. Reactions to these conflicts did not generally accuse bicameralism as such but rather the generally monarchical character of these governments and particularly the dependence of the aristocratic councils on executive and royal authority.[15] Consequently, most state constitutions established strict separations of powers, eschewed interbranch checks, and depended heavily on popular elections to regulate political power.[16] The upper houses were not, in the main, exceptions to these rules. Their powers were strictly legislative, and in ten of the eleven bicameral states, senators were popularly elected (NH, VA, SC, NY, NJ, DE, NC, MA, RI, CT).[17] Within this common framework, these constitutions employed various means to distinguish their senates from the lower houses. In some states, the democratic character was modified by property qualifications for electors or candidates, but these were high in only two (SC, NJ), and they were not always rigorously enforced.[18] Some used larger districts (NH, NY, DE, MA). Some gave their upper houses longer terms (DE, three years; NY, four; VA, four), and three instituted a gradual rotation (VA, NY, DE).

The most complete provisions for a distinctive and prudent senate were Maryland's, whose fifteen senators were far more removed from popular influences and were left, as the constitution stated, "at full liberty to exercise their judgment in passing laws." This independence was achieved through indirect elections; those eligible to elect the lower house elected persons who would then meet to elect "men of the most wisdom, experience and virtue" to be senators. This mode left senators free from any particular and enduring constituency, and this independence was enhanced by a term of office five times longer than the one-year terms for representatives and the governor.[19]

As positive examples, these constitutions were of limited help to later framers. In addition to a general interest in enhancing the prudence of the legislature, there were concerns about democratic majorities, about the ambitions of the legislative power, and about protecting the right of property. But how are these various purposes reconciled in principle and form, and which of them, if any, should take precedence? As Main argues, moreover, many of the variations in purpose and form arose not from deliberate and coherent models of a liberal republican senate but rather from heterogeneous local circumstances such as regional and economic differences, the varying character and influence of elites, and so forth.[20] Obviously, these sorts of considerations also entered into the framing of a national constitution and senate, but they were secondary to the problems of reconciling, in principle and form, the central considerations in the design of a bicameral legislature: popular control, representation, separation of powers, checks, and prudence. With the partial exception of Maryland, the state models provided little clear and positive guidance on these questions.

We do know, however, that prominent figures in this era drew important lessons from the *failings* of these constitutions. Jefferson's criticisms of the Virginia constitution and Madison's detailed account of the "vices" of the state constitutions are discussed below. In brief, though, the list of ills is dominated by legislative shortcomings: abuses of power, including violations of rights (particularly property rights), violations of the separation of powers, frequent revisions of the laws, and unwise laws and policies.[21] The remedy for many of these ills seemed to be a redesigned senate, but how could this one institution meet the broad range of political and constitutional needs: wisdom, stability, a check on legislative power, a check on the executive power, a check on democratic will, and a bulwark for property? Which ends should be given priority? What form could accomplish any one or any mix of these functions?

In a critique of the Pennsylvania constitution, Benjamin Rush acknowledged a general lack of maturity in the designs of early state constitutions. For proper guidance, he argued, would-be reformers should turn from Locke, "an oracle as to the *principles*" of government, to Harrington and Montesquieu, the "oracles as to the *forms* of government."[22] Yet as discussed in chapter 2, these oracles "as to the *forms*" do not agree on either the general constitutional structure of separated powers or the purpose and design of an upper legislative house. Nonetheless, at the outset of the founding era, John Adams attempted a reconciliation of these contradictory models.

ADAMS'S SYNTHESIS:
THE SENATE AS PRUDENT CHECK

Scholars generally agree that Adams's widely circulated letter, *Thoughts on Government*, was influential in bolstering support for a bicameral legislative branch.[23] In making his case, Adams sketches a synthesis of seemingly incompatible principles and forms to arrive at a constitutional design that is liberal and republican. The first step involves a modification of the democratic republic that Montesquieu had faulted for its dependence upon improbable civic virtues.[24] Adams's constitution, moreover, incorporates Montesquieu's separation of powers while dispensing with any hard class division in his bicameral legislature. Instead, Adams recommends a modified form of Harrington's and Hume's senate.

Adams's brief essay is mainly devoted to the means of securing the fundamental and liberal ends of government: "ease, comfort, security, or, in a word, happiness, to the greatest number of persons." Those means are, in sum, the "institutions" of government. To get there, he must dispense with what was generally understood to be the foundation of a democratic republic: civic virtue.[25] Adams begins, however, by embracing virtue; because the happiness and "dignity" of human beings depend upon virtue, he argues, we should prefer the form of government that has virtue as its foundation. He also borrows Montesquieu's analytical scheme to argue that the form based on virtue, on the "noblest principles and generous passions in our nature," is a republic. Yet Adams then dodges the virtuous republic that Montesquieu describes and turns to other authorities—for example, Locke, Sidney, and Harrington—whose modern republics are more in accord with "our nature" and do not, therefore, depend on a rigorous civic devotion.[26] So what happened to the virtue Adams acknowledged was essential? The virtues Adams identifies are not the hard discipline of the republican patriot but rather the more relaxed qualities of the ideal liberal individual: industriousness, frugality, and civility. Rather than being the basis of the political order, moreover, these *liberal* republican virtues are instead the result of the institutional structure of popular government. This constitution gives its citizens the "conscious dignity becoming freemen" and fosters these necessary elements of good character.[27]

This stress on institutions agrees with Harrington's and Montesquieu's accounts of a constitution of liberty, and Adams agrees with these two authorities in arguing that the "best of republics" perpetuate an "impartial and exact execution of the laws." In the general constitutional structure that will secure this result, however, he more closely follows Montesquieu. The "legislative, executive, and judicial" powers must be separated, and hard checks are necessary to control, in particular, the legislative power. Unchecked, the legislature will tend to clash with, and dominate, the executive and the judiciary, undermining the separation. One check is an independent executive, shorn of "prerogative" but armed with a veto. As with Montesquieu, though, the crucial provision for maintaining an effective separation and "balance" between the powers is a second legislative house. Adams then parts ways with Montesquieu. He does not worry about a dangerous clash between classes, and his constitution does not use sharp and formal class distinctions as a way to invigorate the bicameral check. It employs instead a form of senate that is in many significant ways akin to Harrington's and Hume's.[28]

This senate arises from irreducible deficiencies in a representative assembly. Adams does not attribute these deficiencies to the imprudence of the representatives, who he assumes will be "extremely well qualified." Prudence, he argues, should be a characteristic of all officers; political power in general ought to be exercised by "a few of the most wise and good." Thus, representation is not a mere substitute for direct democracy but rather a way of elevating those more fit than the general citizenry to make sound political judgments. Nonetheless, direct representation is designed to secure democratic control of government, and the assembly of representatives ought to be "an exact portrait of the people at large."[29] Adams does not raise any possible contradictions between these two characteristics. Indeed, when Adams argues that this assembly by itself should not be trusted to legislate well, he expresses no concern about its democratic character. The deficiencies of the representative assembly are attributed instead to the arrogance of the legislative power and to the instability and collective imprudence of the necessarily large representative assembly. The list of shortcomings nicely anticipates some of the actual failings of new state constitutions: "hasty results and absurd judgments"; usurpation of executive and judicial powers they are unfit to exercise; exemptions from the law; evasion of accountability; and arbitrariness in the making and execution of laws.[30]

The remedy is a second house. Adams adopts an indirect form of selection similar to Hume's: members of the upper house are to be elected by the representative assembly. This mode seems to be designed to refine even further the personal qualities of these legislators insofar as those in office and familiar with the problems of government would tend to select the more experienced and knowledgeable in these matters. The body of senators ought to be small, "twenty or thirty," presumably to foster more steady and thorough deliberation.[31] Adams also follows Hume's revision of Harrington in giving the upper house the power only of approving or vetoing proposals, denying it an independent power to initiate legislation. Adams departs from both in maintaining a fairly strict separation of powers. The small qualifications of the separation of powers—for example, the upper house must consent to an executive veto, and it is to act as an advisory "council" to the executive—seem to be designed principally to lend that office greater prudence and stability.

Adams's spare sketch, while clear on general principles, leaves important details unexplained and the probable character of the upper house in doubt. To fulfill its function, the judgment of the senate must be, he argues, "free and independent." It must, moreover, have the will to resist the ambition and imprudence of the lower house. Again, following Hume, Adams employs neither Harrington's nor Montesquieu's main provisions for independence. Montesquieu argues that separation will be effective only if the upper house is independent of the lower in origin and is motivated by a distinct set of interests. Harrington's senate would have full control over initiation and deliberation, giving it much greater leverage, and each election would displace only one-third of the senators, insulating it from the popular will of the moment.

Adams argues for quite the opposite. Abiding by the "infallible" maxim that "'where annual elections end, there slavery begins,'" Adams gives senators only one-year terms. Although he allows that a society might find it "productive of its ease, its safety, its freedom" to extend the terms of office to three years, seven years, or life, this allowance is not readily reconciled with his assertion that strict accountability fosters in political officers "the great political virtues of humility, patience, and moderation." How then could his senators be expected to check the house that elects them? This problem is evident in Adams's explanation of the governor's motives. Adams argues that the executive's veto power will not be dangerous because annual elections will tie the governor closely to society's interests and discourage any abuse of power. He assumes, nonetheless, that when the "public utility" of a veto is "conspicuous" the governor will employ that power against the body that elected him. The problem doubles in the case of the upper house. It would have to be disposed to resist the electing assembly and an executive elected by that assembly. Adams seems to rely on (unexplained) virtues of character to resist the pull of personal interest in reelection and to tip the contest toward the public good.[32]

Variations: Long Terms and Independence

Carter Braxton's critique (1776) of Adams's bicameralism revolves around these problems. Braxton agrees with Adams on the major political and constitutional principles: individual liberty as the end, separation of powers as the general organization of government, and a senate as both a check and a provision for prudence. Adams's constitutional plan, however, is flawed in the mismatch between aims and form. The most distinguishing features of Braxton's alternative arrangement are long terms of office, which are meant to secure an independence of judgment and a surer check.[33]

Braxton argues, with Adams, that institutional arrangements should and can replace the improbable civic virtue upon which republics had been grounded. Yet for this project to succeed, the democratic character of the liberal republic must be more qualified than Adams allows.[34] Braxton turns for support to Montesquieu's account of the British constitution as a valuable model. He does not, however, adopt anything like Montesquieu's means. His upper house is not designed around a distinct, interested, and privileged class; it is far closer to Harrington's and Hume's alternative. In general, like Adams, Braxton assumes that adequate checks on democracy and the legislative power do not require hard class antagonisms. An upper house can be designed instead to refine legislative judgment and policy. This improving influence requires superior practical knowledge, the independence to apply this knowledge to public affairs, and the disposition to do so. Although it was designed with the same specifications in mind, Adams's model, Braxton argues, would be deficient in these essential qualities.

As a first step toward generating a prudent upper house, Braxton employs the same refining mode of election as Adams: members are to be elected by the assembly of representatives.[35] The term of office, however, is the defining feature. Indeed, officers "exposed to the uncertain issue of frequent elections" would tend to forsake their duties and the public good out of "fear of giving offense" and for the sake of an "increase in popularity."[36] Braxton's alternative, life terms for members of the upper house, would secure the desired independence of judgment. This extraordinary term of office is intended to refine senators in two other ways. The one is quite simple and obvious: by guaranteeing extensive on-the-job experience in political affairs. The second is more complicated.

A well-designed institution must provide the means and the *motive* to fulfill its constitutional and political functions. The means, and the powers and skills to use them, are more readily provided and attained.

The motive to apply those powers and skills to the right objects and purposes poses a greater challenge. If human beings were strongly disposed to do their duty, no particular provision for institutional character and disposition would be required. Braxton faces an especially difficult challenge because he has dismissed two standard sources of motives, electoral accountability and class distinctions. Precisely the democratic character of Adams's senators was a defect that life terms were to remedy. Class interests and pride are simply passed over, possibly because no sharp class antagonism was present in American society and probably because this class character would corrupt the other desired characteristics. In any case, Braxton's independent upper house needs a character and disposition fitting its functions. How can an institution dispose the wise and experienced to resist the unjust and imprudent measures of the other branches and otherwise devote their resources to the good of the whole society?

Life terms, Braxton argues, will foster in the upper house a distinctive and fitting character. Members of the upper house "should be *induced by the permanence of their appointment* to devote their time to such studies as may best qualify them for that station." These senators will, moreover, "*acquire* firmness from their independency, and wisdom from their reflection and experience, and appropriate both to the good of the state."[37] The upper house is not, in other words, to be filled by a preexisting "senatorial" class. Life terms will, in a sense, *create* a class of dutiful career public servants by "inducing" members of the upper house to live up to the extraordinary institution and office they have the honor to occupy. The members' terms, rather than their social or political status, will impose an expectation, generate a sense of responsibility in individuals, and foster an *esprit de corps* in the body as a whole. This will, Braxton assumes, be sufficient to secure an assiduous and disinterested application of knowledge to law and policy.

If Braxton is, nonetheless, assuming some preexisting virtuous motive, it need be only a very modest one because he has removed many temptations. Members of his upper house would not be distracted and narrowed by reelection concerns. The term of this office, moreover, is likely to filter out those whose ambitions would not be satisfied by such a career and status. The parallels with the purpose and effect of similar terms for justices of the Supreme Court are instructive. Unlike the Court, however, this upper house cannot act alone. Although it is authorized to initiate proposals as well as review those of the lower house, it must accommodate the concerns of representatives, whose shorter term is meant to tie them faithfully to society and the public will.

Thomas Jefferson proposed similar solutions to similar problems. His arguments in the *Notes on the State of Virginia* begin with the defects in Virginia's highly democratic postrevolutionary constitution. In particular, Virginia's bicameral legislature was "too homogenous." Because members of the house and the senate were "chosen by the same electors, at the same time, out of the same subjects," the two houses did not have "different interests or different principles." To achieve an effective check on the dangerous legislative power, the senate's character and motive must not be generated by popular will.[38]

Jefferson suggests that a bicameral division could be based on the distinction between the "honesty" of the general populace and the "wisdom" of a few—a distinction also used by Hume. Following Hume's reasoning closely, Jefferson argues that election by the people "is not generally distinguished for it's [*sic*] wisdom"; "to get the wisest men chosen," the senate should be elected by the lower house. Elsewhere, he allows that election by a temporary body of special electors would be an acceptable alternative, and this alternative is evident in the draft constitution (1783) later appended to the *Notes*. In either case, following Braxton's rationale, senators should be elected for a long term to secure independence of judgment in applying that greater wisdom. Jefferson would acquiesce even to life terms—"anything rather than a mere creation by & dependence on the people"—but this would sacrifice the advantages of an awareness in senators that they must at some point return to being "governed." Instead, a term of nine years followed by a permanent disqualification from that office will "make them perfectly independent when chosen."[39]

The Special Case of Property

The models of Adams, Braxton, and Jefferson have much in common—in particular, upper houses elected by lower houses with the purpose of securing practical wisdom and independent judgment as a check on democratic will and the legislative power. Senators in these American models are not distinguished by, and cannot be motivated by, any distinct social or economic status and interest. Braxton's model especially suggests that the desired qualifications and dispositions can be fostered to a great degree by the institutional design. These models do not depend upon clearly defined social or political classes. Although property qualifications for electors and officials were common in state constitutions, none of these models includes them. Jefferson opposes basing the upper house on a representation of property because wealth and "integrity," the desired quality, are not generally found together.[40]

The use of property qualifications might, therefore, indicate the presence of a competing form of constitution, one closer to a traditional mixed form.[41] Yet property and property qualifications enter constitutions through a number of distinct principles and concerns, only one of which is what might be called the pure principle of mixed government: the incorporation of powerful and antagonistic classes into different institutions of government. This form was almost never advocated in America, and drawing parallels between the House of Lords and various uses of property in American constitutions is more misleading than helpful.[42]

A variation on this theme is derived from Montesquieu, who recommends a type of mixed government as a means of securing a separation of powers and liberty. As Jefferson noted, the search for a principle to distinguish the dispositions of the two legislative houses could lead to wealth as a substitute for a formally privileged class. The elevation of the wealthy to a particular office would invest it with a distinct interest that would resist some legislative and democratic excesses.

A third argument justifies property qualifications, not as an indirect means of securing general liberty but rather as a direct means of securing the specific and universal right of property, which would not be safe in the hands of a single and popularly elected legislative assembly.[43] A popular assembly would be inclined to shift private and public burdens of debts and taxes onto the wealthy, and this sort of policy would violate the principle of an equal and broad right to acquire and dispose of property. One solution would be an upper house more sensible to and more directly interested in the rights of property, and this sort of body could be attained by drawing members, or at least their electors, from those with a significant property interest.

A fourth set of arguments would use a property distinction not as special provision for property rights but rather as a means to secure the general aim of a prudent upper house. If the wealthy tend to be more educated and more deeply involved in public affairs, then property thresholds, especially for candidates, would tend to produce a politically knowledgeable and experienced upper house. Wealth may not be the most precise indicator of the desired qualities, but it can be readily incorporated into a mode of election.[44]

Property, Class, and Prudence in a Senate

These peculiar roles for property in an upper house are woven into another important variation found in the *Essex Result* (1778), commonly attributed to Theophilus Parsons. This astute report on a proposed constitution for Massachusetts builds on familiar liberal republican principles.[45] Safe and free government must also be prudent government, and Parsons's model is informed by this desideratum. Yet his account of the specific dilemmas facing liberal republican constitutions and their remedies departs significantly from the foregoing models. Although Parsons sees society divided not into two classes but rather into multiple interested parties, he proposes an explicitly class-based upper house.

Naturally selfish human beings, Parson argues, tend to compete for political power and to use that power to exploit others. Liberal republican constitutions must manage this selfishness so that government pursues the "good of the whole" while also treating "the interests or professions of all individuals" impartially. Establishing this impartiality requires what he calls a mixed and balanced government. In free societies, however, selfish interests neither arise from nor form into large classes. Free societies produce a wide diversity of particular "interests or professions." Consequently, the particular interests that cause the problems are not related to the elements that Parsons's constitution mixes and balances.[46]

Indeed, he proposes a mix, not of social or economic classes, but rather of the three positive ingredients of just and prudent government: a "disposition to promote" the happiness of the whole; "wisdom" to provide the means to this end; and adequate "power" to execute the decisions of the government. Derived entirely without regard to the claims of the partisans and implemented without their direct or organized input, these elements must be mixed because a good disposition may lack knowledge of the right means to its ends, and neither power nor wisdom will necessarily tend to serve the good of the whole. This mix is then grafted on to a standard separation of powers, and the separation of powers will, in turn, enhance the three characteristics of good government.[47]

The first element of the mix, a disposition to serve the common good, is secured through a representative assembly, which is the vehicle for majority consent to each law. This body "should think, feel, and act" as would "the people at large." To ensure that representatives have "political honesty, probity, and upright intentions to the good of the whole," elections ought to be annual. Nevertheless, Parsons's representatives are to be far more removed and refined than the ones discussed earlier in this chapter. They ought to be drawn from large and populous districts, and election should be by electors. The resulting body ought to be small, one hundred members, in order to avoid the factions and confusion that attend large assemblies.[48]

These refinements notwithstanding, Parsons follows Adams closely in arguing for an upper house to check the representative assembly's ambitious threats to the separation of powers and to check and refine its rash and otherwise imprudent proposals. Like Braxton and Jefferson, though, Parsons wants this senate of "coolness and wisdom" to be fully independent of the representative assembly.[49] He sees the need for distinctly senatorial qualities of mind, but he does not rely on long terms of office to foster them. His constitution, like Harrington's, relies instead upon a preexisting class of sorts, one whose members have already acquired the essential senatorial qualities: learning, experience, and independence of mind. This class can be located with sufficient reliability because, in general, those with a certain degree of wealth tend to have the desired qualities. This class does not, however, include those absorbed in making money. The upper house should be filled with persons of "fortune," those wealthy enough to pursue a refined education and take on the responsibilities of public life and office. Settled in life, such leisured individuals will also tend to have the "firmness and consistence of character" necessary for independent judgment.[50]

While fortune, measured by property ownership, is treated as a good gauge of learning and experience, other provisions are designed to refine the choice of senators. For example, election by electors is recommended, and only those with high-level experience in public office should be eligible for election.[51] These refinements notwithstanding, Parsons does not assume that the leisured few will be adequately disposed to serve the common good. Consequently, Parsons recommends additional provisions, the most important of which is the size of the body. The smaller the body, the more closely its individual members can be observed. Close observation will engage a person's concern for his reputation, and this concern will tend to moderate the influence of merely personal interests and concentrate the mind on measures that could win approbation. The senate ought, therefore, to have around thirty members.[52]

While provisions for independence and prudence dominate the design of this senate, a concern for securing in practice the right to private property leads to a secondary purpose, a representation of property. The idea of a representation of property has roots in Locke, who argues that, when the legislative power is not vested in a representative assembly, the constitution must create a representative assembly for the express and limited purpose of consenting to measures, like tax laws, that would take property.[53] In this manner, Locke allows for a distinction between the general rights or liberties of persons and the particular right of property ownership. Although the *Result*'s representative lower assembly seems to simplify matters, it actually complicates them. A majority within a popular assembly will necessarily represent the majority of society and, therefore, provide effective defense of the rights of "persons," which all enjoy more or less equally. Yet the majority of representatives may not, at any one time, represent the majority of property, which all do not hold equally. The importance of this distinction is amplified by the fact that personal rights, such as the liberty of conscience, can be defended by specific and absolute limits on the legislative powers. Because the government needs revenue and, therefore, ready access to personal wealth, the right to property is less readily protected in practice. An ordinary majority of representatives thus may fail to provide adequate security for private property. Parsons consequently embeds the distinction between personal and property rights in his bicameral legislature by arguing for a separate "representation of property."[54]

This representation is achieved through a property qualification, but it is important to distinguish the purposes of the different property thresholds he uses in his constitution. The high property qualification for senators themselves is designed, as discussed above, to elevate those with learning and practical experience. The high qualification for candidates for governor, however, is intended to make this important office less susceptible to "bribery or undue influence." *Electors* for the governor have no extraordinary property qualification because, as Parsons states, there is no specific property question involved in this office. Electors for the senate, on the other hand, do. Yet the senate, Parsons argues, should represent property generally rather than property holders as such. To achieve this, senators should be apportioned to counties based on the taxes paid by the county, and the electors should be required to meet a threshold of wealth, measured in taxes paid. To guarantee the broad representation of property, this threshold must be "moderate."[55]

The *Result* argues for this representation of property in the senate only because there is no other adequate means for securing property rights. Wealth as such, however, is not used to establish a contrast of character and interests between house and senate. The defining characteristics of a senate must be its coolness and wisdom. Indeed, the small size Parsons recommends seems intended to reduce the degree to which this upper house acts like an estate or faction. Rather than a large group intended to comprehend a distinct class and its peculiar interests, the senate should be small so that individual actions can be observed closely. Senators, moreover, will be held to account for their actions annually.[56]

Yet this feature also poses a problem. Close accountability ties senators to a distinct, if also broad, class of wealthier citizens who would tend to use this influence to advance their particular interests. The representative assembly would be able to frustrate the designs of an interested senate, but it would not be able to prevent the coolness and wisdom of the senate from being corrupted by this influence. With the additional function of defending property rights, Parsons's senate highlights the difficulties with combining and harmonizing distinct purposes and dispositions in one body, and American senates tended to be burdened with a complex of purposes. As the following chapters explore in detail, the framers of the national senate tried to secure in one body not only wisdom, coolness, and a defense of property, but also a representation of states.

THE TALENTED AND DANGEROUS FEW IN ADAMS'S MIXED CONSTITUTION

The difficulties of harmonizing various responsibilities in one institution is more starkly evident in John Adams's *Defense of the Constitutions of Government of the United States of America*, the first volume of which was published and widely discussed in the months leading up to the Philadelphia convention. Adams's unabashedly mixed constitution and class-based senate marks one extreme on the spectrum of possible models, and the *Defense* helps delineate more precisely the problems and questions faced by delegates to the convention. In particular, Adams poses a challenge to both American framers and his earlier *Thoughts:* Unless the ancient antagonism between many and few has been thoroughly subdued, then a liberal republican senate must also serve its traditional function as part of a mixed constitution.[57]

As in the other American models, the constitutionalism of the *Defense* is modern, liberal, and republican. Although the rights of property, "rights of mankind as really as liberty," are of particular concern to Adams, they are part of the more general and equal liberty of individuals to pursue happiness.[58] Among the modern improvements in the "theory and practice of government" are "checks and balances," an independent judiciary, a free press, commerce, and religious toleration,[59] and his model republic is a cosmopolitan, commercial regime that is in accord with "human nature" in serving happiness and protecting universal rights.[60] Adams affirms the dependence of liberty on the rule of law and the dependence of the rule of law on a separation between the "naturally distinct" legislative and executive authorities.[61]

Yet when he combines the principle of separation with the mixed form, the separation of powers seems to take a back seat to the independence and balance of "orders": the monarchical, the aristocratic, and the democratic.[62] This type of mixed constitution is necessary, in part, because even a cosmopolitan and commercial republic will divide into two parties, the many and the few.[63] In general, the many have less education, status, and property, while the few have more of everything. Our "moral and political equality" does not entail equality "in natural and acquired qualities, in virtues, talents and riches," and a relative few persons will reap the benefits of the "sources of inequality . . . common to every people." Those born of "illustrious" families, moreover, will tend to have "advantages in education and opportunities and exposure to public affairs."[64] This greater experience and learning can be, as in the *Result,* a boon to government. But where Parsons sees diverse and diffusive interests, Adams sees two antagonistic classes. Neither of these classes is "honester or wiser." Both aristocrats and democrats are infected with a "thirst for power" that arises from "rapacious and ambitious passions" common to all. A constitution must "compel all to respect the common right, the public good, universal law, in preference to all private and partial considerations."[65]

Restraining the few is a particularly difficult task. The more wealthy, prominent, educated, and respected will tend to develop into an oligarchic menace. When mixed in a single legislative assembly, the learning, "cunning," and rhetorical skills of this elite will overwhelm the "plain sense" of the modest commoner. Popular representation and democratic authority will diminish, leaving in control only "a few rich and honourable families, who have united with each other against both the people and the first magistrate." Unless it is "judiciously managed in the constitution," this aristocracy will "destroy *all equality and liberty with the consent and ac-clamations of the people themselves.*"[66] The constitution, therefore, must remove these few from the representative assembly and "tie their hands" by collecting them into a "senate." This senate will fail in its purpose if it merely represents the few and if members of this class are free to sit in the representative assembly. The senate must actually circumscribe the entire class.

A few other features of this upper house are clearly articulated. Once the classes are separated, balance between them requires a separation of powers; all executive powers, for example, must be removed from the senate and vested entirely in "a single person."[67] Drawing on the British constitution, "the most stupendous fabric of human invention," Adams favors life terms for senators. Life terms are necessary not to establish an institutional character but rather to avoid the dependence, instability, and faction that attend elections.[68]

At this point, though, Adams's defense of America's bicameral legisla-tures becomes, at least in effect, a critique of American senates, including his own earlier model. The designs of these relatively democratic upper houses took for granted America's broad and relatively equal distribution of property. In other words, they had assumed away the antagonisms that would necessitate a balance of social and economic classes. These circum-stances, Adams argues here, are evanescent. The degeneration in America "might not be very rapid," but hard class divisions will emerge. Then demagoguery, corruption, and faction will come to mark elections, and senates to any significant degree dependent upon popularity will fail to serve their essential functions of checking democratic will and containing oligarchic ambition.[69]

Up to this point, Adams's upper house resembles Montesquieu's. In addition to protecting democratic control from the rich and well born, this institution would establish in the legislature a clash of interests that would check democratic will and control the legislative power. Yet unlike Montesquieu, Adams wants his upper house also to be a provision for legislative prudence. Once the interest and ambition of the rich and well born are confined within a senate and checked by a representative branch and an independent executive, he argues, the government and society can benefit from this elite's "abilities and virtues." He is confident that a strictly class-based check will serve as the necessary "reservoir of wisdom" and will be inclined to apply that wisdom to general goods. "The aristocratic part of the community . . . are noble patriots when they are kept under; they are really then the best men and the best citizens."[70]

These seem more like Rome's nobles than Montesquieu's, and Adams does argue that inadequate separation and checks had allowed Roman nobles to follow their grasping passions. Roman nobles, however, held a position of power and status that could satisfy great pride and ambition, and they were supported by a regime of honor that has been replaced by modern republican principles.[71] Roman patricians could claim to be the finest embodiments of virtues admirable in themselves and essential to the nobility, power, and even survival of the republic. America's circumstances and principles, on the other hand, would not tend to sustain a class pride and status that might encourage a public spiritedness. Liberal principles do not establish for emulation standards of public honor or nobility. Instead, they lower and diffuse standards of excellence and, in the main, privatize them. These problems are only heightened by Adams's insistence on life terms, which weaken public approbation as an inducement to serve the general good. Adams's senate, moreover, would be quite large, thereby sacrificing whatever good effects a small body might have on individual responsibility and character.

The difficulties of integrating prudence and public spiritedness into a class-based, class-conscious senate argue for simplifying and harmonizing the senate's functions, but these difficulties cannot, by themselves, justify abandoning the hard checks of a mixed legislature. Adams's scheme certainly was, in republican America, an impracticable extreme. Yet his challenge remained. If the conflict between many and few continues to threaten democratic liberty and individual rights, then it must be controlled, and a class-based bicameral legislature would be the most eligible remedy. Even if liberal republican America had or could meliorate class antagonism enough to forgo a deliberate mixing of class interests into the institutions of government, problems remain. Additional responsibilities, as we have seen, threaten to make the liberal republican senate an unworkable hybrid of functions and motives. Even a senate with uncomplicated responsibilities requires some provision for character and motive.

What could move knowledgeable and experienced senators to employ these qualities in service to common interests?

UNMIXING THE PRUDENT SENATE: THE NATIONAL CHARACTER OF MADISON'S UPPER HOUSE

This problem of competing motives, and the sad fact that the narrower interests tended to dominate, was a leading lesson James Madison drew from his experience in the Continental Congress, a body responsible for national legislation but composed of representatives of state governments. These state representatives frequently ignored their national responsibility and advanced instead the particular interests of their states. Madison's study of the ills in national and state constitutions gradually converged on a senate as the principal institutional cure. Along the way, he addressed the complications and quandaries of class, property, multiple functions, compound character, and virtue. Although a complete account of this senate was not articulated until he wrote as Publius in the *Federalist Papers,* his thoughts leading up to the Constitutional Convention sketch the main features of a coherent liberal republican senate that could serve as the "great anchor of the Government."

The Special Case of Property

Dogging this development, though, was a discrete concern over property rights. Madison shared with Adams a fear that wealth would eventually be concentrated into the hands of a few, generating a potentially destructive conflict between those with much more and those with much less.[72] Madison articulates this concern in response to a request for ideas concerning a constitution for Kentucky, a "state in embryo." In his discussion of the legislative branch, Madison turns first, however, to the need for "wisdom and steadiness," the priority in all of his thinking on the legislatures: "The want of these qualities is the grievance complained of in all our republics." He suggests a number of provisions for prudent scrutiny of law and policy, "as a valuable safeguard both to public interests & to private rights," and a senate with a long term, four or five years, is the most important of them.[73] The property problem arises in response to a question about the basis of representation. The specific difficulties of protecting property rights lead him to a distinction between the rights of persons and the rights of property.

As with Adams, the property problem cuts two ways; those with little property may either abuse their power, presumably through attacks on the wealthy, or "sell" that power to the rich, "who will abuse it." Neither a generally restricted suffrage nor a generally unrestricted one will protect the legitimate powers and rights of both parties. Madison's compromise— provisional, qualified in principle, and limited in scope—is broad suffrage for one house and restricted suffrage for the other. His aim is not exactly, it seems, a representation of property; he does not recommend a property restriction on candidacy for the senate, and he does not depend on an interest in property to animate the upper house. He insists, though, that the "rights of property . . . be respected as well as personal rights in the choice of Rulers." Restricted suffrage for one house might give some "influence" to those with property without violating the principle of equality by endowing the propertied with "legal privileges."[74]

These concerns about class conflict and property rights would re-emerge in the convention and after, so it is striking that in the period leading up to the meeting in Philadelphia, Madison's ideas for a new national constitution do not include similar defenses against threats to property. Certainly other concerns dominated his thoughts at that time; he continued, for example, to worry over parochial influences, and his sketch of a new national government eliminates state influences on national institutions and officials. Yet this is only the beginning of an explanation. The other side of this coin was Madison's confidence in the just and impartial character of the national government, which is most evident in his radical proposal for a national veto over state laws. That confidence rested not on a superior mix and balance of classes but rather on the expectation that the national government would not be similarly susceptible to the influence of interested or factious majorities. Madison had, it seems, found an answer to Adams's challenge.

Parochialism and Imprudence in the Confederation and Its Small Republics

In the period leading up to the Constitutional Convention, Madison concentrated on a glaring defect of the Articles of Confederation: the tendency of its government to sacrifice the long term and general needs of the nation to the interests of the states. In both the Continental Congress and the legislature of Virginia, Madison had been exasperated by the "predominance of temporary and partial interests over . . . just & extended maxims of policy." The ill-effects of this disregard for "National Character" and "national credit" were apparent in all national policies, from revenue requisitions to foreign policy.[75] In anticipation of a convention to amend the Articles, Madison drafted a detailed diagnosis, his *Vices of the Political System of the United States,* which explained the necessary and desirable qualities of a just and prudent national republic. Subsequent letters began to delineate the institutional features of a new national constitution. When the diagnosis and the remedies are read together, the large role of the senate in this new order becomes evident.[76]

In general, the *Vices* is an examination of the defects of the small, state republics, both as independent polities and as constituents of the whole. The latter character, in particular, helps explain Madison's vociferous and relentless objections in the convention to a representation of states in the national legislature. As constituents, the states were not complying with national laws and treaties, a problem "inherent" in confederacies.[77] Worse, they tended to encroach, by omission and commission, on national authority at the risk of national "calamities." Particularly in the sphere of foreign policy, this was due to "the sphere of life" from which most state legislators were taken and "the circumstances under which their legislative business is carried on."[78] In other words, these legislators had limited and mainly local experience and were under the influence of primarily local interests. This parochialism extended to relations between the states; trade restrictions and debtor relief policies, for example, were rarely informed by any "spirit of the Union" or prudent concern for the general and long-term welfare of the nation. Overall, the "national dignity, interest, and revenue," and the specific needs of a regular and prosperous economic life, had been "defeated by the perverseness of particular states."[79]

The state constitutions, moreover, were themselves flawed. Instability in state legislatures generated "mutability" and "multiplicity" in their laws, and these "pestilent" qualities undermined the rule of law, liberty, and, more specifically, economic prosperity. Each of these ends, and good government generally, requires stability and system in law and policy.[80] Many laws enacted by these highly democratic governments were also simply unjust, and this potentially "greater evil" was calling into question the fundamental principle of republican government—that the people are the "safest Guardians both of the public Good and of private rights." Indeed, the more "fatal" of the causes of injustice was "the people themselves." If a majority is animated by the same interest, it will use its control over the government to oppress the remaining minorities.[81]

Here was plentiful evidence of an incompatibility between majority rule and just government, and yet Madison's sketch of a new national order concentrates instead on refining prudent deliberation. This focus on what seems to be a secondary concern can be explained, at least in part, by the fact that Madison had already understood the moderating effects of a large republic on majority will. Democratic majorities are less dangerous in a larger, more populous republic because "a common interest or passion is less apt to be felt" as society "becomes broken into a greater variety of interests, of pursuits, of passions." The dispersion of those with similar interests will frustrate the organization of factions, and those that do form will tend to "check each other."[82] Society in a large republic will, therefore, be marked not by a general antagonism between broad classes but rather by competition between relatively small factions. The diversity of interests would reduce in particular the threat of majoritarian attacks on property. By relieving the senate of the complications that troubled the models of Parsons and Adams, these general and specific effects pave the way for a more focused and harmonious institution.

A large republic, however, does not supply the positive conditions for steady and prudent deliberation about national interests. The diversity of interests that solves the problem of partisan majorities makes the object of deliberation—common interests—more difficult to locate in practice. The *Vices* attends to this problem in its discussions of the qualities and motives necessary to attain prudent attention to national affairs. Although these characteristics are not assigned to any particular institution, Madison's account of the conditions that promote and foster them outlines a senate in fair detail.

Prudence and National Character

Just and wise legislation will not emerge, other than by accident, from the unmitigated calculation and contention of particular interests. Legislative deliberations ought to be guided, at some point, by a broader perspective and more general aims. At least some legislators need to be endowed, in Madison's modest terms, with a "prudent regard to their own good as involved in the general and permanent good of the Community."[83] This enlarged perspective, as in Harrington, sits between mere selfishness and self-abnegating virtue but is far closer to the former. It is a practical understanding that one's own safety and prosperity depend upon the safety and prosperity of the whole and that the pursuit of particular and immediate interests will tend to harm those very interests in the long run. In a regime of liberal individualism, however, even this approximation of disinterestedness is rare.

This prudence is also rarely in a position of sufficient influence in human affairs. Knowing human nature, Madison does not expect this prudent understanding alone to rule over the urgent demands of an individual's interests and passions. What, moreover, could motivate a legislator to enforce the commands of this practical knowledge against the immediate demands of the citizenry? Madison seems, at this point, to fall back on extraordinary and preexisting characteristics: just and prudent government requires a "process of election" that elevates the "purest and noblest characters."[84] This appeal to virtue, however, is modified by Madison's other arguments. His account of prudent self-interest has already established a modest standard of purity. Nobility, moreover, is defined more precisely as a "respect for character," a strong desire for the good opinion of others.[85]

A sensitivity to the praise and blame of a discerning and critical audience, Madison suggests, would deter narrowly interested and otherwise neglectful uses of power and encourage the responsible application of practical knowledge to public affairs. This argument appears less odd and contrived when put in the context of the problem Madison is trying to solve. He needs to locate a disposition not only to acquire practical political knowledge but also to press its conclusions in the face of imprudent majorities and fellow legislators. That motive must be situated somewhere between heroic virtues, which are improbable, and class interests, which are corrupting.

Madison recognizes two obvious problems with his solution. First, where is the audience to animate this concern for personal reputation? Modern republics, he notes, tend to foster concern only for the opinions of the general public. In this circumstance, a respect for the opinion of others would hardly serve to check or refine the ill-considered demands of the majority. Madison assumes, however, that individuals with "extended views," a cosmopolitan perspective, will be aware of another source of reputation—how the nation's policies fare in the court of international opinion. If these cosmopolitans are also imbued with "national pride," they will be personally sensible to disdain or contempt of other nations, and insofar as these opinions will be more disinterested, they will tend to be an improving guide to domestic deliberation.[86]

This solution leads to the second problem. What makes persons of this sort desirable as legislators is their unwillingness to appeal to popular passions and interests. As a consequence, they "will never be followed by the multitude." They will, in other words, rarely be successful popular politicians.[87] Although Madison does not offer a specific "process of election" that would elevate the desired types, we know it cannot be the direct popular form used for representatives. We also know that for these prudent legislators to have a sure effect, they cannot be mixed into the larger mass of representatives. The assembly of prudent cosmopolitans, moreover, would need to be small. The *personal* responsibility that engages a respect for character, Madison argues, is weakened when observation of individual actions is obstructed by "multitudes" sharing "the praise and the blame." Altogether, these thoughts leave us but a small step from a model senate.

Madison's Model Senate

Three letters Madison wrote around this time sketch the institutional order that follows from the vices of states and confederation.[88] It should be noted that they recommend no particular provision for defending property. Although the threat to property was one of the principal concerns in the *Vices*, that threat issued not from majorities as such, but from majorities in the small republics of the states.[89] Basing national offices on proportional representation of the national citizenry would shield the national government from the influence of parochial and minority state interests. Consequently, Madison anticipates that the national government, given the right design, could meet the "great desideratum which has not yet been found for Republican Governments": the need for a "disinterested & dispassionate umpire in disputes between different passions & interests" in society. He is confident enough in the superior qualities of a national government to recommend that it be given a veto over state laws to defend its authority and the rights of individuals.[90]

Madison's upper house, consequently, arises not from a concern about the injustices of a *democratic* assembly but rather from a concern about the imprudence of a "numerous" assembly. The second house, therefore, should be a small, more stable, and "select" senate. The stability will be instituted through longer terms and a gradual rotation that will "leave in office a large majority of old members." His high expectations for this institution are most evident in his recommendation that the senate in particular control the veto over state laws. This strongly suggests that more than any other national institution the senate is to embody the rare qualities of a "dispassionate & disinterested umpire" that he discusses here and in the *Vices*.[91]

These principles and forms were introduced to the Constitutional Convention through what has been called the Virginia Plan.[92] Although a mere skeleton of a constitution, this plan fills a crucial blank: a mode of election for the senate. Senators were to be selected by the house of representatives, and its choices would be confined to nominees submitted by the state legislatures.[93]

Insofar as senators would not be elected by the people and would not be required to represent particular and equal constituencies, this form seems to violate the requirement that national representation be proportional to population, a fundamental principle of Madison's national constitution. One explanation for this apparent anomaly is correct, as far as it goes: "the Senate's representative character was incidental to its substantive functions and deliberative qualities," and this form of election is designed to serve the latter.[94] Pushing this point a bit further, the senate's being a legislative institution does not require, in principle, that it also be directly representative, and Madison's senate was not intended to be representative of any particular constituencies. As long as it is attached to the general national good, it no more violates a principle of proportionality than does the judiciary. Even so, this senate would not in fact violate proportionality because it would be elected by the proportionally representative house. Its membership would reflect that proportionality as much as would any law passed by the same assembly.

This arrangement is burdened by more serious doubts. Why in the world would Madison choose a mode of election that threatens this crucial institution with two viruses: a potentially ruinous dependence of senators upon the lower house and a narrowing dependence upon parochial state governments, the mortal disease of the confederation? Madison was obviously aware of the dangers; the plan urges a term of office that is "sufficient to ensure" the independence of senators from the lower house, and it prohibits senators from holding "any office established by a peculiar State" during their terms and for some number of years thereafter.[95] Given the importance of this institution to a sound national government, he must have had good reasons for adopting this apparently risky form.

The most obvious defense of selection by the lower house, as argued by Hume, Adams, Jefferson, and others, is a more select election, one that would have a tendency to elevate the cosmopolitans who would not be favored in popular elections. Yet why not use, as did the Maryland constitution, temporary bodies of electors to secure a select election without any risk of dependence? Madison apparently was seeking certain qualities of judgment that only a lower national house would have. In general, sitting legislators are particularly aware of the skills and character appropriate to a senate, and at least some representatives would have significant experience in the national legislature. The lower house of a large republic, moreover, would also be moderated and broadened in its views by the diversity of interests it represented. It would be led by that diversity to take a more or less comprehensive view of the problems the government would need to address. This national assembly would, therefore, be more fit than local bodies of electors to judge the qualities and experience appropriate to a national senate.

Two other considerations argue for using national representatives as electors. Because members of the lower house would have a personal interest, not necessarily shared by temporary and local electors, in the authority and reputation of the national legislature, they would be interested in electing a senate that would enhance their status. Selection by the lower house, moreover, would make election to the senate a high and strictly national honor, thereby enhancing the attractiveness of senatorial service.

Election by the lower house, however, risks the distracting turmoil of electioneering as ambitious representatives employ intrigue, faction, and corruption to secure election to the senate. This danger helps explain the restriction on candidacy, as in Harrington's *Oceana*. Because only some number nominated by the state legislatures would be eligible for election, electioneering would be complicated by the need to secure the favor of at least two independent and quite different bodies. A limited list of state nominees would also prevent a majority coalition in the lower house from filling the senate with persons from one region of the country. That a state legislature cannot directly influence even the probability of its nominee(s) being elected qualifies the risk of state influence that attends this mode of nomination. Indeed, the one way a state could improve the chances of success would be to nominate candidates with the broad views and other qualities that would appeal to a diverse body like the national house of representatives. Certainly narrow state partisans would tend not to fare well.[96]

The great advantage of this complicated mode of election is that it "*obscures* constituency" and even obliterates it.[97] It thereby achieves a goal crucial to Madison's whole plan for a national government. At the top of his list of criticisms of the existing national and state legislatures is the debilitating "spirit of *locality*" with which their forms and circumstances infected them. Legislators with local ties tend to "lose sight of the aggregate interests of the community."[98] The mode of election prescribed in the Virginia Plan removes senators about as far as possible from any sort of locality. Nor is its character defined or determined by the interests of a particular social or economic class. The plan does not recommend property qualifications for senators, and it recommends that senators be paid a "liberal stipend."[99]

On the other hand, the spirit of locality is unavoidable, and is even desirable, in representatives. The Virginia plan's provisions for direct elections, term limits, and voter recall of representatives during their terms constitute a highly democratic lower house. Madison's liberal republican legislature is divided, then, into two essential but incomplete contributions to the general good: a representative house that ties the government securely to the particular circumstances and general interests of society and a prudent senate that is national in character and free to deliberate about the interests of the nation as whole.

A few general themes emerge from this survey of early American senates. One is the common foundation: a strictly modern, democratic republicanism serving strictly liberal principles and purposes. Another is the agreement that senates are essential provisions for stability and prudence in legislative deliberations. The last theme is the variety of forms sharing these foundations and aims. The variations are generated not by ideological paradigms but rather by thoughtful attempts to resolve unsettled *practical* questions: about the good and ill effects of democratic accountability and representative assemblies, about the importance of prudence and how to establish it in the legislature, about the degree to which antagonistic class divisions could be ameliorated and mixed forms avoided, and about the need for special provisions to protect property rights.

Even though the Philadelphia convention opened with Madison's refined model, the delegates would revisit these thorny questions. Indeed, Madison struggled throughout for even the rudiments of his "great anchor," and what emerged from the convention's quarrels and compromises was a convoluted hybrid. Before descending into an examination of that decisive event, it is worth pausing to recall Madison's benchmark: a liberal republican senate of prudence, relieved of dependence on improbable virtues and free from the complications of either a direct representation of property or an interested check on democracy. This principal provision for wise and steady deliberation about national concerns was to be above the partiality of any particular constituency or class and attentive to national interests without regard to short-term personal concerns like reelection. How and why did the Constitutional Convention resist and revise this model? Did it discover and repair critical flaws and omissions? Or was its version merely an unavoidable compromise?

FOUR

The Constitutional Convention
The Senate and Representation

The structure of legislative representation was the most vexing issue of the Constitutional Convention. The convention came close to collapsing against this obstruction; once it was overcome, although other difficulties remained, the convention appeared certain to produce a final document. As James Madison lamented during the debates, "The great difficulty lies in the affair of Representation; and if this could be adjusted, all others would be surmountable."[1] At the center of this struggle was the composition of what would be called the Senate. Though this is common knowledge, the richness and complexity of how the Senate affected, and was affected by, the struggle over representation are lost or obscured in many accounts of the process.

As we pointed out in chapter 1, in most accounts the goal is to describe or explain the politics of the convention more generally, not those of the Senate in particular. Even in the few accounts that emphasize the Senate, a more complete picture often escapes a focus on either the clash and compromise of various geographic and material political interests, including those between large and small states, or on the alleged class interests of the framers in producing an antidemocratic Senate. Political deals and elite sentiments played significant roles, but the emphasis on such interests neglects the part that republican ideas and principles played in shaping the compromise. While it would be stretching the truth to argue that the representational compromise came into existence because of the Senate, or more precisely, because of the near consensus on the need for an upper house, we demonstrate the significant ways in which the widespread agreement on the need for a Senate in a stronger national system helped to shape and produce the compromise, rather than the other way around. A republican Senate was crucial to the new system, regardless of any political compromises. The problem, however, was that the Senate would become essential as well to the resolution of the question of federalism; that is, the extent to which the new constitution would embrace or eliminate the role of states as sovereign actors. As a result, despite the agreement on a senate in principle, and for republican purposes, the actual

Senate that would emerge from the convention was the complicated and compromised product of the most important and bitter struggle of that summer.

SETTING THE AGENDA:
THE VIRGINIA RESOLUTIONS AND A SENATE

The Constitutional Convention began with a mandate from the Congress of the Confederation to meet "for the sole and express purpose of revising the Articles of Confederation" to "render the federal constitution adequate to the exigencies of Government & the preservation of the Union" (*Records*, 3:14). The problems and weaknesses of the Confederation were such that, at least at an elite level, many believed change was necessary. Congress's lack of power and frequent inability to act (often due to a lack of quorum or the need for a supermajority for certain decisions) demanded reform. Although many among the political elite favored reform, two rather different paths could be followed. The route suggested by Congress's authorization and the one in the minds of most Americans who were mindful of the situation was a strengthening of the Confederation, mostly of the powers granted to Congress, without altering the fundamental basis of confederation. As we have seen, Madison, and others, had been laboring to cut another path. This one led toward consolidation; that is, a truly national government to replace confederation. Did either of these paths to reform imply the need for a Senate? A reformed confederation, with an enhanced but still very circumscribed role for the national government, did not. Perhaps a more clearly defined executive was necessary to run the day-to-day business and enforce the laws, but a second legislative chamber was not. Consolidation, however, did at least imply a second legislative chamber. Consolidation meant a real government with significant powers, and a real government entailed all the features of a properly constituted government that were part of liberal republicanism, including a tripartite separation of powers and a divided legislature. With the power came the attendant balances and safeguards against the abuse of that power. All this and more was evident in Madison's writings prior to the convention.

After the first delegates arrived in Philadelphia in early May 1787, a quorum would not be attained for nearly two weeks after the scheduled starting date of the fourteenth. Madison made sure that Virginia was there in force from the beginning, and he used the potentially idle time to meet with his state delegation and draft a plan for a new constitution to be used to set the agenda for the convention. The results were what have come to be known as the Virginia or Randolph resolutions, or the Virginia plan. On May 29, just after final agreements on the rules of procedure for the convention, Edmund Randolph of the Virginia delegation presented "sundry propositions," which became the opening business for the deliberations of the Committee of the Whole on May 30 and set the agenda for the summer's work (*Records*, 1:16, 18–22).

In contrast to the final product of the convention, the Virginia plan can seem more like a skeleton than a blueprint of a constitution. It was relatively short and not very specific about many of the powers or institutional structures of the new government. Madison, however, knew that the few fundamentals in the Virginia plan were the "ground-work" for the creation of a truly national system. Immediately after the one-sentence introduction resolving that the "Articles of Confederation ought to be so corrected and enlarged" as to accomplish their stated objectives, the second article of the Virginia resolutions stated "that the right of Suffrage in the National Legislature ought to be proportioned to the Quotas of contribution, or to the number of free inhabitants, as the one or the other may seem best in different cases" (*Records*, 1:20). Here was the change in the principle of representation upon which Madison staked the rest of his project of reform. The Articles of Confederation had defined but one governmental institution: Congress. The Confederation Congress was unicameral, and representation was apportioned on the basis of state equality; states sent delegations of varying size to Congress, but votes were taken by state, each state having one vote. Just as Madison envisioned, the Virginia plan altogether eliminated the representation of states as corporate or sovereign units and sought to substitute the direct representation of citizens in the first branch of his proposed national legislature. Madison's thinking about legislative design went a step further when he and the Virginians proposed a second branch for the national legislature.

The next, or third, resolution stated "that the National Legislature ought to consist of two branches" (*Records*, 1:20). Although some details were left unspecified, the contrast between the two branches of the legislature was stark. If one keeps in mind that the Virginia plan was designed for an unprecedentedly large republic, the provisions for direct election, recall, and mandatory rotation, envisioned a *radically* democratic lower house. While some of these stipulations might not have been to Madison's liking, during the convention he defended the democratic nature of the first chamber and even moved to double the number of representatives.[2] In sharp contrast, the upper house was to be selected by the lower out of nominations made by state legislatures and was to consist of a smaller number of members with a long tenure and staggered terms to "ensure their independency" (*Records*, 1:20).

Proportional representation based on direct elections and a smaller, insulated Senate were Madison's two fundamental features of institutional reform in the new government. They were in tension automatically by the dictates of republican theory. But there was a practical tension as well. Could Madison get both institutions as he envisaged them, or did the characteristics of the two chambers in their ideal forms make them, in practice, mutually unattainable? Proportional representation was not essential to the republican purpose of the Senate, which was its independence and detached judgment.[3] While proportional representation was explicitly tied to what would become the House of Representatives, the representative basis of the Senate was rather different and did not require proportionality among the states. The fifth resolution stated that "the members of the second branch of the National Legislature ought to be elected by those of the first, out of a proper number of persons nominated by the individual Legislatures" (*Records*, 1:20). Proportionality was not mandated in outcomes but rather only in the influence on the selection process, and even this was tempered by the states' role in nominations. In fact, the nomination by the state legislatures, though intended by Madison to be part of the process of senatorial elevation, independence, and detachment, instead immediately introduced the idea that the Senate was tied, more than the House, to the states, as states (though in theory the House could pick whomever it wanted from the nominations).[4] In this way, two of Madison's primary republican objectives—direct representation of national citizens and a refined selection process for the Senate (which were to provide tension and balance in the actual workings of government)—immediately came into conflict in the attempt to design the government. Madison, as he would discover, was in danger very early in the convention of being hoisted by his own republican petard.

More than any other delegate, Madison had "gamed" the convention beforehand by anticipating the divisions based on state size and counting the probable votes accordingly. Madison could do this because unlike the other delegates, he had a plan by which to judge potential reactions. The only evidence we have shows that Madison's strategic calculations centered on the change in the basis of representation with proportional representation at its core. Anticipating an equal vote by each state at the convention, Madison predicted a victory for the new principle of representation based on a coalition between the currently large states and the prospectively large states.[5] States would be for or against this new principle, not so much on the basis of abstract principles, but because of rather straightforward calculations of political advantage and disadvantage. Power and principle mixed freely in Madison's view of the crux of the matter. It is worth bearing in mind that for Madison proportional representation was a logical corollary to the representation of national citizens as individuals; it was not simply or even primarily a power grab by the large states.

Not everything in the Virginia plan had to be accepted simultaneously, but Madison seemed to think that once the grand (and most controversial) principle of the new basis of representation was accepted, the Senate would follow as a derivative of that acceptance (with bicameralism taken for granted). What Madison did not foresee, at least publicly, was how delicate the relationship was between his two key goals (the basis of representation and a select, insulated Senate). Madison apparently did not anticipate that the change in the principle of representation would not find its serious opposition in general principle or even in its application to the lower chamber, but in the specific application to the other chamber of the legislature. In particular, he did not anticipate how an alteration in the basis of the selection of the Senate could upset everything else in the bargain.

In no other institution did power and principle come together in such a direct way. The institution that enjoyed a near consensus on its desirability on pure republican grounds (so much so that Madison perhaps did not think as carefully about its constitution as he should have), nevertheless became the principal point of contention during that summer. Thus did the power struggle that he anticipated, and the institution he took for granted, collide. Once it became clear, early in the convention's proceedings, that most of the delegates were amenable to a centralizing alternative to the Articles of Confederation, the real difficulty became the place of states as corporate entities in a more national system, and the key to resolving that problem was in the structure of the legislature. The devil was in the details when the agreement in principle on bicameralism and a strong and independent Senate confronted the political realities of constitution making.

CONSENSUS

Though they confronted a daunting task, the delegates who convened in Philadelphia had some advantages. The formidable talents of many of the participants notwithstanding, it just so happened that the formidable talents who were opposed to the project of fortifying the national government decided to boycott the meeting, partly in the expectation that it would collapse under its own weight. The convention was, as a result, populated by many of the most nationally minded among the political elite (table 4.1). This not only greatly enhanced the prospects for something more than a mere reformation of the Articles of Confederation, it broadened the level of agreement on several features of a good government. The delegates shared similar conclusions based on their republican beliefs and experiences in their state governments. One such conclusion was a widely shared belief in the desirability of a two-chamber legislature, with an upper house to check the more popular lower house.

At several points during the debates, the delegates expressed confidence about the self-evident appeal of bicameralism. As Virginia's George Mason argued, "Much has been said of the unsettled state of the mind of the people. He believed the mind of the people of America, as elsewhere, was unsettled as to some points, but settled as to others. In two points he was sure it was well settled: 1. in an attachment to republican government. 2. in an attachment to more than one branch in the Legislature" (*Records*, 1:339). Even the democratic soul of the convention from unicameral Pennsylvania, James Wilson, vigorously defended the need for a two-chamber legislature: "Is there no danger of a Legislative despotism? Theory and practice both proclaim it. If the Legislative authority be not restrained, there can be neither liberty nor stability; and it can only be restrained by dividing it within itself, into distinct and independent branches. In a single house there is no check, but the inadequate one, of the virtue and good sense of those who compose it" (*Records*, 1:254).

The extent of this accord on bicameralism is evident from the opening actions of the convention. The Virginia resolution for a two-house legislature was the opening item on May 31, and it engendered no debate or

TABLE 4.I. States and Their Delegations at the Constitutional Convention

Three Most Populous	Geographically Large and Prospectively Populous	Less Populous
Massachusetts	*North Carolina*	**Connecticut**
Gerry, Elbridge	Blount, William	Ellsworth, Oliver
Gorham, Nathaniel	Davie, William	Johnson, William Samuel
King, Rufus	Richardson	Sherman, Roger
Strong, Caleb	Martin, Alexander	
	Spaight, Richard Dobbs	**New York**
Pennsylvania	Williamson, Hugh	Hamilton, Alexander
Clymer, George		Lansing, John
Fitzsimmons, Thomas	*South Carolina*	Yates, Robert
Franklin, Benjamin	Butler, Pierce	
Ingersol, Jared	Pinckney, Charles	**New Jersey**
Mifflin, Thomas	Pinckney, Charles	Brearly, David
Morris, Gouverneur	Cotesworth	Dayton, Jonathon
Morris, Robert	Rutledge, John	Houston, William
Wilson, James		Churchill
	Georgia	Livingston, William
Virginia	Baldwin, Alexander	Patterson, William
Blair, John	Few, William	
Madison, James	Houston, William	**Delaware**
Mason, George	Pierce, William	Basset, Richard
McClurg, James		Bedford, Gunning
Randolph, Edmund		Broome, Jacob
Washington, George		Dickinson, John
Wythe, George		Read, George
		Maryland
		Carroll, Daniel
		Jenifer, Daniel
		Martin, Luther
		McHenry, James
		Mercer, John Francis
		New Hampshire*
		Gilman, Nicholas
		Langdon, John

Note: States with substantial slave populations are italicized.
*New Hampshire's delegates did not arrive until after the Great Compromise.

opposition. As Madison recorded in his notes, "The Third (3d) Resolution 'that the national Legislature ought to consist of two branches' was agreed to without debate or dissent, except that of Pennsylvania, given probably from complaisance to Doc. Franklin who was understood to be partial to a single House of legislation" (*Records*, 1:48). Yet Pennsylvania's dissent on this issue disappeared thereafter. This effectively unanimous vote on bicameralism took place even after it was clear that the Virginia plan would end the equal representation in both houses, a change to which at least Delaware, the smallest of the small, took exception only the day before. Yet Delaware, with its explicit instructions to protect state equality, did not object on this first vote on bicameralism. Small states, it would seem, at first saw the need for bicameralism, not the threat to state representation. It would take more debate before the intractable relationship between these two facets of the convention's work—the number of legislative chambers and the ratio of representation—became apparent to the delegates and became the crux of the proceedings. After the connection was made and the battle begun between the so-called large and small states, bicameralism faced its only threat in the form of the New Jersey plan and its adherence to a unicameral legislature based on state equality. The turn against bicameralism came when the small-state coalition realized it could only hope to preserve state equality in a one-chamber legislature similar to that of the Confederation. There was no chance of agreement to equal representation in both chambers. As we shall see, the delegates rejected the largely tactical unicameral threat rather easily.

The accord on bicameralism was based in no small part on the delegates' widely shared assumptions about the distinct and special purposes of the upper house. While the lower house was to be simplicity itself in its democratic form and purpose, a carefully constructed Senate was essential to balancing and enhancing the legislative process. To demonstrate the nature of the consensus on the general design and functions of a republican Senate, we found and categorized every remark or speech that referred to a desired or ideal trait or purpose of a properly designed Senate.[6] From the beginning of the proceedings to July 16 and the vote on the Great Compromise, nineteen delegates, most of the active participants during the period, offered at least some opinion about what they felt were the important characteristics of a Senate. Some only hinted at their preferences; others expounded repeatedly and at some length. The total number of remarks or speeches on the subject is forty, citing sixty-five preferred traits or purposes of a Senate (table 4.2).[7] The table displays the list of speakers in chronological order and the classification of their comments. The comments are classified first by whether the speaker was referring to a preferred characteristic (or trait) of the proposed Senate or to a purpose (or goal) the Senate was to serve, and second by the specific characteristic or goal.

Though the delegates cite a number of desired characteristics, the list is a harmoniously interrelated one, and the level of agreement is evident. The trio of traits—small size, select appointment, and independence—account for nearly half the references to an ideal upper house and elicited no dissent beyond John Dickinson's claim that small size was not important (see below). At fourteen references, small size is the most frequently invoked trait, and we shall discuss its central importance as the debate over legislative apportionment unfolds. The remarks about size manifest concern for producing the quality of debate in which only a small group can engage. Madison would provide this trenchant summary of the logic of numbers: "In all very numerous assemblies, of whatever characters composed, passion never fails to wrest the scepter from reason. Had every Athenian citizen been a Socrates, every Athenian assembly would still have been a mob."[8] Most delegates seem to have agreed with this judgment. The small size, length of term, and process of selection would also mitigate the passions and precipitation to which more numerous assemblies are prone. A small number of senators, who would be, by and large, better men because they had achieved their positions through some refining mode of selection, and who were independent of any other branch of government, could best achieve the purposes or goals of a Senate. All three traits promoted superior deliberation, characterized by dispassion, wisdom, and a respect for stability. This stability and wisdom would be primarily a check on the democratic excesses of the lower chamber (the comments on stability often implied a check on democracy). A properly constructed Senate would provide some institutional memory and a knowledge of and experience with various proposals and policies; as a result, it would reduce the likelihood of constantly fluctuating laws and policies.

The tabulation also clarifies what most of the delegates did *not* believe was the essence of the Senate. First, the Senate was not a second chamber intended merely to provide a mechanical check on the legislative process. While several delegates linked the Senate to a general or bicameral check,

TABLE 4.2. Comments on the Ideal Characteristics and Purposes of a Senate, from the beginning of the proceedings to the representational compromise on July 16th

		TRAITS				PURPOSES				
Speaker	Page	Small size	Select appointment	Independent	Quality of deliberation	Wisdom	Stability	Check on democracy	Bicameral check	Represent property
Randolph	51	1			1			1		
Butler	51	1								
King	51	1								
Wilson	52	1		1						
Madison	52		1							
Dickinson	86								1	
Madison	120	1		1						
Dickinson	136		1	1			1			
Pinckney	150	1								
Dickinson	150		1							
Williamson	150–51	1							1	
Read	151		1							
Madison	151	1			1	1				
Gerry	152			1	1			1		
Wilson	154		1			1				
Madison	154		1				1			
Pinckney	155	1		1			1			

Randolph	218								
Madison	218–19								
Madison	233								
Butler	233								
Madison	233								
Sherman	234								
Wilson	254								
Hamilton	288–89								
Ellsworth	406								
Williamson	407								
Randolph	408								
Madison	421–22								
Sherman	423								
Hamilton	424								
Wilson	426								
Madison	426–27								
Gen. Pinckney	426								
Dayton	428								
Mason	428								
Baldwin	469–70								
Davie	487								
Wilson	488								
Morris	512								
		14	8	8	2	8	8	6	7	4

Note: Page numbers refer to *Records*, vol. 1.

a few of the comments we have so categorized are ambiguous. The vast majority of comments explicitly or implicitly designate a properly designed Senate the sine qua non of a republican legislature rather than simply a necessary check. In most of these comments, the lower house is taken for granted as being the essential democratic component but is never accorded any real respect, except through fear of its power. A small and independent Senate is required to balance and refine the legislative process. Second, the balance represented by the Senate was not simply the counterweight of property against the masses. Though four delegates linked the Senate to representation and protection of property, their views constitute a minority, even amid the secret deliberations. Some were not so obvious in their preferences. For example, by the end of Gouverneur Morris's speech on this topic, he has implied that the rich should have their own chamber so that others can watch and check them (*Records*, 1:512). No doubt, men of property were implicit in the refined selection, but not simply to represent the interests of property; instead, their possession of property imbued them with the wisdom and independence to form an effective Senate. Most delegates believed that property, independence, education, and breadth of experience came together as a package in society.

The delegates were all but united on bicameralism as a principle of good government, and not because it offered a solution to the dilemmas of geographical representation. A broad agreement on the need for a bicameral legislature preceded the Great Compromise, and though challenged, was never seriously endangered. Because the Senate was the linchpin of the compromise that resolved the problem of state representation in the new government, and thereby saved the convention, there is a mistaken tendency to conflate the origins of the Senate with the Great Compromise. The vast majority of delegates agreed on the need for a two-chamber legislature even as state representation in the legislature became the pivotal issue that summer. They likewise shared views about the purposes of an upper house. But the idea of an upper house designed to carry through the principles of republican government, as we shall see, was muddied by the issue of legislative apportionment. Despite the general agreement in favor of a bicameral legislature and a strong and independent upper house, legislative design was the central issue from the start because the basic nature of the republic would be embodied in the form and structure of legislative representation.

CONFLICT

Movement toward what would become the Great Compromise, and the role of the Senate in solving the convention's central dilemma, developed quickly but indirectly at first. The delegates initially resorted to the tactic (perhaps a necessary one) of delaying the issue of proportionality or equality of representation in favor of resolving as many of the other issues of legislative structure and powers as possible before having to confront in any final fashion the crucial issue. This strategy was only partially successful insofar as the apportionment issue refused to disappear—it was important to, or implicit in, the other issues of legislative design. Nevertheless, this bit of indirection may have helped the compromise develop and impress itself on the delegates in a manner that tempered opposition, as will be shown. This long gestation of the compromise also forced the delegates to reveal their sentiments about the form and functions of a Senate. In short, the debate shows how the Great Compromise was not only a settlement between state or regional interests but also a compromise of many delegates' vision of a properly constructed upper house.

The conflict and the indirect approach to compromising over representation arose almost immediately. On May 30, the first day of substantive deliberation, the proposal to end equal state representation in the national legislature as a whole sparked the initial controversy. After circling around direct language about proportional representation, the delegates closed in on a more general resolution that called for an end to the "equality of suffrage established by the articles of Confederation . . . and that an equitable ratio of representation ought to be substituted" (*Records*, 1:36). This was, perhaps surprisingly, agreeable to most, but George Read of Delaware objected and reminded the delegates of Delaware's explicit instructions to adhere to equal representation—in general—or abandon the proceedings. Though Madison responded with the first speech on why equal representation was no longer necessary or justifiable, the delegates decided to postpone the resolution due to Delaware's resistance (*Records*, 1:36–38).

This evasion did not get the delegates very far. The next day, the issue quickly resurfaced in the discussion of how the House and Senate would be selected, a discussion that *preceded* any explicit discussion of equal representation in any part of the legislature. The Virginia plan called for the people of the states to elect the first branch and for the first branch to select the membership of the second from nominations submitted by the state legislatures. After some debate about the merits of direct public participation and democracy, the delegates agreed to popular election of the first branch (*Records*, 1:50–51). However, according to the notes of Georgia's William Pierce, before they had even voted on this, an objection was raised by delegates who thought the two chambers so interrelated that they could not vote on the mode of selection of the first without knowing the mode of selection of the second. Pierce records that Richard Spaight of North Carolina interrupted the discussion of the first branch to argue that the mode of selection of the upper house was linked to any decision on the lower house, and he proposed that the second branch be selected by the states, no doubt to ensure that at least one branch would be tied to the states as corporate entities. South Carolina's Pierce Butler seconded the proposal and insisted that he could not decide on the mode of selection without knowing more about the "number of Men necessary for the Senate" (*Records*, 1:58).

Whether this debate actually preceded the vote on House selection or came after (according to Madison's notes) is not crucial; either way it shows that delegates began to protect the place of states within the system prior to an explicit discussion of equal representation (and Spaight and Butler *opposed* state equality during the convention). Madison's and Pierce's notes agree that Butler's objection took the delegates off in a somewhat different direction. In his demurral, Butler asked Randolph to explain his resolution and, in particular, "the number of members he meant to assign to this second branch" (*Records*, 1:51, 58). Why Butler felt the number of senators was crucial to determining the mode of appointment is unclear, but it allowed Randolph to provide the first endorsement of a Senate whose membership "ought to be much smaller than that of the first [branch]; so small as to be exempt from the passionate proceedings to which numerous assemblies are liable. He observed that the general object was to provide a cure for the evils under which the U.S. laboured; that in tracing these evils to their origin every man had found it in the turbulence and follies of democracy: that some check therefore was to be sought for against this tendency of our Governments: and that a good Senate seemed most likely to answer the purpose" (*Records*, 1:51).

Massachusetts delegate Rufus King drew the logical conclusion: If Spaight's proposal to have the state legislatures select the second branch were adopted, the Senate would be, from the outset, too numerous, unless "*the idea of proportion* among the States was to be disregarded" (*Records*, 1:51). The concern that the Senate would get too big apparently caused Spaight to withdraw forthwith his proposal for state selection. James Wilson then offered a radical alternative. To Wilson state nominations and selection by the first house were objectionable: the second branch "ought to be independent of both." Wilson, the convention's most ardent democrat, favored election of both chambers by the people, but with the smaller and more select upper house created by combining states into larger districts, analogous to the combination of counties used to select New York's upper house. Madison immediately objected on behalf of the small states that would be ignored when combined with larger states. But the point about independence was made: selection of the Senate by the House would compromise the Senate's independence. The debate concluded with a three-to-seven vote rejecting the Virginia plan resolution to have the first branch select the second from state nominations (*Records*, 1:52).

Two problems have thus far emerged to undermine Madison's principle of proportional representation for the new government, at least as far as the Senate is concerned. The first problem is the mode of selection and its relation to the independence of the second branch. Selection by the first branch would create too close a connection and undermine the bicameral check. It was rejected partly on that basis and, of course, partly on the basis of delegates from large and small states alike wanting to give states direct representation. Having eliminated selection by the lower house, the delegates were pushed toward election by the states as the obvious solution. Any scheme such as Wilson's district system, however abstractly sensible, was unworkable and probably unacceptable to the country.[9] Moreover, the Virginia resolutions had already proposed that state legislatures nominate the candidates for the upper house. If states' legislatures were to choose senators, then the Virginia plan's implicit proportionality for the upper house would have to be made explicit because each state would have to be allocated its share of the Senate membership. Hence the second and more intractable problem: the adverse impact on the size of the Senate that would be produced by any form of proportionality. This will surface several times during the debate, showing the strong sentiment for a small Senate, significantly smaller than strict proportional representation would produce. Thrown back to the states for the primary role in selection and constricted by the nearly universal desire for a small Senate, the delegates were on the road toward the Great Compromise whether they knew it or not at the time. As support for proportional representation in the Senate was eroded by the problem of size and the role of state selection, equal representation emerged as the only viable alternative. As it did so, the nature of the nascent Senate began to change as the ideals of independence, elite membership, and the checking function merged with the direct representation of states. To Madison and his allies this potential perversion of the Senate was anathema. However, to the nascent coalition of those interested in protecting states—especially small states—state selection became a wedge for redefining and expanding the purpose of the Senate to accommodate state influence.

The idea of combining state selection with state equality in the Senate evolved rapidly. As early as May 31, Connecticut's Roger Sherman made the initial, brief, and unpursued suggestion that each state legislature select one senator. For Sherman this was no spur-of-the-moment idea. He had suggested essentially the same bicameral arrangement during the 1776 deliberations of the Second Continental Congress on the Articles of Confederation, advocating the need for concurrent majorities of both citizens as individuals and states as units.[10] This was followed on June 2 by John Dickinson's foresight: "As to the point of representation in the national legislature as it might affect States of different sizes, he said it must probably end in mutual concession. He hoped that each State would retain an equal voice at least in one branch of the National Legislature" (*Records*, 1:87). Neither of these suggestions was considered because the primary issue was still the mode of selection not the ratios of representation. In fact, Dickinson, Sherman, and other advocates of state equality made their case for state selection primarily in terms that did not demand or even evoke equality. The first goal was to secure direct state selection as one way of assuring state influence, even if some delegates, including Sherman and Dickinson, were merely laying the groundwork for making Senate equality an inflexible demand.[11] As the two features—state selection and equality—merged, the small-state advocates developed a new logic for the Senate, one that attempted to combine what Madison and others saw as oil and water: state control of the Senate and the Senate's role as an independent upper house.

Dickinson began the amalgamation by uniting state selection with a core principle of Senate design, the elevation or refinement of membership selection: "Mr. Dickinson considered it as essential that one branch of the Legislature should be drawn immediately from the people; and as expedient that the other should be chosen by the Legislatures of the States. This combination of the State Governments with the national Government was as politic as it was unavoidable. In the formation of the Senate we ought to carry it through such a refining process as will assimilate it as near as may be to the House of Lords in England" (*Records,* 1:136). Dickinson saw selection by state legislatures as fully compatible with the principle of an elite and independent Senate. In the same speech he acceded to concerns about possible Senate dependence on the states by suggesting a long and "irrevocable" term of three, five, or seven years. He was supported by Sherman and, more importantly, Massachusetts' Elbridge Gerry who likewise argued: "It was necessary on the one hand that the people should appoint one branch of the Government in order to inspire them with the necessary confidence. But he wished the election on the other to be so modified as to secure more effectually a just preference of merit. His idea was that the people should nominate certain persons in certain districts, out of whom the State Legislatures should make the appointment" (*Records,* 1:132).

William Pierce then summarized the emerging principle by advocating "an election by the people as to the first branch and by the States as to the second branch; by which means the Citizens of the States would be represented both *individually and collectively*" (*Records,* 1:137). South Carolina's Charles Cotesworth Pinckney (or General Pinckney) and Roger Sherman raised one more point in support of state selection. They asserted that state selection would help interest the states in the national government and preserve harmony between the two types of government (*Records,* 1:137, 150). In this way a small number of delegates attempted to merge the ideal with the necessary and pragmatic, much to the chagrin of Madison and his allies.

On the decisive day for Senate selection, June 7, Dickinson proposed selection by state legislatures, with Sherman seconding the motion. Neither of these small-state stalwarts suggested anything about the ratio of representation, but Charles Pinckney immediately noted that proportionality would produce too large a Senate, even if the smallest state only got one senator. Dickinson responded with another attempt to blend state representation with a powerful and elite upper house:

Mr. Dickenson had two reasons for his motion. 1. because the sense of the States would be better collected through their Governments; than immediately from the people at large. 2. because he wished the Senate to consist of the most distinguished characters, distinguished for their rank in life and their weight of property, and bearing as strong a likeness to the British House of Lords as possible; and he thought such characters more likely to be selected by the State Legislatures, than in any other mode. The greatness of the number was no objection with him. He hoped there would be 80 and twice 80 of them. If their number should be small, the popular branch could not be balanced by them. The legislature of a numerous people ought to be a numerous body. (*Records*, 1:150)

Dickinson, the only delegate to express a lack of concern for the size of the Senate, again posited a unity of purpose between state selection and his ideal Senate, obviously without equal representation foremost in mind. (His cavalier comments about eighty and twice eighty left plenty of room for proportional representation.) Hugh Williamson of North Carolina replied by endorsing a small Senate of twenty-five, with each state getting at least one senator. Madison expanded on Williamson's idea in a blunt attack on Dickinson's logic:

If the motion (of Mr. Dickenson) should be agreed to, we must either depart from the doctrine of proportional representation; or admit into the Senate a very large number of members. The first is inadmissible, being evidently unjust. The second is inexpedient. The use of the Senate is to consist in its proceeding with more coolness, with more system, and with more wisdom, than the popular branch. Enlarge their number and you communicate to them the vices which they are meant to correct. He differed from Mr. D., who thought that the additional number would give additional weight to the body. (*Records*, 1:151)

Though he would resist equal state representation to the end, Madison was painting himself and his allies into a corner. Equal representation was inadmissible and a large Senate was inexpedient, but others had pointed out forcefully that proportional representation and a small Senate were mutually exclusive. The Senate would simply become too large under any form of proportional representation. A large Senate violated the first principles of republican legislative theory, which insisted that the second chamber be more deliberative, and to most delegates this required that it be smaller. This dilemma worked in favor of the Great Compromise. It made exact proportional representation all but unacceptable, even to a few of the staunchest large-state delegates, though some like Madison would hold fast on the issue. The contradiction between size and proportional representation may have been influential in pushing some other delegates toward compromise, as we shall see. Again, however, the discussion had strayed from the issue on the floor, which was the mode of selection. So the relationship between size and proportionality was pushed aside to make the final decision on selection. As a last alternative, Wilson offered his proposal for direct election of the Senate by the people combined into large districts (to keep the Senate small). This was defeated ten to one. Not only were new districts thought by some to be politically unacceptable and impracticable, the proposal was inextricably linked to popular election, which clearly a majority of the delegates were against when it came to the Senate. This remaining option eliminated, the delegates voted eleven to zero in favor of state selection (*Records*, 1:149, 155–56).

Once decided, state selection was here to stay. The delegates would later, amid the rancor and peril of the representation debate, reaffirm their support for state selection of the Senate by a nine-to-two vote, with only Pennsylvania and Virginia in opposition. This shows that many large-state delegates believed that state selection was the best way to pick the Senate and that state representation (the emerging principle of federalism) was vital, despite the obvious opening this gave to equal representation. Commitment to state selection was, for many of these delegates (Gerry and Pinckney among them) a matter of conviction rather than political expediency. For Gerry, this conviction would help push him to compromise; for others like Pinckney, the belief in state selection did not require the abandonment of a proportional Senate. Pinckney, as we shall see, tried until the last moment to salvage proportional representation for a state-selected Senate.[12]

CRISIS AND COMPROMISE

With the issue of who would select senators settled, deciding the ratio of representation loomed even larger and could not be long postponed, although the delegates attempted to settle other matters. As each day passed, however, the delegates had less success trying to do other business. The issue of apportionment in the Senate intruded with increasing persistence until it threatened to break up the convention. The proceedings circled in an ever-tightening gyre toward an uncertain vortex—either resolution or dissolution. The actions from June 9 to the July 16 compromise can be divided into two stages of roughly two weeks each: first, the spiral toward the five-to-five-to-one deadlock on Senate representation and the subsequent creation of the compromise committee on July 2; and second, the debate of the compromise committee's proposal, ending with the Great Compromise vote. The debates and decisions from each period show, first, how the consensus on bicameralism was tested but survived with broad support, and, second, how shared principles of the ideal Senate continued to move the delegates toward compromise.

Following the decision to have state legislatures elect the Senate membership, the delegates could not manage even two days of business without returning to the issue of representation. The meeting on June 9 began with the issue of the selection of the executive but ended with William Patterson of New Jersey calling for a return to the issue of suffrage in the legislature. During his long speech that day, Patterson most vehemently opposed a system he believed would be dominated by the large states (Virginia, Massachusetts, and Pennsylvania, in his view) and declared that New Jersey "will never confederate on the plan before the Committee . . . He had rather submit to a monarch, to a despot, than to such a fate." "If N.J. will not part with her Sovereignity," retorted Wilson, "it is vain to talk of Govt." (*Records*, 1:179–80). The next day of business, Monday, June 11, foreshadowed the ensuing five weeks. Rufus King and South Carolina's John Rutledge opened the day with a motion to affirm the Virginia resolutions' call to scrap equal representation as established by the Articles of Confederation and substitute for the first branch "some equitable ratio" of suffrage. This passed seven to three to one, and was immediately specified by Wilson and Pinckney's motion to base the ratio on the number of free citizens "and three fifths of all other persons." This sectional compromise and bit of circumlocution was familiar to the delegates because it used the same method of dealing with the representation of slaves as the ultimately unratified 1783 rule of revenue contributions passed by Congress under the Articles of Confederation.

The convention accepted this basis for House apportionment by an easy vote of nine to two. Two members of the Connecticut delegation,

Roger Sherman and Oliver Ellsworth, followed the quick and decisive victory of proportional representation in the first branch with a motion that each state have one vote in the second branch of the national legislature. This lost five to six, despite Sherman's warning that "Every thing . . . depended on this. The smaller States would never agree to the plan on any other principle than an equality of suffrage in this branch" (*Records*, 1:201). James Wilson and Alexander Hamilton immediately proposed that the second branch have the same rule of representation as the first branch. This passed six to five, in a mirror image of the previous vote, thus establishing the close division between the "large" (Massachusetts, Pennsylvania, Virginia, North Carolina, South Carolina, and Georgia) and "small" state coalitions (Connecticut, New York, New Jersey, Delaware, and Maryland). *Large* and *small* are, of course, overly simplistic terms: "[T]he average population of the large states, exclusive of heavily populated Virginia, was 307,000; of the small states, excluding tiny Delaware, it was 278,000, a relatively small difference."[13] An important part of the large/small dimension of conflict was not current population but prospective population based on current physical size. The geographically large states, especially ones with western lands, were assumed to be, sooner or later, the most populous. A direct reference to this assumption was made by Delaware's Gunning Bedford, who in commenting on Georgia's alliance with the large states noted that "Though a small State at present, she is actuated by the prospect of soon being a great one" (*Records*, 1:491).[14]

Despite the initial victory of proportional representation, Madison's nationalist Senate had been significantly distorted by the victory of state selection, the first step in what would become a process of combining and confusing the structure and purposes of the upper house. Moreover, the temporary vote in favor of proportional representation in the Senate was based more on principle than practicality; the advocates of proportional representation had not solved the problem of size.

Only after the six-to-five vote in favor of proportional representation in the Senate did the small states rally and offer an alternative to the Virginia resolutions; William Patterson presented the New Jersey plan on June 15. Up to this point, the opposition had no clear alternative. In part this was because there was broad agreement on the overall thrust of the Virginia plan—the only point of significant dispute had been the issue of equal representation of states. The need for a more effective response to this bone of contention necessitated a more complete alternative, and until this point there had been no significant opposition to bicameralism. The New Jersey plan, which called for a moderately strengthened Congress of the Confederation, retained the unicameral, equally apportioned legislature of the Articles. This aspect of the design did not imply a philosophical preference for a single-house legislature. Patterson offered the plan in reaction to the convention's initial and narrow support of proportional representation in both legislative chambers. The small states had voted, it should be remembered, for bicameralism at the beginning. Nevertheless, Patterson and his allies, chiefly Sherman, New York's John Lansing, and Luther Martin of Maryland, did have a principled argument against the need for a two-chamber *national* legislature. The Virginia resolutions were objectionable, first, because they exceeded the powers delegated to the convention by proposing a wholly new kind of government and because the people or states would not accept such an innovation. Second, the problem with the current Congress was not its structure (unicameral) or basis of representation (state equality), but rather its lack of power, which the New Jersey plan sought to remedy without proposing an untested and unsought new governmental structure. Third, a second legislative chamber was not necessary in a confederacy of states. The states served as a sufficient check on one another, and, implicitly, a confederation government did not act on individuals, which obviated a house to represent the people directly. Finally, Sherman contributed a note of caution—adding a popularly elected chamber would be an embarrassment to the new government as few citizens would interest themselves in the elections in large districts, and as a result designing men would be able to control the outcomes.[15]

Despite these arguments, this protest against proportional representation was rejected fairly easily on June 19 by a seven-to-three-to-one vote (*Records*, 1:322). The opposition to a two-house national legislature ended on June 21, with the consideration of the revised Virginia plan and the final vote on the bicameralism resolution (with dispute over the ratio of representation still to be resolved). This final endorsement of bicameralism reproduced the seven-to-three-to-one division that rejected the New Jersey plan two days earlier (*Records*, 1:358).

With unicameralism eliminated, the remaining battleground was the Senate. Sherman once again reminded the delegates that: "If the difficulty on the subject of representation can not be otherwise got over, he would agree to have two branches, and a proportional representation in one of them, provided each State had an equal voice in the other" (*Records*, 1:343). The issue of representation in "the other" intruded with increasing persistence until it threatened to break up the convention. While some delegates would keep the door to compromise open, others threatened to slam it shut and gave intransigent expression to their willingness to end the proceedings on this issue.

As the figurative temperature rose and the members of the convention sensed the desperation of their plight, three sets of voices were heard repeatedly. Some from the large states, principally Madison, Wilson, King, and Pinckney, though open to a modified version of proportionality in the Senate, were irreconcilable to state equality in any part of the government. During this period Madison and company made several long speeches in a fruitless attempt to persuade their colleagues that equal representation in the Senate was neither "just, nor necessary for the safety of the small States agst. the large States" (*Records*, 1:446). Madison tried to show that small states and large states did not form distinct and natural coalitions on the material issues that would be before the government. It followed that equality was an unnecessary precaution, in addition to being manifestly unjust (*Records*, 1:446–49, 455–56). King and Wilson used similar logic but could be quite blunt. Both ridiculed state sovereignty. As Wilson put it: "Can we forget for whom we are forming a Government? Is it for *men*, or for the imaginary beings called *States?*" (*Records*, 1:483, 489).

Some small-state delegates took umbrage at having to endure what they saw as arrogant and dissembling lectures from the large-state representatives. New Jersey's Jonathon Dayton retorted that "When assertion is given for proof, and terror substituted for argument, he presumed they would have no effect, however eloquently spoken." The large-state advocates had failed to show that state equality was the source of the Confederation's problems and had substituted "an amphibious monster" which "never would be received by the people." Luther Martin would "never" confederate unless on the principle of equality. Delaware's Gunning Bedford, however, stoked the hottest fire by telling his large-state colleagues, "I do not, gentlemen, trust you," and that if the Confederation were dissolved the small states "will find some foreign ally, of more honour and good faith, who will take them by the hand, and do them justice" (*Records*, 1:490, 492, 500). Though they said almost nothing, New York's Robert

Yates and John Lansing were alienated utterly. They didn't even stick around for the compromise vote and left the convention for good on July 10.

Interspersed amid the unyielding remarks of the stalwarts, the voice of exigency and reconciliation could be heard from both large- and small-state delegates. Foremost among the moderate voices in the small-state group were Connecticut's Ellsworth and Sherman along with Dickinson. Ellsworth reasoned that "If an equality of votes had been given to them in both branches, the objection [from the large states] might have had weight." Ellsworth seemed to be urging caution by pointing out that they were in danger of "running from one extreme to another. We are razing the foundations of the building, when we need only repair the roof." They were joined, certainly with some reluctance, by key large-state delegates, principally Gerry and Williamson, whose votes would be instrumental in producing the ultimate compromise. Williamson, supporting the formation of a compromise committee, warned that "If we do not concede on both sides, our business must soon be at end. He approved of the commitment, supposing that, as the Committee would be a smaller body, a compromise would be pursued with more coolness." Likewise, Gerry thought "Something must be done, or we shall disappoint not only America, but the whole world . . . We must make concessions on both sides" (*Records*, 1:484, 515). Benjamin Franklin, though he could not change Pennsylvania's vote, was another large-state delegate in favor of compromise.

Amid this acrimony, Madison was showing signs of desperation. The day before the convention would deadlock on the representation issue, he unleashed a new argument. The true division of interests in the country, he said, did not lie between small and large states but between north and south on the basis of slave labor, "and if any defensive power were necessary, it ought to be mutually given to these two interests." This "important truth" had compelled him to search for "some expedient that would answer the purpose," and he suggested, but did not propose, a modified version of proportional representation with one branch apportioned counting free inhabitants and slaves (according to the three-fifths ratio) and the other free inhabitants only. Madison's reluctant reference to the slave issue evinced his anxiety (*Records*, 1:486).[16] The tactic did not seem to help; in fact, it might have augmented the sentiment for equal representation in the Senate by invoking a way in which state equality might be a safeguard against regional interests.[17]

Just after Madison's speech, Benjamin Franklin proposed, unsuccessfully, that the delegates seek divine intervention by beginning each day with a prayer. Another unsuccessful request was made to hasten the arrival of the New Hampshire delegates. This phase ended on July 2 with another vote on the issue of equal representation in the Senate. This time, however, the states deadlocked in a five-to-five-to-one vote, in which Georgia (hitherto a firm vote for proportional representation) cast the crucial indecisive vote, the only change from the six-to-five victory for proportionality on June 11.[18] The gravity of the situation vividly expressed itself in the immediate and almost desperate decision of the delegates to appoint a committee of one member from each state to produce a compromise proposal. The committee, comprised of moderates from the large states and some staunch advocates of small-state interests, was stacked in favor of equal representation in the Senate.

The committee produced, in Gerry's words, the "ground of accommodation" that paired state equality in the Senate with vesting the House with the exclusive power over the origination and amendment of money bills (leaving the Senate with the equivalent of a veto power) (*Records*, 1:527). This compromise is generally seen as having little effect on the eventual agreement to Senate equality, and not without good reason. To begin with, three weeks earlier the delegates had rejected the money bills provision on its own merits. At that time, Gerry proposed to "restrain the Senatorial branch from originating money bills." This was raised not as part of a potential compromise but as an aspect of Gerry's vision of good government, with Great Britain as the example. Several delegates spoke against the proposal, and Pinckney labeled it "premature" and asserted that should the ratio of representation change, he would favor it, but if it stayed proportional then the two houses should have equal say in money bills. Gerry's proposition lost three to eight, with Delaware, New York, and Virginia voting in favor. At this earlier stage, money bills were not clearly tied to large- and small-state interests or a possible compromise (*Records*, 1:233–34).

So it is somewhat odd that this should have resurfaced as the basis of compromise, the concession by small states, the quid pro quo to save the convention, and it is not surprising that it was greeted with scorn by several delegates, including Madison, Butler, Williamson, Wilson, Pinckney, and Gouverneur Morris. Even Gerry, presenter of the compromise committee's work, noted that "he had very material objections to it."

Wilson and Williamson (who ultimately becomes a key vote for the compromise) remarked that if one house should have exclusive rights of origination, it should be the more deliberative Senate. Pinckney reminded the delegates that "the restriction as to money bills had been rejected on the merits singly considered by eight States against three; and that the very States which now called it a concession were then against it as nuga-tory or improper in itself." The delegates quickly voted—albeit by one of the most divided votes of the convention—to keep the money bills provi-sion as part of the package, by five to three to three, with Massachusetts dividing and North Carolina voting in favor (*Records*, 1:527–32, 543–47).[19]

Having retained the committee's package deal, the delegates con-fronted the decision on equal representation. Two other important votes preceded the final decision. The first vote, analogous to the vote on money bills, was whether to retain equal representation in the Senate as part of the compromise committee's report, which the convention did by a six-to-three-to-two vote. Though Madison explains in his notes that "several votes were given here in the affirmative or were divided because another final question was to be taken on the whole report," the vote was a fairly clear indication of what was to come (*Records*, 1:551). In fact, take away New York's vote in favor (the New York delegates left three days later), and the only difference between this vote and the Great Compromise vote is divided Georgia. On July 14, after heated debate and uncompromising words from both sides, Charles Pinckney offered the final motion to salvage proportional representation for the Senate with his modified plan to give the states one to five senators each, which Madison supported as a reasonable compromise (*Records*, 2:5). This was defeated by the slim mar-gin of four to six. Maryland, now joined by Daniel Carroll, voted for this compromise, while North Carolina and Massachusetts voted against it. This was the last action of the convention prior to the Great Compromise vote on Monday, July 16, when by a five-to-four-to-one decision the con-vention accepted equal representation in the upper chamber of the legisla-ture. In this vote, with New York gone from the convention, the small-state core of Connecticut, New Jersey, Delaware, and Maryland was joined by North Carolina, and with Massachusetts divided, the large states of Pennsylvania, Virginia, South Carolina, and Georgia fell short.

As some have argued, the Great Compromise was a compromise in name only. From this perspective (perhaps a largely Madisonian perspec-tive), there was no compromise; instead, the large-state interest simply lost.[20] The Great Concession is perhaps a more apt moniker. A real compromise took place only if one believes that the New Jersey plan supporters were serious about a unicameral legislature. As we have shown, bicameralism received broad support whenever tested. Once bicameralism was accepted, the contest was between proportional representation as the proper form of representation for the government as a whole, and some retention of state equality and corporate representation. We think, however, for many who had mixed ideas about the matter, and certainly for most small-state representatives, this was a compromise. What the term "compromise" does tend to inflate is the simplistic view that this was simply a political deal between contending interests, a quid pro quo. For some delegates, and Madison was not alone, this was not a compromise because it sacrificed the coherence of the system, the new basis of representation, the independence of the Senate, and the national perspective. An analogous claim can be made for many delegates who favored state equality in the Senate: The elimination of state equality would have threatened the viability of states themselves, which were still the working models of republican government.[21] Deeply held values about good government, not just parochial state interests, were at stake in the compromise.

The motivations behind the key vote changes that produced the Great Compromise vote remain somewhat of a mystery. Decades of scholarship have produced a list of usual suspects but no smoking guns. The general problem is that the Great Compromise is simultaneously over- and underexplained. It is overexplained insofar as several plausible (and not mutually incompatible) theories have been advanced to show why the large-state coalition fragmented. It is underexplained insofar as many of the theories do not attempt to address the change of particular votes that were crucial to the compromise. Most explanations for the Great Compromise vote fall into two categories. The first and most common is the "save-the-convention" school of thought, which centers on the conflict between large- and small-state coalitions and the coercion or compromises involved. The small-state coalition's insistence on equal representation in the Senate, to the point of putting the whole convention at risk, compelled some large-state delegates to agree to a compromise to salvage the project, with the reluctant and last-minute votes of a few delegates producing the compromise and saving the day.[22] Those from the large-state coalition who changed their votes are generally portrayed as men willing to compromise to insure the completion of constitutional reform. There is certainly truth to this, as we will see, especially when it comes to Massachusetts and the behavior of Gerry and Strong. It may have been a factor for North Carolinians as well, though the evidence is weaker. Even so, the theory of successful coercion by the small-state coalition has some trouble explaining why only certain votes in the Massachusetts and North Carolina delegations changed, or why Georgia changed back to opposing a compromise.

The second set of theories sees the compromise arising from the effects of other geographic or economic cleavages and related deals. The wheeling and dealing on side issues include the conflict between North and South over slavery (eased by the three-fifths compromise on slavery and representation in the House),[23] conflict over the disposition of western lands (eased by Congress's timely agreement on the North West Ordinance),[24] and the particular situation and interests of North Carolina.[25] Also cited are some circumstantial changes—mostly involving the comings and goings of delegates.[26] The substantiation for each of these interest-based arguments is slim and often based on assumptions or deductions about their effects rather than direct evidence.[27] The record of the convention offers little support for them, especially when it comes to the crucial changes in voting.

We do not seek to construct a new explanation for the compromise vote. Instead, we have shown how widely shared principles about bicameralism and a senate's role helped to shape the compromise rather than the Senate simply being shaped by the compromise. Concerns about Senate selection and size pushed the delegates toward the compromise, and the agreement on bicameralism withstood the counterattack by the small-state coalition. This put the delegates at the brink of the compromise, but did not compel them to agree to it. In addition, these shared principles may have influenced some of the key vote switching that produced the compromise vote.

After New York's departure (a solid vote for equal representation), the crucial changes were the division of the Massachusetts vote and the switch by North Carolina to favor equal representation. The North Carolina vote made up for the loss of New York, and the Massachusetts division prevented another tie vote. There is significant evidence that key members of the North Carolina and Massachusetts delegations were increasingly inclined toward compromise, with equal representation as the only viable alternative. Part of the evidence comes in the expressions of concern, voiced as the dilemma became apparent, by the four crucial delegates whose votes produced the compromise: Elbridge Gerry and Caleb Strong of Massachusetts and William Davie and Hugh Williamson of North Carolina.

The division of Massachusetts on the Great Compromise vote is not that surprising, given the record of the delegation on earlier votes and the remarks of delegates like Gerry. Massachusetts had divided on thirteen votes prior to the Great Compromise, and "whenever the individual votes were recorded Gorham and King stood against Gerry and Strong."[28] Gerry, in particular, was one of the early supporters of state selection on the dual merits of preserving independence from the other chamber and preserving a strong role for the states. State selection of the Senate, for Gerry, was also a way of elevating senatorial selection and producing a more fit body of men (*Records*, 1:132, 152). Though the Massachusetts delegation stayed with the large-state coalition through the July 2 deadlock vote of five to five to one, it is clear that Gerry and Strong decided thereafter that equality was all but inevitable and probably necessary to save the convention. So firm was their conviction that Gerry and Strong voted against Pinckney's eleventh-hour modified proportional scheme. Massachusetts was (with King voting *yes* and Gorham absent) the crucial vote against it. At least in Gerry's case, support for the compromise was made relatively easy because of his clearly expressed political philosophy and his desire to save the convention. Gerry seems to have wanted any sort of concession to hide behind in order to keep the process going. When the crisis came, Gerry and Strong backed the compromise as imperfect but the only way to preserve the convention. Gerry was on the compromise committee and delivered its report. Both Gerry and Strong expressed their belief that the concession on money bills was a significant compromise by the small states.[29]

The behavior of the North Carolina delegation is more mysterious and subject to more elaborate explanations based on more complicated motivations. North Carolina was the only southern state to shift ground completely on the crucial question. With William Blount absent, and Spaight voting against the compromise, North Carolina's decision was determined by Williamson, William Davie, and Alexander Martin. While Martin apparently said nothing of his motivations either during or after the convention, his colleagues Williamson and Davie evinced strong concern for the problem that plagued proportional representation from the start—that it would produce too large a Senate. Though troubled by the same dilemma, some delegates, such as Pinckney, King, and Madison, did not change their votes. For Williamson and Davie, who did vote for the compromise, these concerns might have been more influential.[30]

Hugh Williamson, a defender of proportional representation, "preferred a small number of Senators, but wished that each State should have at least one. He suggested 25 as a convenient number. The different modes of representation in the different branches, will serve as a mutual check" (*Records*, 1:150–51).[31] Later, as the pressure built, Williamson professed that he wanted to preserve state governments but "was at a loss to give his vote as to the Senate until he knew the number of its members," and he moved to add language that would have mandated a set ratio of membership size between the two branches to guarantee a smaller Senate (*Records*, 1:407). Though he was not seconded in this motion, it shows the extent of his concern for a small Senate. Moreover, Williamson expressed some conflicting sentiments with regard to the need to compromise and the quid pro quo produced by the committee. Williamson spoke in favor of forming the compromise committee and called for concessions on both sides, or "our business must soon be at an end" (*Records*, 1:515). However, after the committee produced the trade, Williamson said that "He was ready to hear the Report discussed; but thought the propositions contained in it, the most objectionable of any he had yet heard" (*Records*, 1:532). The proposition he specifically criticized was not equal representation, but the money bill monopoly. As was noted earlier, Williamson argued that such an exclusive power was better vested in the more deliberative Senate rather than in the popular House. This would seem to contradict his later remark (on August 9 as the money bill provision was significantly weakened), which is sometimes taken as an explanation for North Carolina's vote: "The State of N.C. had agreed to an equality in the Senate, merely in consideration that money bills should be confined to the other House" (*Records*, 2:233).

Likewise, William Davie gave passionate voice to his concern for a small Senate. Indeed, when faced on June 30 with the choice between equality and proportionality in the Senate, he seemed nearly vexed:

> Mr. Davy was much embarrassed and wished for explanations. The Report of the Committee allowing the Legislatures to choose the Senate, and establishing a proportional representation in it, seemed to be

impracticable. There will according to this rule be ninety members in the outset . . . It was impossible that so numerous a body could possess the activity and other qualities required in it. Were he to vote on the comparative merits of the report as it stood [with proportional representation], and the amendment [Ellsworth's equal representation motion], he should be constrained to prefer the latter. (*Records*, 1:487)

Later in the same speech, Davie changed his perspective: "On the other hand, if a proportional representation was attended with insuperable difficulties, the making the Senate the Representative of the States, looked like bringing us back to Congress again and shutting out all the advantages expected from it. Under this view of the subject he could not vote for any plan for the Senate yet proposed" (*Records*, 1:488, 498).

Though ultimately indecisive in his remarks, Davie clearly considered the size of the Senate to be a central concern that outweighed proportional representation almost to the extent of agreeing to equal representation. Davie was also North Carolina's representative on the compromise committee, and this may have reinforced his role in bringing North Carolina around.[32] Size does not provide the smoking gun in North Carolina's case. But Williamson and Davie were clearly influenced by the size dilemma as well as the need to compromise, and were not obviously swayed by the money bills concession.

While perhaps not decisive, the widely shared sentiments of an ideal Senate—independent to be an effective check, small to promote deliberation, and selected (rather than elected) to enhance both deliberation and the check—pushed the convention toward the compromise in the ways we have described. Efforts to elaborate purely interest-based explanations mistakenly overlook this evidence from the record. We cannot, given the limited evidence, conclude that ideals or principles of good government were decisive, but among the factors that shaped the compromise and swayed the votes of a few individual delegates, these shared principles manifested their importance throughout the deliberations, even at the brink of compromise.

The Senate was a product of multiple forces and motivations (often as much within individual delegates as among them), and the product reflects this mixture. In the end—as far as the larger argument of this book—we would argue that knowing the exact balance of the framers' motivations is less important than understanding the consequences of the sometimes confused deliberations, sharp disagreements, and grudging compromises. Whatever the exact motivations that produced the compromise, the Senate was, as a result, a compromised institution, intended to embody two potentially incompatible purposes, and no one felt this more keenly than Madison. Rufus King reminded the delegates of this dilemma on the last day of debate before the compromise vote: "According to the idea of securing the State Govts. there ought to be three distinct legislative branches. The 2d. was admitted to be necessary, and was actually meant to check the 1st. branch, to give more wisdom, system, & stability to the Govt. and ought clearly as it was to operate on the people to be proportioned to them. For the third purpose of securing the States, there ought then to be a 3d. branch, representing the States as such and guarding by equal votes their rights and dignities" (*Records*, 2:6–7). Did the compromised Senate represent the states, or was it still the national institution and steward of governmental policy? Could the two functions be combined? Confusion and disagreement on the former question were evident throughout the rest of the convention. The latter question was never addressed and would have to be answered if and when the new constitution was put into practice.

Immediately following the compromise vote, the delegates considered the powers to be granted the legislature. After a few motions and comments were made on the subject, Randolph argued for an adjournment. He said that "The vote of this morning (involving an equality of suffrage in the second branch) had embarrassed the business extremely. All the powers given in the Report from the Committee of the Whole were founded on the supposition that a Proportional representation was to prevail in both branches of the Legislature" (*Records*, 2:17). Rather than discuss powers further, he urged an adjournment so "that the large States might consider the steps proper to be taken in the present solemn crisis of the business, and that the small States might also deliberate on the means of conciliation" (*Records*, 2:18). Although his colleagues agreed to adjourn for the day, Randolph was wrong about either side seriously contemplating "steps proper to be taken" or "means of conciliation." The next morning, large-state delegates—with some small-state representatives in attendance as well—met informally to discuss the "solemn crisis." Madison noted that opinions at the meeting ranged from calling for the dissolution of the convention to accepting equality and moving on to complete the project. As a result no definite proposal was made, and Madison concluded: "It is probable that the result of this consultation satisfied the smaller States that they had nothing to apprehend from a union of the larger, in any plan whatever against the equality of votes in the second branch" (*Records*, 2:20). Randolph was right, however, about the relationship between the decision in favor of equality and the powers to be granted the Senate. The legislative powers anticipated by the Virginia plan did presuppose proportional representation. State equality in the Senate would not bring the convention to a premature and unsuccessful conclusion, but it would help motivate a reconsideration and revision of the powers to be given to the Senate as the convention sought to make up for lost time.

FIVE

Completing the Compromised Senate
Composition and Powers

The Great Compromise—the decision to pair equal representation in the Senate with proportional representation in the House—did not end the controversy over the Senate. To a certain extent the compromise created new problems because it resolved only two compositional elements of the Senate: the method of selection and apportionment of representation. However crucial, this agreement left many other important issues of composition and institutional powers unsettled and, for the most part, to be resolved amid the sometimes acrimonious feelings and ambiguities precipitated by the Great Compromise (table 5.1).

Both sets of decisions—the completion of the Senate's composition and the specification of Senate powers—manifested three fundamental consequences of the convention's work. First, despite the various favorable references to the House of Lords, the Senate was not going to be a House of Lords in its composition or powers. As South Carolina's Charles Pinckney argued, "the United States contain but one order that can be assimilated to the British Nation.—this is the order of the Commons." Pinckney's lengthy and eloquent speech carried one message: The United States are not Great Britain, particularly due to the lack of a nobility, and we should not and cannot imitate that government though it is the "best Constitution in existence" (*Records*, 1:397–404). Every decision the delegates made was an affirmation of Pinckney's argument. Second, the apportionment compromise, along with the emergence of an independent executive, prompted the convention to shift power away from the Senate and toward the presidency. Because of equal representation in the Senate, some delegates were motivated to diminish the powers that they had assumed would belong to the upper house. This shift was also a consequence of the delegates' sincere deliberations as they became more comfortable with the idea of a single, independently selected executive, and as they worked out the nuances of a system of "separated institutions sharing power." Finally, though republican, the Senate would emerge from the convention an ambiguous institution, with more than one built-in contradiction, a kind of catchall of the Constitution.

TABLE 5.1. Important Decisions in the Construction of the Senate

Composition	Senate	House
Apportionment*	Equal representation	Proportional representation
Selection process*	By state legislatures	Popular election
Length of term	Six years	Two years
Pay	National pay (versus by states or no compensation)	National pay
Property qualifications	None	None
Age requirement	30	25
Length of citizenship	9	7
Delegation size	2 senators per state	At least one, proportional to population
Method of voting	By senator (versus by state)	By representative
Vice president	President of the Sentate	Elects own speaker
Power over Composition of Other Branches of Government		
Presidential selection	No role	Votes by state if no electoral majority
Judicial and executive appointments	Advice and consent (simple majority)	No role
Impeachment and removal	Trial of all impeachments	Sole power of impeachment
Special Policy-making Powers		
Money bills	May not originate but can amend	Power of origination
Treaties	Advice and consent (two thirds majority)	No role
War	Shares in declaration of war	Shares in declaration of war

* Covered in chapter 4.

COMPLETING THE COMPOSITION OF THE SENATE

As the representation crisis brewed in early June, the delegates attempted to take care of other matters in an effort to postpone the inevitable showdown. The process of evasion and indirection was not without its successes. Though the delegates kept coming back to the ratio of representation, they were able to resolve (or nearly resolve) other aspects of the Senate's composition prior to the apportionment compromise, including a final decision on the length of term. Most other elements, though sometimes discussed and refined before the July crisis, were not settled until after the Great Compromise. Though the delegates would agree on many issues, including a long term for senators, the early decision in favor of state selection injected a powerful dose of confusion and debate into the decision making on these other issues. That the Senate would in some way represent the states clashed with notions of that body's republican purpose when it came time to define the rest of the Senate's structure.

Length of Term

The first issue to manifest these disputes and clarify the nature of the upper house was the length of term for members. The Virginia plan did not specify a length of term for either branch of the legislature. The members of the second branch were "to hold their offices for a term sufficient to ensure their independency" (*Records*, 1:20), which implied only that the term of the second branch should be longer than that of the first. The delegates first discussed term length only a few days after the decision for state selection of senators, as it was becoming increasingly clear that the ratio of representation would be the key issue. Some, including Edmund Randolph, James Madison, George Read, Gouverneur Morris, and James Wilson argued for the duration and stability a long term would provide; the Senate's primary purpose was to temper democracy and refine policy, especially as it emanated from the lower house, as well as to provide stability, particularly in foreign affairs. Others, including Roger Sherman and Pinckney, argued that too long a term would alarm the public and insulate the members from influence by or sympathy with their states, and, after all, the primary purpose of the upper house was to represent the states.

Long terms for the Senate *and* the House won the initial victories on June 12. Three years, the longest period suggested, was adopted for the House, and seven years prevailed for the Senate. The debate over House term length bounced back and forth between the philosophical and practical. Some, like Madison, preferred the longer term of three years because it minimized the mischief and instability of frequent elections and because annual terms were impractical in a large republic where representatives would travel great distances with little compensation. Others, like Sherman and Elbridge Gerry, held fast to the principle of annual elections for the people's branch of government. A House term of three years prevailed by a seven-to-four vote but was later eliminated on a seven-to-three-to-one vote, and two years was agreed to on June 21 without a recorded vote (*Records*, 1:214–15, 360–62).

The June 12 debate over the Senate term paralleled and contrasted with the House debate in telling ways. As was noted, the Virginia plan did not specify terms for the Senate or the House, but the Senate term was intended to be longer, and no delegate disagreed with this principle. Having agreed to three years for the House, the convention had already set a high standard for the Senate term. Seven years was moved by Richard Spaight and defended by Randolph and Madison as essential to providing the "firmness and independence" necessary to balance the popular branch. No one objected to this argument, but Sherman and William Pierce worried that seven years was longer than was necessary or prudent. Nevertheless, seven years prevailed on a vote of eight to one to two (*Records*, 1:218–19).

When the convention returned to the issue of Senate terms, having reduced the House term from three to two years, Nathaniel Gorham suggested four years for the Senate with the innovation that one-quarter rotate out every year.[1] Hugh Williamson proposed six years, as closer to the length already agreed to (seven years) but more convenient for rotation. The delegates first struck seven years by a seven-to-three vote, but then tied five to five to one on six years and on five years. The debate and voting on this issue cut across regional lines and blended the various concerns about senatorial independence and state representation. Only a few, such as Sherman and Pinckney, believed in short terms to tighten the bonds between states and senators. While the majority favored a term longer than four years, only Read (seconded by Morris) called for life appointments. This was resolved the next day when Gorham reintroduced six years with a one-third rotation. South Carolina's other Pinckney, Charles Cotesworth Pinckney, or General Pinckney (cousin of the more talkative Charles Pinckney), countered with four years to keep senators mindful of the states that appointed them. Read still preferred "during good behavior" but "being little supported in that idea, . . . was willing to take the longest term that could be obtained." He suggested nine years with a three-year rotation and was supported in this by Wilson, the convention's principal democrat, but was decisively defeated three to eight, with Delaware, Pennsylvania, and Virginia voting in favor. Then the delegates approved six years by a seven-to-four vote, with New York, New Jersey, South Carolina, and Georgia in opposition (*Records*, 1:408–9, 421–26). Life terms never had the support of more than a few delegates and were never given a vote. In fact, greater sentiment existed for shorter terms, as an electoral check and as a link to the states. The issue of term length, settled before the Great Compromise, was complicated by the conflicting views of the Senate, and this cut across the large/small schism of the apportionment compromise.

That anything truly akin to the House of Lords was far from the mind of the vast majority is reinforced by one of the curious features of the convention's work—the nature and intent of Alexander Hamilton's long speech on June 18, during the debate on the New Jersey plan. Hamilton's exact motives for stepping into the breach as the Convention was faced with choosing between the Virginia and New Jersey plans are less important here than that his speech drew no tangible support. Its effect, if not its intent, was to appear so radical and unacceptable that the Virginia plan looked downright moderate by comparison, and the New Jersey plan seemed little more than an ineffectual modification of the Confederation. Hamilton suggested things that, as he noted, "went beyond the ideas of most members." The three that stood above all the others were (1) his musings—not a proposal—that states be abolished; (2) the idea that the Senate be elected to serve during good behavior; (3) likewise the executive. In the end, Hamilton did not include abolition of states in his outlined constitution, but he did propose a few items that went beyond the supremacy clause in the New Jersey plan, including national appointment of all state governors who would have veto power over their state legislation (*Records*, 1:282–311). While the convention did move in the direction of federal power by adding the New Jersey plan's supremacy clause and other express powers, it never even voted on lifetime tenure for the Senate, as we have seen. Hamilton's isolation shows just how alien the notion of an elected lifetime Senate was to delegates, even when deliberating in secret.

Pay and Property Qualifications

Directly following the determination of term length, the delegates nearly resolved the issue of compensation. Just as the uncertain role of states in the nascent system caused much of the confusion and conflict over term length for the Senate, the same uncertainty prevented quick resolution of compensation for *both* the House and the Senate. The controversial issue was not whether either or both types of legislators would be paid, but who would pay: the states or the national treasury? The Virginia resolutions specified that members of the two branches of the national legislature were "to receive liberal stipends by which they may be compensated for the devotion of their time to the public service" (*Records*, 1:20). Both were to be paid, implicitly from the national treasury.

Prior to the apportionment compromise, the delegates decided that states should pay the legislators in *both* chambers. This concern over the source of pay applied equally to the House and the Senate. Several delegates endorsed the idea that Senate service receive no compensation, but the first such direct proposal was defeated by a decisive three-to-seven-to-one margin (*Records*, 1:219). The issue was revisited on June 26 when General Pinckney moved to strike the provision for a salary. He argued that the Senate "was meant to represent the wealth of the Country, it ought to be composed of persons of wealth; and if no allowance was to be made the wealthy alone would undertake the service" (*Records*, 1:426–27). After Benjamin Franklin provided a noble motive for no compensation—that, as many among them would probably be senators, they did not want to appear to be giving themselves jobs—the states divided five to six against General Pinckney's motion. This was followed by a ten-to-one vote (with South Carolina against) in favor of compensation.[2] Oliver Ellsworth immediately moved to strike payment by the national treasury in favor of payment by the individual states, in part to help bind the loyalty of the states to the new national government. Madison and New Jersey's Jonathon Dayton objected, arguing that this would make the upper-house members slaves to their states and thereby vitiate the very independence and stability that were the main reasons for a Senate. Ellsworth's proposition lost five to six. Then George Mason raised the need for a property qualification for senators insofar as the Senate's duty was "to secure the rights of property." He made no motion, but the implication was that pay was not necessary. His speech was followed directly, and somewhat mysteriously, by a vote on whether to keep the national treasury as the source of compensation. This was also defeated by a five-to-six margin, with North Carolina the only state to vote against both sources of payment (*Records*, 1:371–75, 377–79, 385, 391, 426–28). As with the House, the delegates left the issue of Senate pay in a partially resolved state prior to the Great Compromise: Senate service would be compensated, but by whom?

The issue rested there until August, after the apportionment compromise, when the Committee of Detail produced its draft, which somewhat surprisingly specified that compensation for both chambers be determined by the respective states. This sparked a final round of debate, in which the disagreement about the Senate's purpose was evident. At one point, two Marylanders flatly contradicted each other about the nature of the upper house. Luther Martin's assertion that "As the Senate is to represent the States, the members of it ought to be paid by the States" caused Daniel Carroll to reply that "The Senate was to represent and manage the affairs of the whole, and not to be the advocates of State interests. They ought then not to be dependent on nor paid by the States." Was the Senate to represent the states, the national interest, or, somehow, both at the same time? Although the delegates would never square this circle, by August more of them had rallied around the national system. For example, Ellsworth, earlier the repeated sponsor of motions to strike national pay, had a change of heart and made the motion to substitute national pay for state pay for both houses. His motion won nine to two, with Massachusetts and South Carolina the dissenting votes. As this change of heart followed the Great Compromise, one might suspect that it can be attributed to the victory on equal representation, which then allowed Ellsworth and others more latitude to back other aspects of a more national system. The pivotal battle was over national or state pay, and that issue—the source of the pay—affected some of the votes on compensation; in direct votes, compensation won easily. National pay, while tilting in favor of a more national Senate, hardly resolved the ambiguity and Janus-like quality of the Senate (*Records*, 2:290-92).

The delegates also showed no serious interest in another pecuniary distinction between the legislative chambers. Property qualifications, though seriously discussed as a necessity for all office holders in the national government, legislative, executive, and judicial alike, were not considered separately as a distinctive requirement for the Senate.[3] On July 26, during debate that had been devoted to the executive branch, Mason moved that the Committee of Detail receive a clause that would establish "certain qualifications of landed property and citizenship in members of the Legislature," including disqualification for persons having unsettled accounts or debts with the United States. This motion was quickly amended without objection to include the judiciary and the executive. Most of the discussion was about the inadvisability and dangers of the debt disqualification, and about the difficulties in formulating a national property qualification. One of the strongest condemnations of property qualifications came from John Dickinson, the only delegate to repeatedly invoke the image of the House of Lords in earlier debates on the Senate. Dickinson "doubted the policy of interweaving into a Republican consti-tution a veneration of wealth . . . It seemed improper that any man of merit should be subjected to disabilities in a Republic where merit was understood to form the great title to public trust, honors, and rewards." The delegates removed the disqualification clause but agreed to instruct the Committee on Detail to produce "certain qualifications of property and citizenship, in the United States, for the executive, the judiciary, and the members of both branches of the legislature" (*Records*, 2:121–26).

The Committee on Detail's August 6 report, however, essentially evaded the issue by giving the national legislature the power to create property qualifications for legislators of both houses. A brief debate re-vealed general distaste for this mechanism, and several delegates deemed property qualifications either unworkable or undesirable. Sentiment was so clearly against the idea that the convention refused even to vote on a motion to specify the property qualifications for both houses and then dropped any mention of property qualifications altogether (*Records*, 2:248-51). In the end, as far as property qualifications, the Senate was less aristocratic than most state upper houses, which had varying levels of property qualifications for senatorial candidates.[4] The debates on pay and property qualifications show that although parallels to the House of Lords were present in some delegates' thinking, neither came close to creating a bicameral distinction. Senators would be paid, and there would be no national property qualification.

Age and Length of Citizenship

Although always attuned to the differences between the upper and lower houses, the convention failed to draw a meaningful distinction between them with regard to two other electoral qualifications: age and length of citizenship. As with many such details, the Virginia plan left these matters unspecified, leaving a blank space for the minimum age and not even mentioning citizenship. The age blank was filled early on, well before the apportionment compromise, when the consensus on the characteristics of an ideal Senate still drove the process. The convention decided initially to strike any age qualification for the first branch by a ten-to-one vote, but by a three-to-six-to-two vote failed to strike the same clause about the Senate. Instead, thirty years was chosen as the minimum age for senators by a seven-to-four margin. The unspoken logic was clear: Let the voters decide for the first branch, but a minimum age is prudent for the Senate. The convention amended this ten days later when the delegates by a seven-to-three-to-one vote decided to specify twenty-five years as a minimum age for members of the House (*Records,* 1:375).

Decided much later, length of citizenship was a more controversial factor than age. Citizenship qualifications did not appear until the Committee on Detail presented its August 6 draft, which required three years for the House and four years for the Senate, an insignificant difference. Length of citizenship for both chambers then went through bidding wars between those delegates who sought the highest possible number of years and those who thought minimal requirements would do or were even unnecessary. Mason began the debate by moving that the requirement for the House be raised from four to seven years. This was quickly passed with only one dissenting vote. Wilson, once again the voice of the people, got support for reconsideration, and the bidding started. Proposals to merely require citizenship, or to require four, five, or nine years of citizenship all failed to draw a majority, and seven years remained (*Records,* 2:216, 230–31, 251, 268–69, 272). The Senate qualification drew slightly more debate when Gouverneur Morris "moved to insert 14 years instead of 4 years citizenship" for Senators. Whether or not Morris got fourteen by doubling the House's seven is unclear but logical. Several remarks about the excessiveness of this proposal led quickly to a series of votes in which fourteen, thirteen, and ten years all failed decisively, and nine years passed six to four to one (*Records,* 2:235–39, 272). Again, the Senate, particularly because of its role in foreign affairs, might require a greater term of citizenship, but it was only a modest difference. In the end, rather stringent citizenship requirements adhered to both chambers.[5]

The Number of Senators and Method of Voting

Two final compositional issues with potentially profound consequences were solved rather easily, but once again the effects of the apportionment compromise were woven into the debate and decisions. First, states would be represented equally, but how many senators per state? Second, state equality implied that state representation in the Senate would be corporate as in the Confederation Congress. If there were more than one senator per state, would they vote by state or per capita as individual senators?

These profoundly important details were settled simultaneously on July 23 with relatively little debate and near consensus on the final votes. After considerable attention to unrelated articles in the Virginia resolutions, including the mode of ratification, Gouverneur Morris and Rufus King moved "that the representation in the second branch consist of____members from each state who shall vote per capita." One could surmise that this was part of the counterattack to limit the damage done by the equal representation compromise. By specifying that senators vote as individuals, these large-state delegates were trying to insure that the Senate would not be a replication of the Confederation Congress and to minimize the chances that senators would act simply as mouthpieces for state legislatures. This approach to voting also was closer to the ideal of a senate composed of fewer and wiser men for better deliberation. Morris then moved to amend his motion by filling the blank with three Senators per state, arguing that if "two members only should be allowed to each State, and a majority be made a quorum the power would be lodged in 14 members, which was too small a number for such a trust." Clearly, no one considered one per state a safe number, not only for purposes of deliberation but also for the purely pragmatic reasons of absence, illness, and death. The Confederation Congress had been plagued by failures to achieve quorum. Nathaniel Gorham, a supporter of per capita voting, called for two senators per state because a small number was best for "deciding on peace & war &c, which he expected would be vested in the 2d. Branch. The number of states will also increase." Mason agreed that three, with the addition of new states, would produce too large a Senate. Three per state was defeated by an eight-to-one vote, and two per state was agreed to unanimously. Luther Martin immediately objected to per capita voting "as departing from the idea of the *States* being represented in the 2d. branch." However, the delegates quickly voted on the whole motion, including two per state voting per capita, and gave their approval by a nine-to-one vote, with only Maryland in opposition (*Records*, 2:94–95).[6] This decision shows that even most small-state delegates, though committed to state equality, also wanted to retain some of the Senate's original purpose. Equality of votes might have been a political necessity but not at the cost of a complete sacrifice of senatorial independence. Perhaps for some small-state delegates this was their own compromise of interests and principles in the making of the Senate.[7]

DETERMINING THE SENATE'S CONSTITUTIONAL POWERS

Its composition was not the only thing that would distinguish the Senate and define its special place within the new constitution, nor was it the only thing that would cause controversy over the Senate. The Virginia resolutions outlined overall institutional structures rather than specifying the exact distribution of powers and said very little about defining the separation of powers and the checks and balances of those powers. In the Virginia resolutions the Senate was simply the differently constituted second branch; it had no special powers. Prior to the Great Compromise almost nothing had been done to define the institutional powers of the Senate, that is, any exclusive legislative powers and any exclusive role the Senate would play in the system of checks and balances. However, it was clear from the debates even before the apportionment compromise that many delegates presumed the Senate would be endowed with special features or powers that would distinguish it from the House.

The contrast between the House and the Senate was clear throughout. The nature of the House was more settled and often taken for granted. The House was the people's legislature, the repository of all things democratic in the Constitution. With the exception of its ultimately meaningless power over money bills, the House was given no special legislative powers. The Senate, however, was not simply the second legislative chamber. In chapter 4, we discussed the special characteristics the delegates attributed to an ideal upper house, including its small size and independence to facilitate deliberation. Largely because of these characteristics, the delegates, in different combinations and proportions, also ascribed to the Senate powers that not only made it a more potent legislative chamber but also put it at the intersection of the not completely separated system of powers. The Senate, more than any other institution, was to possess what we will call the *boundary powers* in the new Constitution, that is, those powers that directly affect the separation of powers.

The problem was that the Senate was no longer, in the minds of a number of delegates, the ideal upper house envisioned in the early proceedings. The Great Compromise had compromised the Senate. As a

result, the delegates and their debates over these powers were often ambivalent and confused. Many delegates adhered to the Senate as still being
the more deliberative, experienced body for special decisions (like war and
treaties) and nonlegislative powers (like appointments). These included,
of course, small-state delegates who may have been influenced as much by
interest as by principle, as well as some large-state representatives who
had opposed the apportionment compromise. Some of their colleagues,
nearly all from large states, opposed giving special powers to the Senate
because the Senate was to be a product of state legislatures and unrepresentative. In particular, the Great Compromise had changed the attitudes
of some vocal delegates from the large states, including Madison, Randolph, Wilson, and Williamson about the wisdom and fairness of giving a
Senate, now that it would represent the states, too many powers.[8] Confusion, ambivalence, conflict, and some consensus mixed freely as the convention attempted, after the apportionment compromise, to finish its
work on the Senate.

A triangular set of tensions was at work consistently in the debates
leading to these decisions on Senate powers. First was the battle over the
separation of powers—how was the Senate to be involved in the composition of the other branches and in the making of foreign policy? Second
was the debate over whether the Senate, as the smaller and more deliberative body, was the better qualified branch to be granted such boundary
powers. Third was the tension caused by the Senate's role as the locus of
state power and federalism, which strengthened the commitment of some
to the Senate's special place in this system of boundary powers, while
causing others to rethink that special place by involving either the House
or the presidency.

This mixture is evident in debate over items in several areas of the
emerging document, including the selection of the executive, appointments to the executive and judiciary, the vice presidency, impeachment,
the origination and amendment of money bills, the making of treaties,
and the declaration of war. These decisions, big and small, easy and
difficult, produced a Senate that was less than what some had hoped for.
Nevertheless, it was still more powerful than the House and was in possession of most of the unique boundary functions, all on top of its being
the core of the federal compromise between state and national power. The
principal decisions on the powers of the Senate can be divided into two
categories of boundary powers. The first type is congressional involve-

ment in the selection (or removal) of officials from the executive and judiciary branches. The second category involves the policy-making powers, especially in the realm of foreign policy, that came to be shared with the executive.

SENATORIAL POWERS OVER THE COMPOSITION OF THE EXECUTIVE AND JUDICIARY

Picking the President

The selection of the executive was the most troublesome issue for the second half of the convention.[9] Some of the difficulty over this matter stemmed from the vagueness of the office itself. Was the executive office to be Sherman's narrowly confined institution "for carrying the will of the Legislature into effect" or Randolph's "the foetus of monarchy" (*Records*, 1:65–66)? If the former were true, then perhaps the method of selection was not that important. If the latter, then the delegates had every right to worry considerably about the selection process. Such concerns, however, were more important prior to the apportionment compromise. After the compromise, the problem was more about the relative influence of the two houses of Congress in presidential selection, and near the end of the convention "the chief objection to the proposed plan of election was the additional power that it would place in the senate already vested with excessive powers."[10]

For most of the summer, the convention adhered to the method of selection suggested by the Virginia resolutions: election by the national legislature. After debate over options, including John Rutledge's suggestion to give the power to the second chamber of the legislature and Wilson's version of popular election (the first proposal for a system of selection by popularly elected electors), the delegates gave initial approval to election by the national legislature with an eight-to-two vote on June 2 (*Records*, 1:68–69, 80–81). The delegates did not revisit the issue until they reaffirmed this decision by a unanimous vote on July 17, the day after the Great Compromise. This consensus crumbled on July 19 when concerns about executive independence compelled some delegates to suggest selection by electors chosen by state legislatures. Yet the delegates settled again on selection by the national legislature, and this method was included in the Committee of Detail draft (*Records,* 2:29–32, 57–59, 99–101, 108–12, 115, 118-19).

Not until the Committee of Detail's proposal for election by the national legislature is taken up on August 24 are the consequences of the apportionment compromise clearly injected into the process of presidential selection.[11] Selection by the national legislature raised the problem of bicameral choice: Would the two houses choose by balloting jointly or separately? Rutledge moved for a joint ballot as "the most convenient mode of electing." Sherman objected that this would deprive "the *States* represented in the *Senate* of the negative intended them in that house." Gorham argued in response that "it was wrong to be considering, at every turn whom the Senate would represent." The public good was the proper objective, and separate balloting would lead to "delay and confusion," with the House and Senate "each having a negative on the choice of the other." New Jersey's Dayton agreed with Sherman and chided Gorham: "It might be well for those not to consider how the Senate was constituted, whose interest it Was to keep it out of sight." Dayton warned that he could never agree to a joint ballot (*Records,* 2:401–2).

Other delegates weighed in on the issue of state size and its relation to presidential selection. Nevertheless, joint balloting won seven to four, and an amendment offered by Dayton and his New Jersey colleague David Brearly to have joint balloting with "each state having one vote," was defeated five to six with the core of the large- and small-state coalitions on opposite sides (*Records,* 2:403). The day ended, however, with a tie vote on a motion to return to a system of electors; motivated once again by the concern about executive dependence on the legislature, small and large states voted on both sides (*Records,* 2:401–4). The convention was stuck in a voting cycle on the issue of presidential selection, and as long as this was the case, other issues—particularly problems of how to distribute powers between the executive branch and the Senate—proved difficult to resolve. For example, on August 15 the delegates' frustration rose as discussions about the money-bill restriction and executive veto were confounded by their relationship to still unsettled issues, including the other powers of the Senate and the composition of the executive branch. Nathaniel Gorham, who "saw no end to these difficulties and postponements," put his finger on the problem: "Some could not agree to the form of Government, before the powers were defined. Others could not agree to the powers till it was seen how the Government was to be formed" (*Records,* 2:300).

The vital matter of presidential selection was left with the Committee of Eleven, whose solution to the selection problem produced yet another compromise between the concerns of large and small states while address-ing other concerns as well.[12] Each state would appoint electors equal to the number of senators and representatives to which the state was entitled. The electors chosen in the manner decided by their state legislatures would vote for the president, with the Senate to make all selections when the electoral count was not a majority (clearly balancing the advantage of larger states in the initial process against state equality in final selection). Virginia's Mason cut to the quick; this is better, he admitted, but "nine-teen times in twenty" the Senate, "an improper body for the purpose," would make the selection (*Records,* 2:500). His objection was echoed by Charles Pinckney, Williamson, Wilson, and Randolph. With the excep-tion of Delaware's Dickinson,[13] only large-state delegates attacked this provision. Randolph raised the specter of a Senate aristocracy controlling the executive, as did Mason, who said he would prefer the government of Prussia to this aristocracy (formed by putting all the power in the hands of seven or eight men). Sherman reminded these critics of the Senate's sec-ondary position in the process by noting that "if the Small States had the advantage in the Senate's deciding among the five highest candidates, the Large States would have in fact the nomination of these candidates" (*Records,* 2:500–502, 511–15).

After more debate on September 6, the state delegations voted seven to one (the voting stopped after North Carolina) to keep the decision in the Senate. Finally, Sherman produced another permutation: use the House instead of the Senate to select the executive in the event of no electoral majority, "with the members from each state having one vote." Even Mason liked this insofar as it lessened the aristocratic influence of the Senate. Only Delaware voted against this arrangement, which left the Senate to choose the vice president when the electoral count was indeci-sive (*Records,* 2:522–27). To this extent, even the controversy over how to pick the executive was more about the role of states and their power in the Senate than it was a dispute over the nature and purpose of presidential power. Because of that, the solution of that problem smoothed the way for the resolution of other difficulties affecting the separation of powers and the Senate's special powers.

The Vice President: President of the Senate

In the resolution of the presidential selection process, the Senate was left with the dubious distinction of having the power to select the vice president in the unlikely event that after the House selection of the president there was a tie for second place. Yet the Senate's relationship with the vice president was more significant than that. The vice president was to be the presiding officer of the Senate. In this way, though we discuss it here because of its relationship to the presidency, the vice presidency's relevance to the Senate is actually about the Senate's composition rather than its powers (as we indicate in table 5.1). The vice presidency was one of the convention's more interesting efforts to kill two birds with one stone. One of those birds, once again, was a consequence of the Great Compromise and complications caused by state equality in the Senate. The office of the vice president appeared for the first time, without prior mention or discussion, in the Committee of Eleven's September 4 report. The necessity of such an office seems to have been suggested by a couple of problems, one of which was the preservation of equality in the Senate. The Committee on Detail had specified that the Senate would elect its own president, which would deprive a state of one of its two members. As a presiding officer was assumed to be neutral and vote only in case of ties, this would never do, given the Senate's composition. The office also provided a job, presumably, for the person receiving the second-highest electoral vote for president under the procedure that required each elector to vote for two candidates.

When on September 7 the office of the vice president came up for its first and only substantive discussion, it was regarded with suspicion and probably some puzzlement. The members of the Committee of Eleven provided what might seem like less-than-compelling arguments on behalf of the office and its functions.[14] Sherman noted the link to Senate equality by pointing out that if a sitting Senator were to be that body's presiding officer, he "must be deprived of his vote, unless when an equal division of votes might happen in the Senate, which would be but seldom." Moreover, "If the Vice President were not to be President of the Senate, he would be without employment." Williamson, another member of the committee, admitted that "such an officer as Vice President was not wanted. He was introduced merely for the sake of a valuable mode of election, which required two to be chosen at the same time." Gerry,

Randolph, and Mason spoke in opposition. Mason "thought the office of Vice President an encroachment on the rights of the Senate; and that it mixed too much the Legislative and the Executive." Gerry was blunt: "We might as well put the President himself at the head of the Legislature." Despite the sharp objections and the apparently lackluster justification, the delegates voted eight to two to one to make the vice president the president of the Senate (*Records*, 2:536–38; 3:217, 343–44). The easy approval suggests that the preservation of equality in the Senate and the need to deal with tie votes was an important factor for many delegates.

In any event, by helping to patch a couple of holes, one in the method of selecting the executive and the other in the procedures of the Senate, the vice presidency became another element in the balancing act between independence and interdependence that characterized the deliberations over structure and powers during the second half of the convention. More to the point, the Senate got its presiding officer, and though we tend not to think it a matter of much importance for most of American history, Sherman was right: presiding over the Senate was the vice president's only job (unless the president died, was removed, or was incapacitated). That is what the delegates thought, and it turned out to be the reality for early vice presidents, as we shall see in chapter 7.

Appointment of the Judiciary

The power to select the remaining branch of government, the judiciary, was likewise complicated by the apportionment compromise. The Virginia resolutions specified that the national legislature (both houses) would appoint the judiciary. Legislative appointment was the practice of six states during much of the era of the confederation; three subjected a governor's nominations to the advice and consent of the governor's council.[15] In early June, when the subject of judicial appointments was first broached, opinion was divided among three methods: by the legislature as a whole, by the executive, and by the Senate. Madison's argument that the Senate, as the smaller and more knowledgeable body, was more suited to the selection of the judiciary prevailed unanimously on June 13 (*Records*, 1:119-21, 232–33).

After the apportionment compromise, however, Madison turned against his own innovation, and the delegates showed more inclination to involve the executive in judicial appointments. Although Wilson's motion for an exclusive executive power of appointment failed two to six, a motion by Gorham was nearly accepted. Gorham's motion was to follow the model of the Massachusetts constitution, which gave the power of nomination and appointment to the executive with the advice and consent of the upper house of the legislature. This proposal lost on a tie vote of four to four, with Massachusetts, Pennsylvania, and Virginia joined by Maryland in support of the motion (*Records*, 2:44). When the issue came up again on July 21, Madison proposed appointment by the executive with a veto power given to the Senate. Madison adopted the argument earlier advanced by Wilson and Hamilton that the executive was best suited to make such appointments, but he also argued that state equality now made the Senate an improper body for judicial selection. In a clever speech Madison turned the logic of the compromise into a general principle of constitutional design:

> [A]s the second branch was very differently constituted when the appointment of the Judges was formerly referred to it, and was now to be composed of equal votes from all the States, the principle of compromise which had prevailed in other instances required in this that there should be a concurrence of two authorities, in one of which the people, in the other the States, should be represented. The Executive Magistrate would be considered as a national officer, acting for and equally sympathizing with every part of the United States. If the second branch alone should have this power, the Judges might be appointed by a minority of the people, though by a majority of the States, which could not be justified on any principle, as their proceedings were to relate to the people rather than to the States; and as it would, moreover, throw the appointments entirely into the hands of the Northern States, a perpetual ground of jealousy and discontent would be furnished to the Southern States. (*Records*, 2:80–81)

Although not every large-state delegate favored Madison's proposal, not a single small-state delegate argued for a substantial role for the executive in judicial appointments. Madison's motion lost by a vote of three to six, with only the large states of Massachusetts, Pennsylvania, and Virginia in support. The convention voted, instead and by the reverse margin, to return to appointment by the second branch. On August 6, the Committee on Detail presented its draft, which, in accordance with the decisions of the delegates sitting as the Committee of the Whole, gave the Senate sole power of appointment for the judiciary as well as for ambassadors, and the exclusive power to make treaties. The Senate retained these exclusive powers until September 4, when the Committee of Eleven gave its report, which moved all these functions to the article defining the executive, imparting them to the president with the advice and consent of the Senate. The reasons for this change are somewhat mysterious. There was no debate about this in the convention; justifications and compromises are shrouded in the secrecy of the committee's work. As Max Farrand explains, "Apparently on the assumption that a satisfactory method of electing the president had been discovered, the committee further recommended that the president now be given power with the advice and consent of the senate, to make treaties, and to nominate and appoint ambassadors and judges of the supreme court."[16] Gouverneur Morris captured the appeal of the arrangement just before the final approval of the appointment clause: "[A]s the President was to nominate, there would be responsibility, and as the Senate was to concur, there would be security." Whatever the logic, the convention agreed. Following final adjustments to the method of picking the president, and despite final objections by Wilson and Pinckney, the delegations unanimously adopted presidential appointment with senatorial advice and consent (*Records*, 2:41–44, 80–83, 522–24, 539).[17]

The fate of nonjudicial appointments was part of this resolution. The Virginia plan did not specify anything about the appointment of executive branch officers. Madison removed this ambiguity by adding that the executive should have the power to appoint officers whose appointments were not otherwise provided for (*Records*, 1:67). This addendum is somewhat surprising given that no states gave their executives unencumbered powers of appointment.[18] In August, the convention hemmed in the scope of executive authority by adding ambassadors and "other Public Ministers" to the Senate's appointment power, and by specifying that the executive could not create offices on his own authority (*Records*, 2:394, 405). As we have just seen, however, the Committee of Eleven combined all categories of appointments, judicial and otherwise, into the same process of executive nomination with advice and consent by the Senate. Whether thought of as a compromise or not, the committee's solution was a give-and-take as far as Senate power relative to the executive. Though the Senate lost sole authority over the judges and ambassadors, it gained advice and consent powers for all appointments.[19]

Impeachment and Removal

The role of the Senate in the removal of executive and judicial officials also depended on a solution to the problem of how to select the president and appoint the judiciary. Appointment and removal are, of course, mirror images, and during the convention the delegates struggled with the relationship between these concepts. As we have seen, appointment raised substantial concerns about the separation of powers or the "independence," as they often labeled it, of the branches of government. Removal, here meaning impeachment, was the ultimate check and balance, and raised this problem to a new level of difficulty. The delegates seemed to falter between the Scylla and Charybdis of this issue. On the one hand, removal power potentially gave one branch, especially one that was not dependent on another branch for its selection, coercive power over the other. On the other hand, if the body that was to impeach or try impeachments was appointed by the executive (potentially the judiciary), it might be too favorably disposed to form an impartial tribunal. As long as methods of selection and appointment remained undetermined, so would the process of impeachment.

Confusion and disagreement were evident throughout. The Virginia plan called for the judiciary to hear all impeachments, without, it should be noted, specifying who or what could do the impeaching. Yet how could the judges be appointed by either the legislature or the executive, as either mode of selection would seem to bias their judgment (*Records*, 2:41–42)? Some argued for the power of impeachment and removal to be lodged in the legislature. That, however, ran the risk of making the executive the "mere creature of the Legislature," which was a "violation of the fundamental principle of good government" (*Records*, 1:86). The need for a removal power—which some delegates disputed in the case of the presidency—threatened this independence through the possibility of threat and coercion. For example, Charles Pinckney worried that the legislature through the threat of impeachment could "destroy his [the executive's] independence" and render his "revisionary power . . . altogether insignificant" (*Records*, 2:66, 551). One solution was to make the president or judges more independent of the appointing body by a long or secure tenure.

Although the preceding discussion conveys little about the peculiar place of the Senate in all this, it indicates the difficulties that confronted the delegates as they groped toward solutions. The Committee of Detail got close to an answer when it proposed that the House of Representatives have sole power of impeachment and the Supreme Court exclusive power to hear impeachments (*Records*, 2:178–79, 186). This method had the obvious defect of leaving the matter of judicial removals undetermined, and judges were to be appointed for life. The Senate finally appeared in the process when the Committee of Eleven transferred the power of impeachment trials to the Senate, with two-thirds of those present necessary for conviction. This change was part of the general package of boundary powers tied up with the selection of the president. The bicameral division of labor attempted to solve the twin problems associated with judicial trial of impeachments and the threat of legislative coercion of the executive. Thus, the solution of appointments paved the way for final decisions on removal, though the separation of powers problem was never quite resolved.

An Executive Council

The extent to which the delegates were working out new ways of thinking about the separation of powers is illustrated also by the fate of the idea of an "executive council," another potential avenue for Senate influence over the composition of the executive branch. Early American upper houses evolved in part from the councils of the colonial governments. Nevertheless, because most state governments retained separate privy councils to advise the governor, many delegates entered the convention with the assumption that some sort of executive council would be part of the new government. Ideas for such a council took two forms that occasionally intertwined. The first suggestion was for a council of revision, that is, a select group to be given the power of the veto over legislative acts. The second was for an advisory council to the executive, for general consultation or, as some desired, for the specific purpose of making appointments. Proposals for an advisory council often, but not always, involved participation by the Senate in the selection or actual membership of the council. Although references to and proposals for such councils ran through the convention's deliberations, as the summer unfolded with increasing support for a unitary and independent executive and for a generally stronger separation of powers, the perceived need for either type of council diminished. The executive was given the sole power of the veto, and it was accepted that he would seek advice from the heads of his departments rather than a separately constituted council. The failure to provide for any sort of council was another step in refining the separation of powers and thereby accentuating the Senate's primary role as a legislative body. As we have seen with the power of appointments and will soon see with the treaty power, the Senate was still essential to the resolution of difficult boundary problems and was, therefore, still more than just a second legislative chamber.[20]

SPECIAL SENATORIAL POLICY-MAKING POWERS

Money Bills

As we saw in chapter 4, the first legislative distinction between the two chambers was the money-bills restriction, which became entangled in the Great Compromise. Indeed, it is the only aspect of the apportionment struggle that could be labeled a compromise—that is, a quid pro quo—because the large-state coalition simply lost on getting proportional representation in both houses. Yet, as we have seen, many delegates did not see the money-bills restriction as any sort of compromise, and only a few delegates defended the money-bills restriction as inherently valuable. Most derided it, not only because it was not a fair trade for equality in the Senate but also because they believed the Senate should have an equal say on such a fundamental issue of public policy. Full Senate involvement constituted the desirable check and balance of bicameralism, and the Senate would be the more thoughtful and experienced chamber. Nevertheless, as part of the compromise on representation, it had been agreed that all bills for raising or appropriating money should originate in the House and should "not be altered or amended by the second Branch" (*Records*, 1:524).

When this provision came up for consideration following the compromise, Charles Pinckney moved to strike the prohibition from the Committee of Detail report. He was joined by several other large-state delegates, including Madison, Morris, Wilson, and Gorham. Their attitude seems best summarized by Wilson's comment that he "was himself directly opposed to equality of votes granted to the Senate . . . At the same time he wished not to multiply the vices of the system." Likewise, Morris "considered the Section {relating to money bills} as intrinsically bad." Mason, on the other hand, worried that "To strike out the section, was to unhinge the compromise of which it made a part," and raised the specter of a Senate aristocracy, a handful of men able to stop revenue bills. Mason's concerns were definitely in the minority. A broad majority of large and small, north and south joined to eliminate the restriction by a vote of seven to four. The issue was now controlled by a coalition between small-state delegates who were happy to see the Senate fully incorporated into the power of the purse and large-state delegates who felt the restriction was more trouble than it was worth. On the other side were smaller numbers of mostly large-state delegates (including Mason, Franklin, and Williamson) who saw the exclusion of the Senate on this issue as either inextricably linked to the apportionment compromise or intrinsically important as a principle of good government. Randolph and Mason were implacable and moved to reconsider the removal of the restriction, threatening, without much support, to revisit the equality of votes in the Senate. Charles Pinckney spoke for the majority by reminding the delegates that "notwithstanding what had been said as to the compromise, he always considered this section [on money bills] as making no part of it. The rule of Representation in the first branch was the true condition of that in the second branch" (*Records*, 2:224–25, 232–34, 262–63, 273–80).

Following a protracted debate on August 13, the convention rejected the first attempt to compromise on this issue by having the House originate all "money bills" but allowing the Senate the power to amend. Delegates were clearly tired of this troublesome issue. The next day Williamson acknowledged that the restriction "was dead. Its ghost, he was afraid, would, notwithstanding, haunt us. It had been a matter of conscience with him, to insist on it, as long as there was hope of retaining it. He had swallowed the vote of rejection with reluctance. He could not digest it. All that was said, on the other side, was, that the restriction was not *convenient*. We have now got a House of Lords which is to originate money bills" (*Records*, 2:287). On August 15, borrowing from his state constitution, Caleb Strong of Massachusetts proposed precise language for money bills, "which shall originate in the House of Representatives; but the Senate may propose or concur with amendments as in other cases." The convention failed to vote on Strong's language that day, however, because a few delegates remained worried about what *other* powers the Senate might be granted. They had not, for example, made a final decision on the treaty power, which at the time was in the Senate's hands (*Records*, 2:297).

Once again, it was up to David Brearly's Committee of Eleven to produce the package regarding presidential selection and the resolution of boundary powers, to settle the issue of money bills and nearly everything else involving bicameral distinctions and the separation of powers. The Brearly committee adopted the essence of Strong's proposal, and the convention accepted this without debate on September 8 by a vote of nine to two (*Records*, 2:552). The agreement to give the House the power to originate all money bills and the Senate the right to amend them reduced the issue to symbolic importance. As Warren argues, this shows that most of the delegates were not interested in replicating the majority of their state senates or the House of Lords, which were thus restricted.[21] A republican senate that was free from any meaningful association with mixed government did not need to be excluded, for any reason of theoretical propriety, from full participation in the power of the purse. The new Senate was to be an equal body. A bad compromise was not worth the sacrifice of other principles.

The Treaty Power

The Virginia plan, with its emphasis on institutional structure rather than governmental powers, did not specify anything about treaties or treaty making.[22] The implication, as with many other unspecified powers, was that Congress would have this power, as under the Confederation. The New Jersey plan, which was somewhat more concerned with enumerating powers, made ambiguous references to the treaty power, again apparently giving Congress the power of treaty making (though the plan refers only to acts relating to foreign trade) and assigning no role to the executive (*Records*, 1:243–44). Hamilton's speech of June 18, given in response to the New Jersey plan, called for the executive "to have with the advice and approbation of the Senate the power of making all treaties" (*Records*, 1:292). As with many other issues, however, the treaty power was barely discussed and nothing was settled until the resolution of the fight over representation.

On August 6, the Committee of Detail made its report, which provided some of the first details about the legislative powers (in addition to actually naming the legislature Congress and providing the names House of Representatives and Senate). As part of this enumeration or specification of powers, the Committee gave the Senate exclusive power to make treaties. Although the Committee had been given no instructions on this matter, their assignment of the treaty power came as no surprise to the delegates. Some delegates did not agree with the assignment, but this was because of the apportionment compromise and its implications for who would control the treaty power, not because they had fundamentally different ideas about how best to make treaties. With the power to appoint ambassadors and make treaties now in the Senate, perhaps few delegates disagreed with Charles Pinckney's claim that the Senate had the power of "managing our foreign affairs" (*Records*, 2:235). The executive was not yet part of the picture, and the exclusive senate power did not sit well with some delegates. As we have seen, the efforts to resolve the issue of money bills were thwarted in part by fear of the Senate having too much power, especially the treaty power, by which, warned Mason, that body could "sell the whole Country by means of Treaties" (*Records*, 2:297). Mason, a Virginian and opponent of equal representation in the Senate, was issuing the first (at least the first recorded) warning that an improperly constructed Senate was no longer suited for such an important power.

Why? Unlike appointments, the other major special power initially given to the Senate, the treaty power immediately evoked threats to state and regional interests. Here state size took a back seat to the recently inflamed differences between the states in the northeastern part of the country and those in the south with territory extending west to the Mississippi. On the eve of the Constitutional Convention, the Confederation Congress had been embroiled in a bitter fight over negotiations with Spain. The Secretary of Foreign Affairs, John Jay, was under instructions from Congress to reach a settlement with Spain on several disputed or unresolved issues, including navigation on the Mississippi, the western borders of the United States, and trade. The South sought first and foremost to regain the right to navigation on the Mississippi, which Spain had denied since 1784. The Northeast, having no land in the region, and not motivated to facilitate trade or migration in that direction, sought first and foremost to gain a trade treaty with Spain on favorable terms. Northeastern states were willing to go so far as to concede navigation rights (at least for a considerable number of years) on the great river to get a trade deal. In August 1786, with a majority in Congress, the northern states were able to win a vote to instruct Secretary Jay to strike such a bargain. All seven northern states voted for the new instructions; all five southern states voted against them. The southern states were furious and took this as a decisive measure of the threat posed by northern interests and prejudices.[23] The vote was somewhat of a Pyrrhic victory for the North, however. Under the Articles of Confederation, approval of a treaty required a supermajority of nine states, and the southern states vowed not to agree to a treaty that relinquished the right of navigation. This effectively killed Jay's mission. In late April, with delegates already gathering in Philadelphia for the convention, southerners took advantage of a temporary majority and voted, in effect, to void any instructions to Jay.[24] As a number of the delegates to the convention were themselves members of Congress and had recently participated in this acrimony, no doubt there was far more behind Mason's brief interjection than the consequences of the apportionment compromise. To Mason and his allies, the Senate, especially under a simple majority rule, was no place to lodge the treaty power.

With such tensions barely under the surface, the Senate's newfound hold on the treaty power was endangered from the start. Various delegates, mostly but not exclusively from large states, would pull the treaty power in one of two directions, either toward involving the presidency (which the Committee of Detail had only recently defined in its draft), or toward involving the House of Representatives. On August 23, the first day of substantive debate about the treaty power, Madison, echoing his change of mind about the Senate's role in appointments, "observed that the Senate represented the States alone, and that for this as well as other obvious reasons it was proper that the President should be an agent in Treaties." Gouverneur Morris concurred that the Senate was an improper venue and proposed that treaties must be "ratified by a law," which would give the House a veto power. Dickinson agreed even though "he was sensible it was unfavorable to the little States; which would otherwise have an *equal* share in making Treaties." Morris's proposal for approval by the House garnered support only from his own state (with North Carolina divided). The failure to get the House in the treaty power was much more about practical concerns than about state or regional interests. Delegates worried about the difficulties and delays inherent in full legislative action on treaties. Once again, state and regional interests were important but not the only consideration. A role for the House would have assuaged southern concerns at too high a cost to effective government. Treaties were still under control of the Senate, but the delegates referred the power to a committee for further consideration (*Records*, 2:392–94).

As with judicial appointments, the Senate retained the exclusive power over treaties until the Committee of Eleven reported on postponed parts on September 4. The Committee inserted the president into the treaty process. Instead of exclusive Senate control, "The President, by and with the advice and consent of the Senate, shall have power to make treaties." Moreover, no doubt as part of an effort to allay concerns about state equality and regional influence in the Senate, the Committee added that "no Treaty shall be made without the consent of two thirds of the Members present" (*Records*, 2:495). It also moved the description of the treaty power from the sections on the legislature to those on the presidency. The first attempt to alter any of this came on September 7, when Wilson moved to add the House of Representatives to the treaty power. "As treaties are to have the operation of laws," Wilson argued, "they ought to have the sanction of laws also. The circumstance of secrecy in the business of treaties formed the only objection; but this, he thought, so far as it was inconsistent with obtaining the Legislative sanction, was outweighed by the necessity of the latter." The convention disagreed overwhelmingly and Wilson's motion lost one to ten. Even though the Senate would be unrepresentative, it still would be the smaller and more deliberative chamber, and the one more closely linked to the executive. The two-thirds supermajority requirement drew some opposition because it empowered minorities who might block treaties and because it was unnecessary due to the "check" provided by the president's participation. Madison succeeded in adding an exception for treaties of peace to the two-thirds requirement, so as not overly to impede the termination of conflicts (*Records*, 2:538–41).

The final battles on the treaty power came the next day when separate motions were made to eliminate the two-thirds requirement and the exception for treaties of peace. Williamson and Gerry pointed out that a treaty of peace, under a simple majority rule, could be made by as few as eight senators. Such a small number of individuals could be corrupted, and they might represent only a small fraction of the population of the country. Again, in the minds of some delegates, even this issue of the relationship between peace treaties and supermajorities was intimately linked to sectional differences evinced by the Mississippi controversy—a treaty of peace might cede rights to territory, navigation, or trade.[25] The convention first voted eight to three to excise the exception for treaties of peace and then reaffirmed support for the two-thirds requirement by nine to one, with one state divided. After another unsuccessful attempt to modify the majority required to approve treaties and two unsuccessful attempts to insert a higher quorum standard for treaty votes, the convention finally completed its work on this important power (*Records*, 2:547–50).[26]

War Power

Although the treaty power and the war power are closely related as the major constitutionally designated foreign-policy procedures, the two barely crossed paths at the convention. That is, they were only indirectly discussed together, even though treaties of peace were, along with commercial treaties, foremost in the thoughts of the delegates. With the exception of Hamilton's famous June 18 speech, the Senate was never formally proposed as the locus of the war power; whereas, as we have just seen, the treaty power remained an exclusive Senate power until September. The war power was never a source of great controversy, but what limited debate there was on the subject managed to spill over, however briefly, into the relationship between Senate apportionment and the powers such a Senate deserved. On August 17 there arose a sudden and brief debate concerning the Committee of Detail's giving to the whole legislature the power to "make war." Charles Pinckney, who remained an advocate of Senate power despite the Great Compromise, objected to the legislature as too cumbersome for the war power, and that the House of Representatives in particular was too numerous. Instead, "[t]he Senate would be the best depositary, being more acquainted with foreign affairs, and most capable of proper resolutions." Pinckney's South Carolina colleague Butler countered that "[t]he Objections against the Legislature lie in a great degree against the Senate." It was better, he argued, to give the power to the president who "will not make war but when the Nation will support it." Mason agreed that the Senate was "not so constructed as to be entitled to it," and Gerry worried that fourteen or even eight senators could control the process of war and peace; moreover, "[t]he Senate are more liable to be corrupted by an Enemy than the whole Legislature." No vote was taken to shift the war power to the Senate. The convention voted to change the operative phrase from "make war" to "declare war" in order to make it clear that the executive was empowered to repel attacks, and then the delegates voted to keep the war power in the hands of the full legislature (*Records*, 2:318–19). It seems possible that had the Senate not been compromised by equal representation, more delegates—especially from the former large-state coalition—might have been willing, if not eager, to lodge this power in the Senate rather than both houses.[27]

THE CATCHALL OF THE CONSTITUTION

Just before the Senate was to lose its central role in presidential selection, James Wilson lamented the variety of powers concentrated in the Senate: "Mr Wilson said that he had weighed carefully the report of the Committee for remodelling the constitution of the Executive; and on combining it with other parts of the plan, he was obliged to consider the whole as having a dangerous tendency to aristocracy; as throwing a dangerous power into the hands of the Senate, They will have in fact, the appointment of the President, and through his dependence on them, the virtual appointment to offices; among others the offices of the Judiciary Department. They are to make Treaties; and they are to try all impeachments. In allowing them thus . . . , the Legislative, Executive & Judiciary powers are all blended in one branch of the Government" (*Records*, 2:522–23). While the majority of delegates did not share Wilson's stark apprehension, they had produced a Senate that stood at the intersection of the proposed system of not quite separated powers. That a Senate in its idealized form should have such a preeminent position was harmonious with many delegates' republican vision. That the Senate, in its compromised form, should inhabit the same vantage was another matter. Nevertheless, the business of the convention was done.

From start to finish, the issue of Senate representation pervaded the deliberations of the delegates and affected some of their most important decisions. Although the Senate's powers were somewhat reduced by counterattacks on the other elements of its composition and powers, in the final draft it remained an extraordinary institution, and its nature and purpose were crucial issues to the end of the deliberations.

Despite the enhancement of executive power at the expense of the Senate, the Senate was given vital powers in two particular areas, appointments and treaties. From a modern perspective dominated by the assumption of executive prerogative and power, these boundary powers can seem rather passive and reactive. As we have seen, however, convention dele-gates gave initial approval to Senate control over both these responsi-bilities, and though the delegates retracted some of that power, it is clear they intended for the Senate an active role in each. As others have noted, the convention took the phrase "advice and consent" quite literally, and the last-minute placement of the appointment power and treaty power in Article II instead of Article I should not be interpreted as a dramatic shift in the delegates' view of the proper distribution of powers. The Senate was expected to play an active role in appointments, especially those affecting the judiciary.[28] Moreover, given that treaties were part of the supreme law of the land, the Senate's role in the treaty process was, if anything, paramount. The president was to "make" treaties "by and with the Advice and Consent of the Senate." As Jack Rakove notes, it is telling that the delegates failed to discuss the independent virtues of the presi-dent's involvement in the treaty process.[29] The Senate was expected to be involved in the process of initiating and negotiating treaties, not simply ratifying them after the fact.[30]

Even from the perspective of original intent, however, the Senate was an ambiguous institution. The apportionment compromise made the Sen-ate a creature of the states; at the same time it was to be the steward of stability in national policy. The subsequent compromises on the Senate's composition and powers made it far less than a House of Lords but some-thing more than an ordinary legislative institution. In particular, the Sen-ate was placed at the crossroads of the system of separated institutions sharing powers. The Senate was to check the House, share in the executive power of appointments and treaties, and have a potentially decisive role in the composition of the Supreme Court. The politics of the convention added another special purpose—the Senate would be the institutional embodiment of federalism and state power in the national government. In this way, the Senate became the crucible for resolving several of the thorn-iest problems of American constitutionalism. While the other branches were kept relatively pure in form, the Senate was used to forge solutions to the difficulties of the separation of powers and the nation-state problem. These various and potentially contradictory roles shaped the Senate's place within the American system from the beginning. In fact, they shaped the debate over ratification, as we shall see in the next chapter.

On September 15, the busy final day of substantive debate on the pro-posed Constitution, the last successful motion was about equality in the

Senate.[31] A few days before, the convention had added without debate one restriction on the procedure to amend the Constitution: "no amendment which may be made prior to the year 1808 shall in any manner affect" the provisions protecting the importation of slaves and the three-fifths formula on taxation. Roger Sherman noted the addition of this restriction, and thought it "should be extended" such that "no State shall without its consent be affected in its internal police, or deprived of its equal suffrage in the Senate." Sherman's two-pronged proposal failed on a vote of three to eight. Gouverneur Morris, perhaps in a spirit of accommodation, excised the internal police provision, and the second half of Sherman's restriction passed without debate or dissent, "being dictated by the circulating murmurs of the small States" (*Records*, 2:629–31). Thus the only permanent limitation on the power to amend the Constitution was entered into Article V. The Great Compromise, the creation and effects of which had pervaded the deliberations of the convention from start to finish, was not only great, but permanent as well.

SIX

Unfounded Hopes and Fears
The Senate during Ratification

The Senate emerged from the Constitutional Convention as the most uncertain of the institutional innovations produced that summer in Philadelphia. The delegates had used it as a general receptacle for a variety of major problems that had troubled the convention, and the result was a hybrid of potentially incompatible purposes. Ratification was the first stage in defining (or divining) what was created by the convention. Although volumes have been written on the ratification debates in general, only cursory attention has been given to particular subjects such as the Senate. Many accounts of Senate history provide a rather perfunctory treatment of ratification, and histories of ratification cover the Senate in a few pages.[1] Yet the Senate drew considerable fire from the Constitution's opponents, and the richness and significance of the arguments deserve greater attention. The anti-Federalists vigorously attacked the Senate as the clearest indication of the Constitution's undemocratic and centralizing tendencies: an institutionalized aristocracy with authority and influence that violated the separation of powers and threatened to dominate the House and president. Particularly objectionable was the combination of the Senate's small size, elite membership, and considerable powers, while what had been the most divisive issue in Philadelphia—equal representation—nearly disappeared from the debate.

To defend the constitutional plan as a whole, the Federalists had to justify this essential institution and rebut the particular criticisms. Yet some of the defenders were in a difficult position. They had fought for a coherent national senate and were forced to accept a very heterogeneous institution instead. Was the convention's hybrid in fact adequate to its broad purposes in a republican and national constitution? Could the Senate in fact be both nationally minded and representative of the corporate interests of states? Could it successfully combine its executive duties with its role as a second legislative chamber? We will see that, rather than being duplicitous, as some scholars have argued, the Federalists offered a strategic but forthright defense of the Senate. Indeed, the senate presented in the *Federalist* is much closer to Madison's original conception of a truly national senate than to the convention's compromised design.

THE SENATE IN THE RATIFICATION DEBATES

It would be exceedingly difficult to quantify the degree of debate given to each objection to the proposed constitution. We can say that institutional concerns were common and that the Senate was frequently at the center of these. Historians of the ratification campaign agree that the two principal themes pressed by anti-Federalists were:

1. The threat of "consolidation": that the general powers of the new national government and the lack of adequate checks would allow it to centralize power at the expense of state sovereignty.
2. The threats to liberty: that particularly in the absence of a bill of rights, these inadequately checked and broad powers would be exercised at the expense of individual liberty.[2]

Where did the Senate fit into this picture? Jackson Turner Main's assertion that "[a]ttacks on the Senate itself were of relatively minor importance . . . and almost no one objected to the Senate's existence" is misleading because the Senate, as constituted, was the object of a great deal of debate, both on account of its inherent features and for its anticipated role in national consolidation.[3] More to the point is Herbert Storing's observation that the Senate "represented for many of them [the anti-Federalists] all that was wrong with the Constitution."[4]

What was *not* wrong about either the Senate or the Constitution to most anti-Federalists was either bicameralism in general or equal representation of states in one house. Few essayists and delegates to the state conventions objected to these features. A few anti-Federalists argued for a single-chamber *national* legislature, like that of the Confederation, which would guarantee state equality. As Main notes, though, "most of the anti-Federalists—at least those who were writing and speaking—accepted the bicameral principle" that two houses, differently constituted, provided for safer government.[5] Main cites Richard Henry Lee, John Lansing, and Melancton Smith as examples and notes that even the opposition in Pennsylvania did not make unicameralism one of its demands. In fact, we found no positive reference to unicameralism in the Pennsylvania ratification convention debates; the opponents seem to take a senate for granted. The lack of enthusiasm for unicameral legislatures probably tempered some potential opposition to the Senate.

Equal representation of states was accepted by the majority of Federalists and anti-Federalists alike, which of course worked to the advantage of the former. Although distasteful to some Federalists, equal representation bolstered support for the new constitution. The structure of the Senate facilitated early ratification by a series of small states, including Delaware, New Jersey, and Connecticut, and later, Maryland. These small states seemed eager to seal the deal they had gotten. Anti-Federalists were, however, in a rather difficult position. The Senate was the only institutional feature in the Constitution that embodied the federal principle of state sovereignty and power within the national system. Opposition to equal representation was therefore a weak argument for those who were, explicitly or implicitly, defending the Articles of the Confederation. A few anti-Federalists could and did rail against equal representation, but they received no help from Federalists, who had accepted, at least rhetorically, this feature of the new constitution. Among the large states, opposition to equality in the Senate was manifest only in Virginia, and even there it played a secondary role. Edmund Randolph and George Mason, the Virginia convention delegates who did not sign the Constitution, both objected to state equality. Equality in the Senate was also part of a larger argument about the balance of power between North and South in the political economy of the new nation.[6]

Anti-Federalists instead concentrated their fire on other features of the upper house. Brutus captured the common anti-Federalist attitude toward the Senate: "[O]n this principle [state equality] I approve of it [the Senate]. It is indeed the only feature of any importance in the constitution of a confederated government . . . It is to be regretted, that they were not able to have infused other principles into the plan, to have secured the government of the respective states, and to have marked with sufficient precision the line between them and the general government."[7] Brutus then launches into a list of objections to nearly every other feature of the Senate from the length of term to the treaty power. What was a great compromise on behalf of state sovereignty for delegates at the convention was to the Constitution's opponents a mere fig leaf of real federalism, something to be taken for granted, not celebrated.

Thus, one of the ironies of the transition from the convention to ratification was the change of importance of the representational compromise. The most controversial issue during the convention—equal representation in the Senate—was in ratification debates one of the least.[8] What had achieved broad agreement in Philadelphia—the need for a small, select, and powerful Senate as the institutional anchor of republican government—became the focus of strenuous objections. In other words, the anti-Federalists concentrated their fire on the very features the framers valued most.

THE ATTACK ON THE SENATE

Anti-Federalist Objections

Objections to the Senate commenced with the prominent delegates to the convention who failed to sign the proposed constitution. George Mason, Edmund Randolph, Elbridge Gerry, and Luther Martin all included the Senate in their objections. For Randolph, who came from the large state of Virginia, equal representation was a principal objection to the whole document. For small-state residents such as Martin, equal representation was not enough of a benefit to offset the other exceptionable aspects of the Senate. By late fall of 1787, however, the list of anti-Federalist objections to the Senate had been vetted in various forms and forums:

- Election by legislators rather than the people would make the Senate aristocratic.
- The long term of office and the absence of mandatory "rotation" or term limits would free senators from accountability.
- States were given no power to recall senators, as was the case in the Congress of the Confederation.
- An aristocratic Senate should not have the right to alter or amend money bills.
- The small size of the Senate would give a very few senators an effective veto over all policy.
- The vice president's position as president of the Senate was a dangerous violation of the separation of powers.
- Powers shared with the executive would require that the Senate be "constantly assembled" and thereby reduce the importance of the democratic branch.

—These shared powers would also foster an aristocratic cabal between the Senate and the executive.

—The power of appointment would give the Senate the ability to corrupt the House and influence the president.

—The power to try impeachments would make senators the judges in trials of their own appointees.

—The treaty-making power, especially under the control of a small number of Senate votes, was not safely or justly lodged in that undemocratic body.[9]

Based on these sorts of objections, Cincinnatus questioned what he deemed to be "the most exceptionable part of the Constitution":

Is a body so vested with means to soften & seduce—so armed with power to screen or to condemn—so fortified against suspicion and enquiry—so largely trusted with legislative powers—so independent of and removed from the people—so tempted to abuse and extend these powers—is this a body which freemen ought ever to create, or which freemen can ever endure? Or is it not a monster in the political creation, which we ought to regard with horror? Shall we thus forge our own fetters? Shall we set up the idol, before which we shall soon be obliged, however, reluctantly to bow? Shall we consent to see a proud aristocracy erect his domineering crest in triumph over our prostrate liberties?[10]

Cincinnatus was far from alone in finding the Senate at the center of what was flawed in the proposed constitution, in terms of both representation and institutional powers. The fear of an aristocratic Senate arose from what were seen as inadequate ties of accountability; senators would not be faithful representatives of the states that sent them. Long terms, national pay, and per capita voting, without the protection of recall and mandatory rotation, would promote an insulated aristocracy more than a defender of state sovereignty and interests. If we are being assured that senators are to be representatives of the states, some anti-Federalists wondered, then why such long terms? Why no recall? Unsuccessful efforts were made in several states to add a recall provision as one of the amendments to be added after ratification.

This aristocratic institution would, moreover, dominate the government. The constitutional plan as a whole would tend to diminish the influence of the more democratic branch, and by mixing legislative and executive powers in the Senate, the upper house would be given the undue influence over the executive and judiciary (or, vice versa, the undue influence of the executive over the Senate). Altogether, bicameralism would fail as a check. Whatever slim promise of security there was in the House would be vanquished by the overarching power of the Senate and the cabal with the executive. The chamber intended to resist consolidation through equal representation became a symbol of the potential forces of aristocratic union. Some of the main features contributing to this result deserve a closer examination.

Size

What had been at the convention among the Senate's most lauded and guarded features—its small size—became for anti-Federalists one of its principal defects. This is not totally surprising, given the anti-Federalist discontent even with the size of the House of Representatives. Yet the concerns about the Senate's size were completely different in nature. Whereas the problem with the House was that the ratio of representatives to constituents was simply too small to provide for authentic representation and strict accountability, the complaint about the Senate's size revolved around its powers. Too many important powers would be in the hands of too few senators. A small number of senators would be able to control the outcome in questions of great importance to the government and the nation as a whole.[11] The arithmetic of this problem became a sort of catechism regularly recited by the constitution's opponents: twenty-six senators, of which fourteen form a quorum for business, of which eight form a majority. "Your Senate," noted Patrick Henry to his fellow Virginia convention delegates, "is so imperfectly constructed that your dearest rights may be sacrificed by what may be a small minority."[12] This minority would be profoundly unrepresentative, and even if it were not, it would be too small to prevent corruption. A few saw this as a problem with the smallness of Congress as a whole, including Brutus, who argued that "there will be no security in so small a body, against bribery, and corruption."[13] Many more made these charges exclusively against the Senate. Bribery could come from foreign or domestic sources, but the direct influence of money was not the only problem. In a small legislature, influential senators would need to manipulate or deceive only a few members in order to serve their own private interests.[14] Small size, from the anti-Federalist perspective, would not foster sober deliberation so much as opportunism, collusion, and corruption.

Size and the Treaty Power

This math was particularly disturbing when it came to treaties, which would be among the supreme laws of the land. Whereas the Confederation required a two-thirds majority of all states, the proposed constitution required approval by "two thirds of the Senators present." Anti-Federalists envisioned the Senate voting on important treaties with a bare quorum. Two-thirds of a senate quorum would be ten. Throughout the treaty process, there would be no check by the House, and the Senate, or some part of it, could readily be in cahoots with the president. To many anti-Federalists, full participation by the House was needed not only to provide a check on the elite Senate and the presidency but also to approve what were, in effect, laws of the land. Ten senators were all that was necessary to make peace or ratify a commercial treaty. Virginia's William Grayson, for example, worried that "[i]f the senators of the Southern States be gone but one hour, a treaty may be made by the rest, yielding that inestimable right" of navigation of the Mississippi. After all, "[s]even states had already discovered a determined resolution of yielding it to Spain." "Such is my repugnance," he concluded, "to the alienation of a right which I esteem so important to the happiness of my country, that I would object to this Constitution if it contained no other defect." To top it all off, the same two-thirds that could make an execrable treaty would then be able (in a mistaken view of the impeachment power) to block their own impeachment for their actions. "Here will be," warned one anti-Federalist, "a fine field for the intrigues and even the bribery and corruption of European powers."[15]

Federalists addressed this criticism directly. Publius (*Federalist* 64 and 75) argued that the proposed constitution would be better than the Confederation Congress as far as probable numbers of voting members. Madison made much the same points in disputing concerns about the hypothesized giveaway of the Mississippi.[16] Other Federalists at the conventions in Virginia, South Carolina, North Carolina, and Massachusetts also rebutted these charges and defended the Senate's treaty power.[17] In one of the longest of these rebuttals, North Carolinian William Davie, a veteran of Philadelphia and one of the principal compromisers from that summer, chided his anti-Federalist colleagues for their inconsistencies and double binds; they had worried repeatedly about consolidation but at the same time wanted to share the treaty power with the House, "where the idea of consolidation can alone exist." Likewise expressing his frustration with this general anti-Federalist tactic, North Carolina's Governor Johnston noted that opponents "make use of contradictory arguments. The Senate represents the states, and can alone prevent this dreaded consolidation; yet the powers of the Senate are objected to."[18]

Boundary Powers and Union with the Executive

Complaints and anxieties about the Senate's small size were usually linked to those powers it shared with the executive branch. These "blended" powers, anti-Federalists argued, violated the cardinal principle that the three powers ought to be separated. Taken as a whole, these powers spelled disaster: "It has been wittily observed that the Constitution has married the President and Senate—has made them man and wife. I believe the consequence that generally results from marriage will happen here. They will be continually supporting and aiding each other: they will always consider their interest as united."[19] George Mason's sentiment was widely shared by his fellow anti-Federalists.

The treaty power was first and foremost among these dangerous powers. Second in importance was the Senate's "advice and consent" in the appointment power, which also gave the Senate a role in the judiciary.[20] The Senate's appointment power was sometimes linked to the lack of a "constitutional Council" in George Mason's words, or a privy council, which would provide the president with needed advice on appointments without violating the separation of powers. Another questionable power was the Senate's role as the court of impeachment. Senatorial control over the trial of impeachments was objectionable in and of itself as a violation of the separation of powers; many saw impeachment as a judicial function. This impeachment power became especially problematic in combination with the appointment power: Was it fair and impartial to have senators sitting in judgment over the very people they helped to appoint, or over the president who is ultimately responsible for the conduct of his administration?[21] Finally, there was the vice presidency, an office that actually straddled the division between the Senate and the executive. George Mason believed the vice president was "not only an unnecessary, but a dangerous officer," and one of his objections to the proposed constitution was that it introduced an agent of the executive branch into the formal structure of the legislature. In the case of tied votes, moreover, the vice president would provide one state, probably a larger state, with an extra voice and vote.[22]

Reflecting on the multifaceted Senate, Brutus lamented this "strange mixture of legislative, executive, and judicial powers, which in my opinion will in some cases clash with each other." "I can scarcely imagine," he concluded, "that any of the advocates of the system will pretend that it was necessary to accumulate all these powers in the senate."[23] Particularly the powers shared with the executive would require the Senate to sit continuously. These long sessions, according to many anti-Federalists, would facilitate intrigue within the Senate and strengthen the ties between the Senate and president, all with the effect of diminishing the influence of the House. An already inadequately democratic government would become even less responsive to the people. As Centinel I put it: "The President . . . would either become the head of the aristocratic junto in that body, or its minion."[24] Despite fears about the "foetus of monarchy" at the Constitutional Convention, during ratification anti-Federalists complained about the executive's lack of independence—the violation of the separation of powers that gave the Senate such an important role in executive tasks. Indeed, there would be "two executive branches" with the Senate and president forming a "Venetian aristocracy."[25] Richard Henry Lee saw an "[o]ligarchic tendency from the combination of President, V. President, & Senate."[26] The small size of the Senate was important in this and magnified the danger. As Mason put it, "We know the advantage the few have over the many. They can with facility act in concert, and on a uniform system: they may join, scheme, and plot, against the people without any chance of detection. The Senate and President will form a combination that cannot be prevented by the representatives. The executive and legislative powers, thus connected, will destroy all balances."[27]

THE DEFENSE OF THE SENATE

Regardless of their opinions of the representational compromise, those who supported the proposed constitution embraced the Senate and used that feature to their advantage. The Federalists, "seldom missed an opportunity to clothe the future Senators in the full dress of ambassadors sent by the states to defend their sovereignty." While this is, as Michael Malbin has noted, "overstated," there is no doubt that Federalists used the Senate as a selling point to both large- and small-state residents who feared a diminution of state sovereignty.[28] Occasionally, the nature of the Senate could be tailored for the particular state in question, with small-state Federalists emphasizing the Senate's role as protector of state power and large-state Federalists arguing that state attachments would give way to a more nationally minded Senate. For example, while John Dickinson argued to the Delaware convention that the Senate would be just like the Congress of the Confederation, Noah Webster told the Pennsylvania gathering that the Senate, in time, would become a national body. Yet this approach is no different from other debates on sections of the Constitution that involved obvious compromises—such as the arguments about slavery, where the compromises were interpreted differently in the North and South as either allowing eventual abolition or protecting slavery.[29]

Several scholars have seen this strategic rhetoric as a form of deception, as though the Federalists were hiding their true intentions. These scholars have accused Madison and the Federalists of changing their tune about the Senate once the Convention was over and the public debate over ratification began.[30] To sell the Senate, it is charged, Madison and his allies shed their Anglophilic trappings in favor of more democratic garb, by emphasizing how the Senate was nearly as democratic an institution as the House, selected by state legislatures and designed to protect state interests. Gone, it is alleged, were the class-based justifications supposedly so prominent at the convention. As was shown in chapters 4 and 5, class-centered or mixed government arguments were not as prominent in the convention as is sometimes claimed. Arguments that did not shy from extolling the counterdemocratic virtues of the Senate were quite common.

Indeed, the authors of the *Federalist* reminded their audience of the need for the Senate's check on democratic impulses, and they all but ignored the representational compromise. This is also true of the ratification campaign in general. The defense of the Senate was simultaneously honest and strategic just as the Federalist defense of the whole Constitution was a bit of both. Another tactic in the Federalist counterattack was to argue that the proposed constitution was a painstakingly wrought product of compromise in several crucial facets (representation, slavery, the electoral college, etc.) and that, although imperfect in pieces, the sum was better than the parts and danger lay in any attempt to pick it apart piece by piece.[31] In failing to acknowledge the changed circumstances during ratification, these scholarly critics are being somewhat unfair to the supporters of the proposed constitution. The convention was over, and whether or not this was the Senate of their political ideals, its form was now settled in the document. So why should we not expect them to use slightly different arguments than were raised during the debates and compromises of the convention? It was a different Senate.

The defenders of the Senate were not duplicitous in part because most of them typically were not laying out ex ante justifications for the Senate, but rather answering attacks on the Senate. Their answers could be quite honest by (1) using the Senate's role as protector of the states to argue against the fear of consolidation, (2) refuting the predictions of a Senate or Senate-executive aristocracy, and (3) defending the Senate's direct role in the policy-making process as a check on the power of the president and the House.

Madison admitted forthrightly during the Virginia convention that, "When we come to the Senate, its members are elected by the states in their equal and political capacity. But had the government been completely consolidated, the Senate would have been chosen by the people in their individual capacity, in the same manner as the members of the other house. Thus it is of a complicated nature; and this complication, I trust, will be found to exclude the evils of absolute consolidation, as well as of a mere confederacy."[32] Madison's northern ally, Alexander Hamilton, explicated this "complicated nature" for his suspicious New York colleagues. In perhaps the single longest ratification debate devoted to the Senate, Hamilton rebuffed the idea of an amendment to institute rotation and recall for Senators by arguing that "senators will constantly look up to the state governments with an eye of dependence and affection. If they are ambitious to continue in office, they will make every prudent arrangement for this purpose, and, whatever may be their private sentiments or politics, they will be convinced that the surest means of obtaining a reelection will be a uniform attachment to the interests of their several states."[33] Nevertheless, given the objects of the Senate's efforts, especially in foreign affairs, a long term was necessary and prudent.

When his main adversary, Melancton Smith, objected that a contradiction seemed to be developing between the idea of the Senate as a safeguard of states' rights and the need for an independent and insulated Senate, Hamilton responded: "It has been remarked, that there is an inconsistency in our admitting that the equal vote in the Senate was given to secure the rights of the states, and at the same time holding up the idea that their interests should be sacrificed to those of the Union. But the committee certainly perceive the distinction between the rights of a state and its interests." The Senate would protect state rights, Hamilton implied, but not necessarily individual state interests. "Is he [a senator] simply the agent of the state? No. He is an agent for the Union, and he is bound to perform services necessary to the good of the whole, though his state should condemn them."[34] Madison and Hamilton may not have had the easiest time squaring the circle of state representation, but their arguments were honest about the complexity of the Senate.

Other Federalists were more than willing to sell the Senate on its combined functions and virtues, arguing that its structural complexity could achieve a blend of functions. South Carolina's Charles Pinckney defended the Senate on several occasions during his state's convention. He lauded the bicameral check, especially as a way to protect states, and defended the Maryland senate as the best model, with its long terms to promote "knowledge and firmness." "By constructing the Senate upon rotative principles," Pinckney concluded, "we have removed, as will be shown upon another occasion, all danger of an aristocratic influence; while, by electing the members for six years, we hope we have given to this part of the system all the advantages of an aristocracy—wisdom, experience, and a consistency of measures."[35] Up north in Massachusetts, Theophilus Parsons provided a lengthy explication of the delicate balancing act that "most happily extricated" the framers from the "embarrassment" of constructing a senate that was to represent and be dependent on states as well as to conduct national business such as foreign relations. He applauded the combination of a long term with rotation as achieving that balance.[36] In North Carolina, James Iredell articulated a forthright defense of the Senate's fundamental republican purpose that is worth quoting at some length:

> As the representatives of the people may probably be more popular, and it may be sometimes necessary for the Senate to prevent factious measures taking place, which may be highly injurious to the real interests of the public, the Senate should not be at the mercy of every popular

clamor. Men engaged in arduous affairs are often obliged to do things which may, for the present, be disapproved of, for want of full information of the case, which it is not in every man's power immediately to obtain. In the mean time, every one is eager to judge, and many to condemn; and thus many an action is for a time unpopular, the true policy and justice of which afterwards very plainly appear. These observations apply even to acts of legislation concerning domestic policy: they apply much more forcibly to the case of foreign negotiations, which will form one part of the business of the Senate . . . Nothing is more unfortunate for a nation than to have its affairs conducted in an irregular manner. Consistency and stability are necessary to render the laws of any society convenient for the people.[37]

Federalists had no trouble dismissing concerns about a Senate aristocracy. James Wilson went so far as to assert that "perhaps never was a charge made with less reasons than that which predicts the institution of a baneful aristocracy in the federal senate."[38] An "American Citizen" prefaced his point by point defense of the Senate by noting that "As our President bears no resemblance to a King, so we shall see the Senate have no similitude to nobles."[39] The Senate, argued Noah Webster in his lengthy defense of bicameralism, will give us "all the advantages of checks and balance, without the danger which may arise from a superior and independent order of men."[40] Others, including Iredell at the North Carolina convention and Timothy Pickering in Pennsylvania, issued similar refutations and reassurances that the Senate would not dominate the House of Representatives.[41] In this way the debates that did touch on Senate elitism often redounded to the advantage of the Federalists. The overwrought charges set up the obvious responses, especially the idea that the Senate is elected for six years only, with staggered classes, and by democratically elected state legislatures. Under such circumstances there was little need to defend the republican (and to that extent, antidemocratic) function of the Senate, though, as we have just seen, Federalists did not shy from such arguments.

THE FEDERALIST'S NATIONAL SENATE

The Federalist is a special case. Its explanation of the Senate is detailed, methodical, and thorough, and it is set within a comprehensive examination of the whole constitutional plan. A careful analysis of the relevant essays contradicts a common interpretation that Publius, more or less at peace with the compromised Senate, offers a synthetic account of the resulting institution.[42] Like other defenders, Publius uses the confederal features to fend off critics. Yet he also develops an account of a thoroughly national senate as an essential provision for wise and stable government in a liberal republic. He pointedly fails to demonstrate how the convention's "partly federal . . . partly national" hybrid would work in practice and how it would, or could, serve those national ends. In fact, he does the opposite. Publius explicitly isolates state election and equal representation of states from his consideration of the Senate's crucial constitutional and political functions; those confederal features are, in other words, entirely unrelated to, and separable from "the purposes which are to be answered by a senate."[43] He neither develops a synthesis nor explains how the resulting state influence would be overcome by long terms and small size, the Senate's other main institutional features.

Dismissing the Compromise

Publius's explanations of the Senate's confederal features are, in sum, "dismissive."[44] The brief discussion of the appointment of senators by state legislatures is the closest he comes to acknowledging any practical advantage from the confederal composition of the Senate, but this acknowledgement is, at best, equivocal and conditional (*Federalist* 62: 416). His granting that this mode is "probably the most congenial with the public opinion" neatly evades endorsement and the more important questions concerning the effects of state selection on the institution. It will have the advantage, he acknowledges, "of favouring a select appointment," that is, of favoring more politically mature and experienced persons, at least when compared to *some* other modes of election. He omits, however, an account of how this mode would secure the particular qualities required by the Senate's responsibilities.[45] In the absence of a newfound respect for the prudence of the very state legislatures whose parochial views had precipitated the constitutional crisis (*Federalist* 44: 301–2), Publius's failure to address the obvious concerns is glaring. Nothing is said, for example, about the probable effects of equal representation on the quality of the choices. Instead, the best Publius can muster is that the selection of senators gives the states an "agency in the formation of the federal government" and "*may* form a convenient link between the two systems" (*Federalist* 62: 416, emphasis added).[46]

The occasion for a clear affirmation of the convention's hybrid begins and ends with a whimper. Publius's reticence on this point needs to be compared with his lengthy discussion of the modes of selection for other branches. These modes are treated as the *principal* means of locating people with the skills and dispositions appropriate to particular offices.[47] The *Federalist* devotes all or part of five papers to the selection of the House (*Federalist* 35, 52–54, 57), an entire paper to the manner of choosing the executive (*Federalist* 68), and all or part of three papers to judicial and other appointments (*Federalist* 76–78). The Senate, which was to embody rare and essential qualities, receives one vague paragraph that does not even attempt to reconcile the parochial origin of its members with the qualities appropriate to the distinctively national purposes Publius explains at length in papers 62 and 63.

He also passes quickly over state equality in the Senate. In fact, his flaccid affirmations of state selection seem almost laudatory when compared to his defense of the equal representation of states, "which, being evidently the result of compromise between the opposite pretensions of the large and the small states, does not call for much discussion." Why? Because "it is superfluous to try by the standards of theory, a part of the constitution which is allowed on all hands to be the result not of theory, but 'of a spirit of amity, and that mutual deference and concession which the peculiarity of our political situation rendered indispensable.'" The large states were forced to choose between "the proposed government and a government still more objectionable." "Prudence" argued for accepting the "lesser evil." Publius's only attempt to discover some theoretical propriety in this feature results in a strictly conditional and amusingly evasive explanation: "If indeed it be right that among a people thoroughly incorporated into one nation, every district ought to have a *proportional* share in the government; and that among independent and sovereign states bound together by a simple league, the parties however unequal in size ought to have an *equal* share in the common councils, it does not appear to be without some reason, that in a compound republic partaking both of the national and federal character, the government ought to be founded on a mixture of the principles of proportional and equal representation." Publius forgoes "indulging in a fruitless anticipation of the possible mischiefs which may ensue," and so the evils and objections to the compromised form are not explained here. Prudence, again, advises him "to contemplate rather the advantageous consequences which may qualify the sacrifice" (*Federalist* 62: 416–17).

The two qualifying advantages are not exactly earth shaking. The first is that equal representation in the Senate "is at once a constitutional recognition of the portion of sovereignty remaining in the individual states, and an instrument for preserving that residuary sovereignty." Elsewhere, Publius denies any significant threat to state sovereignty even while exploring other ways in which it will be protected.[48] The second advantage seems more substantial and useful. "No law or resolution can now be passed without the concurrence first of a majority of the people, and then of a majority of the states." This form of concurrent majorities is an "additional impediment . . . against improper acts of legislation." As it turns out, of course, the only *improper* acts impeded by this confederal Senate would be ones that disfavored the smaller states, and he notes, there are no common interests among the smaller states that "would otherwise be exposed to peculiar danger." This representation of states is not, then, much of an advantage, and Publius even comments that this check may be "injurious as well as beneficial." Within his discussion of the potentially beneficial effects of the Great Compromise, Publius marshals his most hopeful words in favor of a by-product of equal representation: the extra check such asymmetrical representation in the two houses places in the way of the "facility and excess of law-making," which "seem to be the diseases to which our governments are most liable." Consequently, it is "not impossible" that this arrangement "may be more convenient in practice than it appears to many in contemplation" (*Federalist* 62: 417).

Criticizing the Compromise: State Influences

It is perfectly understandable that amid a defense of the constitutional plan Publius would only allude to possible ill effects from the confederal structure of the Senate. He would not want to expose a fundamental defect in a major institution and thereby risk the gains that even a flawed plan would make over the Confederation. Yet away from the delicate matter of the Senate, Publius is quite frank about the "mischiefs" from state influence in the national government. Any doubts about the seriousness of these "mischiefs" should be dispelled by his arguments in the forty-sixth paper, where he discusses the dependence of the national government on state and local interests. Obviously, such arguments in general would serve to deflect anti-Federalist worries about consolidation. Publius's strong language, however, exceeds the requirements of a rhetorical finesse. Indeed, he sets the stage by arguing that the modes of selection for House, Senate, and presidency are "much more likely to beget a disposition *too obsequious*, than too overbearing towards [the states]" (*Federalist* 45: 311, emphasis added).

As a consequence of the general bias toward the states, a "local spirit will infallibly prevail much more in the members of the Congress, than a national spirit will prevail in the Legislatures of the particular States." The implications, particularly for the Senate's character, are obvious, and Publius then dilates on the baleful consequences of mixing state predilections into a national government. "Every one knows that a great proportion of the errors committed by the State Legislatures proceeds from the disposition of the members to sacrifice the comprehensive and permanent interest of the State, to the particular and separate views of the counties or districts in which they reside. And if they do not sufficiently enlarge their policy to embrace the collective welfare of their particular State, how can it be imagined, that they will make the aggregate prosperity of the Union, and the dignity and respectability of its government, the objects of their affections and consultations?" (*Federalist* 46: 318)

This argument has two implications: the national legislature needs at least one institution that will focus legislative deliberation on general national interests; and the influence of state legislatures will tend to infect the Senate with parochial concerns. Publius's dire conclusion embraces the whole Congress: "the members of the Federal Legislature will be likely to attach themselves too much to local objects . . . Measures will too often be decided according to their probable effect, not on national prosperity and happiness, but on the prejudices, interests and pursuits of the governments and people of the individual States." To illustrate his point, Publius notes that members of the Continental Congress have "displayed the character, rather of partizans of their respective States, than of impartial guardians of a common interest," and "the great interests of the nation have suffered . . . from an undue attention to the local prejudices, interests and views of the particular States" (*Federalist* 46: 318).[49]

That is quite a mischief. Publius then tries to reassure the reader that the national government will nonetheless pursue "a more enlarged plan" than the confederacy and that state and local bias will serve to prevent *only* invasions "of the rights of the individual States, or the prerogatives of their governments" (*Federalist* 46: 319). This, of course, would be the perfect and the only appropriate balance; the confederal character of the Senate would be engaged only by legitimate questions of state sovereignty, and otherwise its national character would dominate all deliberations on national policy. Yet Publius's reassurance is entirely abstract. How is this delicate balance to be achieved in practice? Here, instead of offering an explanation, he argues that there will be many parochial inclinations to overcome. Elsewhere, as we have seen, he avoids the issue and, at least, allows the inference that the constitutional plan's design does not achieve the right balance. Once we see the importance of a strictly national Senate to the promise of an "enlarged" policy, the implausibility of Publius's reassurance will be more evident.[50]

The Purposes of a Senate

Publius devotes a mere 12 percent of his words in *Federalist* numbers 62 and 63 to either equal representation or state selection.[51] The rest are devoted to a direct and detailed examination of "the purposes which are to be answered by a senate" in the national government. The Senate's true and main purposes are derived from an examination of the six "inconveniencies which a republic must suffer from the want of such an institution" (*Federalist* 62: 418).

1. The loss of an important check on any tendency in one legislative house to act without regard to the general good.
2. The tendency of a large assembly either "to yield to the impulse of sudden and violent passions," or to be misled by unscrupulous politicians.
3. The deficit in a popular house of knowledge about the "objects and principles of legislation."
4. The instability of legislation and policy resulting from the rapid turnover of popular representatives.
5. The deficit in local representatives of a sensitivity to the reputation of the national government and nation as a whole.
6. The deficit of responsibility for, and attention to, long-term and national interests that arises from frequent elections.

Absent a remedy, these defects would undermine the wisdom and stability of national government and policy, and only a body with particular characteristics would correct these problems. The principal elements of the institutional design are small size, longer term, and staggered terms. These features were intended to foster stability and wisdom. Yet stability and wisdom will not provide the desired effects, Publius argues, unless the Senate is also strictly national in its outlook. Publius's explanation depicts a Senate that is thoroughly national in character.

Checking the House

The first inconvenience is common to all government: "that those who administer it, may forget their obligations to their constituents" and act without regard to the general good. Publius is not arguing that the Senate will be more faithful to the people than the House. In fact, the "fidelity" of representatives to their constituents was to be the Constitution's main defense against tyranny (*Federalist* 62: 419). Rather, the people's security is *enhanced* by requiring "the concurrence of two distinct bodies in schemes of usurpation and perfidy." Such security is proportional to "the dissimilarity in the genius" of the two houses, and it would be "politic to distinguish them from each other" as far as possible without undermining either cooperation in all "proper measures" or "the genuine principles of republican government." This was a prominent argument, acknowledged earlier by Publius, in favor of a confederal Senate. By reintroducing the need for dissimilar legislative houses *after* dispensing with the confederal elements, Publius implies that state selection and representation do not establish an appropriate dissimilarity.

The second defect requiring the remedy of a senate is "the propensity of all single and numerous assemblies, to yield to the impulse of sudden and violent passions, and to be seduced by factious leaders, into intemperate and pernicious resolutions" (*Federalist* 62: 418). As noted in the discussion of the Constitutional Convention, the framers reached near consensus on the belief that in larger bodies, passions tend to overrule reason, and a few more clever and eloquent members can manipulate the interests of the rest (*Federalist* 55: 374; 58: 395–96). One way, therefore, to establish a proper difference in disposition is to make the second legislative house significantly less numerous.

The framers' apprehensions about the behavior of "single and numerous assemblies" were based on recent experience with American legislatures and the larger historical record, which apparently supported the conclusion that the smaller the body, the broader the participation within it and the more open, rational, and full the deliberation. Publius does not define "less numerous" with a specific number, and he does not provide the reasoning behind this solution. This understanding of size follows Hume's argument about the effects of size on the concern for reputation: "Honour is a great check upon mankind: But where a considerable body of men act together, this check is, in a great measure, removed."[52] The more isolated and visible individuals are, the more susceptible they are to shame and any concern for the good opinion of others. For an institution to have this sensibility to shame and reputation, the praise and blame must be felt by "each individual." This will not happen "in a numerous and changeable body" like the House because the average representative's responsibility is quite temporary, and it is easily obscured by, or disguised in, the crowd of fellow representatives. A sensibility to reputation will be found in a body either "so small, that a sensible degree of the praise and blame of public measures may be the portion of each individual" or "so durably invested with public trust, that the pride and consequence of its members may be sensibly incorporated with the reputation and prosperity of the community" (*Federalist* 63: 423). These two means seem to be presented as mutually reinforcing conditions. The smaller size helps make individuals more sensitive to external praise and blame, insofar as the acts and potential influence of each member are more evident. The long term makes those individuals more sensible to praise and blame concerning the institution to which they belong and the welfare of the whole community.

While the smaller size tends to quell the influence of passion and support the influence of reason, "a tenure of considerable duration" is necessary to foster greater "firmness" in the Senate's resistance to an intemperate House (*Federalist* 62: 419). In his discussion of the presidency, Publius argues that the longer the term, the stronger the individual's personal interest in the authority and honor of the office and the greater his willingness to suffer the "considerable inconvenience or hazard" that might arise from opposing, particularly, the branch with the most "influence . . . over the people." With popularity and future prospects at risk, moreover, most individuals will not expend the considerable effort needed and suffer the criticisms involved in resisting the will of another branch unless they are in office long enough for subsequent events and arguments to demonstrate the soundness of their judgments (*Federalist* 71: 484–85).

Refining the House

The importance of a crucial senatorial quality—practical knowledge of public affairs and policy—is addressed in the discussion of a third defect a senate must remedy: "a want of due acquaintance with the objects and principles of legislation." Serious errors of the "head" will be committed by representatives, *whether or not* they are faithfully pursuing their proper object, "the happiness of the people" (*Federalist* 62: 419). A second branch of the legislature must be designed to provide knowledge of the "means by which that object can be best attained." This knowledge of means will reduce the number of practical errors, errors that otherwise would be recognized, Publius notes, only when the harms became palpable. The *Federalist* argues, forthrightly, that the principal characteristic of the properly senatorial "class" is not a particular socioeconomic status but rather knowledge gained through study and experience of political and policy matters.[53]

The practical nature of this knowledge is evident in the references to, for example, the "science of legislation" (*Federalist* 56: 379–80; 64: 433–34). Assemblies like the House tend to make practical errors because its members are "called for the most part from pursuits of a private nature, continued in appointment for a short time, and led by no permanent motive to devote the intervals of public occupation to a study of the laws, the affairs and the comprehensive interests of their country" (*Federalist* 62: 419). The longer term for senators will help avoid these defects in a number of ways. Obviously, it affords more time for study and experience in public affairs. It will also attract those inclined to dedicate their lives to public life. Publius assumes also that the House's two-year term will not filter out those who remain more permanently attached to private vocations. Those willing to devote six years to an office, on the other hand, would tend to be attached primarily to politics as a vocation. They would have, in other words, a more "permanent motive" to study the principles of law and policy (*Federalist* 62: 419; 84: 433–34). Enhanced knowledge of public affairs would be conditioned as well by the higher age requirement and longer term of citizenship. These requirements were to furnish men demanded by "the nature of the senatorial trust," which requires a "greater extent of information and stability of character" (*Federalist* 62: 415).

Defying the Compromise

While each of these characteristics and functions assumes, to some degree, a national perspective, the distinctly and strictly national character of Publius's Senate emerges from his discussion of the fourth defect of the House: the instability of legislation. Because the opinions of a representative legislature, with short terms and without a gradual rotation of the membership, will tend to change with each election, each election will tend to produce innovations in the law. Such frequent changes are "inconsistent with every rule of prudence, and every prospect of success" (*Federalist* 62: 420). Long terms and staggered elections will remove senators and the Senate from the irregular opinions and frenetic ambitions that animate the House and enable senators to see the consequences of frequent changes in policy. Yet these features do not explain what would dispose senators to use their practical knowledge to foresee the consequences of instability. Furthermore, what would dispose them to pursue the conclusions of this foresight through resistance, often against a clear popular will, to the harmful measures of the House?

The Senate's confederal character would be far from adequate to these ends. Insofar as a Senate representing the states might be moved by distinctive perspectives and inclinations, it would be disposed, in a sense, to disagree with the House's preferences. But that resistance would not be based regularly, if ever, on a prudent assessment of the prosperity of the nation as a whole. Indeed, senators representing states might be just as prone to produce parochial and unstable national law and policy. For it to be a reliable provision against those ills, Publius's Senate would have to be guided principally by a concern for the good of the nation.

Although Publius acknowledges the Constitution's dependence upon virtues of some sort, he certainly does not argue that any institution can assume a strong and reliable public spiritedness. Instead, he argues, the institutional design must direct the good will and the interests of the officers toward the proper objects of their offices. For example, the most potent means of keeping representatives "virtuous" is the two-year term of office. This short term delineates those parts of the public good for which the representative is particularly responsible and the manner in which he is to fulfill this duty. Specifically, the short term ensures a "habitual recollection of [the representative's] dependence on the people" (*Federalist* 57: 386) to the end of securing a House that will represent local concerns in a spirit of "fidelity" to "the happiness of the people" in general (*Federalist* 37: 233–34; 56: 378–82; 62: 419). Yet because this means of enforcing virtue generates the problem of instability, senators must be directed by other means and motives toward the objects appropriate to a senate's responsibilities.

The necessary senatorial sensibilities and motives can be inferred from Publius's account of the consequences of instability in public measures. This instability "forfeits the respect and confidence of other nations," and if the rules that govern a free people's expectations and choices are constantly changing, it is impossible to make long-term plans, that is, to exercise fully liberty in pursuit of happiness. Altogether, these effects will diminish public respect for the national government and the Constitution (*Federalist* 62: 421–22). Any *inclination* to resist the House's instability must, therefore, arise from a high and dominant sensitivity to these consequences. How this crucial disposition can be fostered is addressed in the *Federalist*'s next paper, which examines the two motives that can direct senators to attend to the good of the nation as a whole: a concern for "national character" or reputation, and a sense of "responsibility" for the general, long-term affairs of the nation.

To form its Senate, the *Federalist* relies upon a heightened concern for personal reputation or the good opinion of others. As noted above, the more readily an individual's actions are observed, the more susceptible he is to praise, blame, and, therefore, shame. Yet the use of this susceptibility to foster a distinctly senatorial character poses a dilemma. Publius is aware of the powerful influence of popular opinion in a republic, and if domestic opinion is the only source of good and bad reputation, a concern for reputation would lead senators to follow rather than check the public's unjust or impolitic inclinations.[54] An earlier paper points to the solution: "Those who represent the dignity of their country in the eyes of other nations will be particularly sensible to every prospect of public danger, or of a dishonorable stagnation in public affairs" (*Federalist* 58: 395). Some part of the government should be highly sensitive to how the nation's political character fares in the opinions of other nations. Only by tying the pride of senators to the opinion of other nations can the Constitution use a concern for reputation to check errors and excesses in domestic opinion.

Indeed, a specific consequence of "mutable government" is that it "forfeits the respect and confidence of other nations, and all the advantages connected with national character" (*Federalist* 62: 420). He urges a "due sense of national character" as a remedy, as a check on "variable" and "unenlightened" policy. Although this sense of national character may have the additional purpose and effect of improving foreign relations, the "justice and propriety" of domestic policy are Publius's main concerns. The Continental Congress, as a representation of states, sacrificed the respect of other nations by neglecting the needs of the nation (*Federalist* 62: 420–21). A Senate sensitive "to the judgment of other nations," to the "impartial world," will want the acts of the national government to "appear to other nations as the offspring of a wise and honorable policy" (*Federalist* 63: 423). This heightened susceptibility to political shame would strengthen the voice of practical knowledge, and national policy judgments would tend to be more comprehensive, sound, and sober. Only a "select and stable" branch, Publius concludes, can bring to the government a "sensibility to the opinion of the world" that is necessary to gain the "respect and confidence" of other nations (*Federalist* 63: 422).

Publius's argument is premised on senators understanding themselves as representing "the dignity of their country in the eyes of other nations" (*Federalist* 58: 395). He has not, however, explained how the institutional devices he describes will overcome, in practice, the confederal influences to the degree required by the Senate's national responsibilities. This problem is only compounded in the discussion of the sixth defect, which explains the other peculiarly senatorial motive.

This defect is "the want . . . of a due responsibility in the government to the people" that arises from "the frequency of elections" (*Federalist* 63: 423). While this consequence of short terms might seem "paradoxical," it should be quite familiar to anyone who has wondered how representatives, highly attentive to their districts, could have, as a body, a reputation for failing to attend to the public good.[55] Rather than vainly hoping that representatives would regularly risk their positions for distant and general goods, Publius argues for differentiating the objects of responsibility and designing institutions with incentives appropriate to each.

Of the two "objects" of government, the House would tend to pursue only one: "measures which have singly an immediate and sensible operation," that is, policies with specific and short-run effects, for which credit could be claimed within the two-year election cycle (*Federalist* 63: 424).

Although considered not altogether desirable, this sort of responsiveness was understood to be an unavoidable consequence of the House's design. That design was determined by the basic responsibilities of representatives: to ensure that all relevant "local information" is available and conscientiously introduced into discussions of particular policies; and to protect liberty by tethering government to society so that any tyrannical tendencies of the government can be checked effectively. Publius does not imply, let alone argue, either that the popular will at any moment should be given its proportional weight in legislative deliberations, or that a representative ought to be an advocate for the passions and interests of his particular constituency. Instead, each representative should "possess *due knowledge of*" the "interests and circumstances of his constituents" (*Federalist* 56: 378–79, emphasis added).[56]

A large membership and (anticipated) single-member districts would provide for the adequate local knowledge, while direct election of representatives to short terms of office would protect liberty by imposing on the House an "immediate dependence" upon the people (*Federalist* 52: 355–57). Such a short leash, however, will lead representatives to neglect those problems and objects that depend upon "a succession of well chosen and well connected measures." The House, therefore, cannot reasonably be held responsible for this broader scope of policy: "Responsibility in order to be reasonable must be limited to objects within the power of the responsible party; and in order to be effectual, must relate to the operations of that power, of which a ready and proper judgment can be formed by the constituents" (*Federalist* 63: 424). It is difficult enough, Publius argues, "to preserve a personal responsibility in the members of a *numerous* body," even for discrete policies with immediate effects. It is unreasonable, especially given the short term, to expect constituents to hold or to be able to hold individual representatives responsible for the more remote and national effects of an elaborate policy. Therefore, as constituents are not likely to impose a responsibility that would moderate the House's bias toward serving local and short-term concerns, representatives will not tend to devote themselves to long-term, elaborate, and general policies, of which the "importance . . . to the collective and permanent welfare of every country needs no explanation" (*Federalist* 63: 424).

A senate must be designed with "sufficient permanency to provide for such objects as require a continued attention, and a train of measures." Yet Publius must explain how the design makes it "justly and *effectually* answerable for the attainment of those objects" (*Federalist* 63: 424, emphasis added). Effectual answerability, presumably, would compel senators to attend to elaborate and long-term concerns. If their six-year term, the principal means of *enabling* senators to pursue such objects, was designed to insulate senators from the shortcomings of popularly enforced responsibility, then to whom—and in what manner—would they be effectively answerable for long-term and general national policy? Publius seems to be presenting a distinction between not only the objects for which each house will be responsible but also the ways in which those responsibilities will be enforced.

Whereas the responsibility of the House as a whole is generated and enforced through the direct accountability of individual members, the Senate's responsibility would be imposed first upon the body as a whole and then, as a consequence, on the individual members. Publius's Senate could be held responsible for elaborate and general policies because, he argues, it has "sufficient permanency" *as a body*. Its permanency as a body is established by the continuity of membership achieved through staggered terms and gradual rotation. Thus the body as a whole would be reasonably "answerable" for its responses to general and long-term policy. Add the heightened sense of individual responsibility, and it is reasonable to expect that senators will tend to feel personally responsible for the body's performance. Especially as they are removed from the temptations of popularity, senators would tend to be concerned with their status and reputation *as members of the Senate*. They would worry about the good opinion of the Senate's wisdom and judgment. Poor results would embarrass the Senate and therefore degrade the individual senator's reputation. In sum, the expectations and reputation of the Senate as a whole would enforce broader responsibilities on individual senators.

A Republican Senate and the Deliberate Sense of the People

To direct senators to long-term and national concerns, Publius seems to rely principally on a carefully fostered senatorial pride and concern for the opinions of the larger world. Yet it is worth noting that the last desideratum, the utility of an "auxiliary" check on popular majorities, also argues that public opinion may ultimately support a senate's wise resistance to its momentary intemperance and imprudence. This check is not intended to have the mere *effect* of cooling the democratic coffee;

cooling, as such, requires only delay, which can be achieved by a body of almost any character and without regard to the justice and national import of the measure being delayed. Publius's justification of the Senate's check on majorities assumes that the Senate's second look will refine deliberation and policy significantly. The Senate must also devote itself to persuasion because the sense of the community will ultimately and rightly "prevail over the views of its rulers." In the end, the "cool and deliberate sense of the community" should align with the cool and deliberate judgment of a "well constructed" Senate: "how salutary will be the interference of some temperate and respectable body of citizens, in order to check the misguided career, and to suspend the blow meditated by the people against themselves, until reason, justice and truth can regain their authority over the public mind?" (*Federalist* 63: 424–25).

In sum, Publius's bicameralism establishes not a clash of classes but rather two different representations of the same people. The first, through the House, is characterized by close ties to localities; knowledge of particular circumstances and interests is gathered in a numerous assembly and should be present in any assessment of a policy's impact. The second, through the Senate, concerns itself with the long-term and more comprehensive interests of the people; this representation is needed to generalize, broaden, and refine legislative deliberations.

Most accounts of the framers' design generally assume that the Senate's national functions could readily coexist with its confederal form. Yet Publius's discussion of the Senate's strictly national character and responsibility neither argues away the effects of state selection and representation nor demonstrates a compatibility between these confederal means and the national ends. He certainly does not suggest that state legislatures would hold individual senators responsible for national policies, and he does not expressly argue that the longer term and the small size would overcome a senator's origin in, and effectual responsibility to, the interest of his state. The latter argument would seem to be demanded by the worries expressed elsewhere in the *Federalist* about the influence of narrow state interests and by the fact that the actions of individual senators would be quite visible to their electors.

Lacking such an explanation, the *Federalist* does not describe how the upper house would function in practice. In declining to provide a synthetic account, it instead exposes the great distance between the convention's "partly federal . . . and partly national" hybrid and an appropriately national senate. Given that this institution was to have a broader array of constitutional roles than any other branch and was to have the most deliberate and comprehensive responsibility for national interest and policy, the *Federalist*'s account of the Senate may also delineate the significant distance between the convention's work and a well-ordered national government.

FROM RATIFICATION TO REALITY

Publius's attempt to rescue and reassert the functions and character of a national Senate was only one of the many voices heard during the ratification process. The alarmist predictions of anti-Federalists twisted the Senate into a nightmare of aristocratic domination. The sober and strategic realism of most Federalists defended the hybrid Senate that was written into the proposed constitution. Insofar as the debate on the Senate influenced the outcome, the Federalists held most of the high cards, as they did in the debates more generally. They could defend the Senate honestly against its attackers, while the anti-Federalists were compelled to conjure demons. Nevertheless, both sides were anticipating something different from what they tended to support or condemn. Just as the Madisons and Hamiltons among the Federalists were hoping for a nationalist Senate to prevail when the new government formed, most anti-Federalists were hoping for the nearest relative of the Confederation Congress. Neither side would get exactly what it wanted.

SEVEN

Reality
The Early Senate

In 1789, the rather small group of men who comprised the national government gathered in New York City to run the country that had just been
created or recreated, depending on one's point of view. In coming together
to manage the new nation's affairs, these men would also be defining the
governmental institutions created by the Constitution. The earliest incar-
nations of the House, Senate, presidency, and Supreme Court would give
life to the words of the document so hotly debated only months before. As
the government moved from New York to Philadelphia to Washington,
D.C.—a migration that symbolized the unsettled nature of much of what
the Constitution created—the institutions took shape. As we have seen,
the Senate was perhaps the most ambiguous among its peers.

During ratification the Senate was harshly criticized by anti-Federalists
and vigorously defended and sometimes lauded by Federalists. The Federalists hoped for a republican anchor, a source of stability and stewardship,
and a cooperative, consultative relationship with the executive branch.
Anti-Federalists feared an institutional aristocracy that would form a cabal
with the executive, dominate the House, and be a motor of consolidation
to diminish the role of states. The contrast was stark and bitter.

The Constitution was approved, but what shape it would take had not
been clarified by the struggle over ratification. Despite, or perhaps because of, the voluminous outpouring of debate and analysis during ratification, little was resolved. If anything, the ambiguities of the Senate were
only multiplied. The real Senate was going to emerge in the interstices
between the multiple and contrasting views, between the various facets of
praise and condemnation. The actual Senate would be less dramatic in
form and function than either the hopes of its creators and advocates or
the fears of its detractors. It would not take long for the Senate, despite
tensions and pretensions, to take its place as a powerful but—from a
modern perspective—ordinary legislative institution.

By 1796, before the end of Washington's presidency, many fundamental
elements of the Senate in action had been arranged. This view of what
could be referred to as *institutionalization* contrasts with the more com-

mon use of this term and with other approaches to the Senate's development. Nelson Polsby's notion of institutionalization, similar to much of
the work on the development of Congress, is teleological. It reaches back-
wards from modern features of Congress or legislatures (party organization, leadership, rules, committees) to the origins and evolution of those
same features.[1] It has been a productive way to look at Congress; however,
our goal is a bit different. Working forward from the contradictory political expectations and constitutional uncertainties surrounding the Senate,
we seek to show when and how these ambiguities and contingencies were
resolved. The goal is not to discover when the Senate first took its modern
form but to see how the operations of the early national government
clarified or eliminated the most significant uncertainties about the place
and purpose of the Senate in the new system.[2]

NEITHER A PERMANENT ARISTOCRACY NOR A REPUBLICAN ANCHOR

Anti-Federalists feared that a permanent aristocracy would take root in
the Senate, but this was not to be the case. By the same token, the Senate
would not become, at least initially, the anchor sought by Federalists.
Whatever pretensions some senators might have entertained, neither the
House nor the president—nor the public—was prepared to indulge those
notions of an aristocratic upper house. For that matter, most early members of the Senate were not disposed to remain in the institution long
enough to provide stability, let alone constitute an aristocracy.

Pretensions

The few initial nonconstitutional attempts to differentiate the Senate
from the House in a Lord-like manner failed utterly. These attempts
ranged from symbolic to substantive. Titles constituted an initial and
utterly unsuccessful symbolic effort. Among its opening items of business,
the first Senate considered what title to affix to the president; it also
considered whether to preface every mention of a senator in the minutes
with "The Right Honorable." Both efforts were vocally supported, if not
instigated, by Vice President Adams, who was president of the first Senate
and defended titles as an element of the dignity and respect necessary to

any national government. Although Adams had some support in this affair, his quite recent and extended stay in Europe may have biased him and facilitated a misjudgment about what Americans thought about such matters. The skirmish over titles produced satire and ridicule instead of dignity or distinction. A senator privately dubbed Adams "Rotundity," and one of the tallest members of the Senate was referred to as "Your highness of the Senate" just as a representative of similar stature was addressed as "his Highness of the Lower House." With some help from the House, the Senate decided against any grandiose title for the president and dropped the matter of Senate titles altogether.[3]

Also unsuccessful was the attempt to differentiate between the ways the two chambers would communicate with one another. The Senate tried to get the House to agree to pay it greater respect when delivering messages than the Senate would have to bestow on the House. According to a plan prepared by a joint House-Senate committee, all communications from the Senate to the House were to be delivered by the Secretary of the Senate. A bill from the House was to be presented by two representatives, and all other communications by a single representative, with a detailed number of "obeisances" to accompany this process. The House was apparently amused and offended by this, refused, and that was the end of it. The House would send its clerk to deliver messages to the Senate; the Senate could send whomever it pleased.[4]

More tangible was the controversy over whether senators should be paid more. Greater pay for the Senate, however, turned out to be as much or more about practical differences than Lord-like pretensions. In an odd contradiction, the institution containing more members who did not need pay (some of whom, in fact, disdained it) insisted that it be paid more as a mark of distinction. Senators also justified their temporarily successful effort to earn six dollars versus five dollars a day for the House with practical arguments about their need to stay in session longer and bear the consequences of a six-year term. Indeed, at least two representatives, James Madison and John Page, made the same argument on behalf of the Senate. Though finally accepted, the pay differential did not go into effect until 1795 (so that it would not be seen as benefiting any of the current senators) and it lasted only one year. When the pay bill came up again in 1796, the House leveled compensation, and the Senate did not resist.[5]

Procedure

Secrecy, or more precisely, the Senate's initial practice of conducting normal business behind closed doors, became the only significant early distinction in the procedure of each chamber. The difficult question is the extent to which secrecy was driven by an aristocratic spirit or by the practicality of precedent. The Senate's practice of closed deliberations is often viewed, at least implicitly, as the exception to the rule and a manifestation of its Lords-like pretensions, when actually most legislatures had operated in a similar fashion, and the openness of the House was the more novel feature of Congress. Parliament in England, both the Lords and Commons, excluded nonmembers from chambers. As Elizabeth McPherson notes, "Prior to 1766 no legislative body in America had admitted the public to its sessions." The Continental Congresses and the Confederation Congress generally operated in secret. In fact, in 1783 the Congress of the Confederation defeated James Wilson's open-door proposal by a vote of seven states to one (and an individual vote of nineteen to five). Many senators were accustomed to secrecy in their legislative practices, and many had seen how well it worked in the recent Constitutional Convention.[6]

The state constitutions produced during and after the Revolution typically specified that each chamber of the legislature was to determine its rules of procedure. Only four state constitutions mandated that the journals of proceedings be published, and three required that votes be recorded if requested by the requisite number of members. These few explicit provisions seemed to presume that legislative sessions, if not actually closed, would not be widely attended or covered by the public and press. Only New York and Pennsylvania required the doors of their legislatures to be open to the public. Many legislators in the House and Senate believed closed doors led to more honest and productive deliberations, and some in the House were not happy with the degree of public scrutiny.[7] The democratic spirit of the first Senate, William Maclay, anticipated periodic secrecy in proceedings, though he stated to his colleagues that he could think of no reason for open sessions that did not apply equally well to their chamber.[8] A relatively inaccessible upper house was apparently taken for granted by those who, in remodeling what would become Federal Hall in New York, provided galleries for the House but none for the Senate. As Philadelphia prepared to receive Congress, they did the same in the conversion of the new county courthouse into Congress Hall. The lack of galleries, in turn, became one argument against changing the policy.[9]

Use of the terms *secret* or *secrecy* to describe this early Senate practice is misleading. The Constitution stipulates only that "[e]ach House shall keep a Journal of its Proceedings, and from time to time publish the same." Recorded votes are not required in either chamber (and many of the House's early votes were not recorded). Moreover, journalistic accounts of floor action were thought to be incomplete and often inaccurate. The first Senate, therefore, probably saw little practical difference between its mode of operation and that of the House, except for the positive benefits that could derive from not playing to the audience.[10] This is not to say that a sense of senatorial privilege or superiority did not play a role. Some of the support for closed sessions simply involved the weight of practice and precedent—senators were used to secrecy and loath to change that habit. Habit and practice also fit with the beliefs of the time about privilege and the limits of democracy. These beliefs no doubt applied more to the somewhat nebulous Senate, which was also seen—mistakenly as it would turn out—as a hybrid between an executive and legislative body. Senators' length of term and other concrete features of the new constitutional regime implied that they should not be as open to public influence.

The assumption in favor of secrecy appears to have been so general that the Senate did not even write it into its standing rules. As Clara Kerr notes, the closed-door policy "was provided for by no rule and seems to have been entered upon without debate and without question."[11] The Senate, according to its records, did not vote in any affirmative manner for the policy until the campaign against secrecy compelled it to. That movement began almost immediately and appears to have been driven by several forces. To many citizens and observers, republicanism, in its increasingly liberal-democratic form, dictated openness, especially for legislative bodies so physically distant from the people. Many state legislators, who saw senators as constitutional creatures of the states, declaimed secrecy because it further attenuated their influence over the actions of their senators. In practice, these two political principles—openness and state control—were joined by nascent factional or party politics. As others have argued or suggested, partisan politics helped to precipitate the end of closed Senate sessions. The push for an end to secrecy can be seen as part and parcel of the rise of partisan politics as Republican strength grew in the South in reaction to Federalist policy emerging from Congress and the Washington administration. McPherson notes that the Federalist North "had little to fear from Congressional legislation and could see little danger in the closed sessions of the Senate."[12] Conversely, as Republicans gained strength in southern state legislatures, they began almost immediately to push for an open Senate. The South could see advantage in opening up the Senate for scrutiny. Some of this seems to have been motivated by the fact that some southern state legislatures had initially picked senators, especially with four- or six-year terms, who turned out to be too Federalist for the emerging state majority. The press allied with the opposition hammered away at Senate secrecy as well.[13]

State legislatures' desire to have more control over their senators brought together the issue of secrecy—which some saw as the ultimate expression of Senate elitism—and the most audacious expression of the view that senators should be answerable to their state legislatures: the doctrine of instruction. Instruction, which we discuss later in this chapter, was the belief that state legislatures could "instruct" their senators on how to vote on particular issues. Republicans, predominantly from the South, attempted to use instructions from state legislatures to compel the Senate to open its doors. In fact, secrecy provoked the very first use of instruction by state legislatures. On December 16, 1789, the Virginia legislature instructed its senators to use " 'their utmost endeavors' to obtain 'free admission' of the American people to the Senate."[14] Virginia was joined by North Carolina, South Carolina, Maryland, and later New York. The two Virginia senators made the first motion to open the Senate on April 29, 1790, but the next day the proposal apparently received only the votes of the two Virginia senators joined by Maclay of Pennsylvania.[15]

Federalists generally resisted efforts to open the Senate and likewise argued against the legitimacy of instruction. There were exceptions, however. Senator Rufus King of New York, an ardent proadministration Federalist, claimed to have voted for an open Senate whenever the opportunity arose.[16] Some Federalists defended a closed Senate with arguments that turned the role of state influence against proponents of change. For example, Charles Cotesworth Pinckney, as a South Carolina state senator, argued that the Senate *and* House should be closed to the public to mitigate the influence of the Pennsylvania state legislature, which met only yards away from Congress Hall.[17] James Monroe was met with a similar sentiment during the war crisis with England in early 1794: "I found it a subject of complaint as I pass'd thro' Jersey that the doors of the H. of R. were not shut as those of the Senate were, because the people were already so hostile to G. B. [Great Britain] that it wo'd be difficult to keep them within bounds if encouraged in that licentious spirit by the discussions in Congress."[18]

The more common obloquy directed at Senate secrecy was not lost on Federalists, however. There was, in the end, a vast difference between being shown respect and deference and being ignored or vilified. The Senate was ignored insofar as the press and public were paying much greater attention to the House, to the extent that the press began to refer to the House as "Congress" as though the two were synonymous. Conversely, the Senate's more pronounced support for Federalist policies allowed opponents to heap scorn on the products of secrecy and cabal, particularly the national bank. Secrecy under such circumstances was detrimental. This inspired some Federalists in the Senate to reconsider the advisability of secrecy insofar as they were in danger of losing the public arguments over the merits of public policy. An open Senate would also allow the reporting of sound Federalist arguments on behalf of specific policies. Federalists, whose grip on the House was weakening by even the Second Congress and lost by the Third Congress, began to realize they needed to compete more effectively in the court of public opinion, and the Senate was their tallest soapbox.[19]

Nevertheless, by decisive and somewhat regionally divided margins, the Senate defeated three open-door motions in 1791, 1792, and 1793.[20] Finally, a motion made by Alexander Martin of North Carolina on January 16, 1794, was passed February 20 by a nineteen-to-eight vote, with only one senator from the South in opposition. To what extent instruction, conversion (principally by states replacing their senators), or changing convictions brought about the final vote, we will not discuss here.[21] Some scholars have attributed at least part of the change in the Senate's disposition to one ad hoc experiment with openness, when it voted to open its doors for the debate on the election of Albert Gallatin to the Senate.[22] Gallatin's eligibility, despite his having been elected by a Federalist state legislature in Pennsylvania, was questioned by Senate Federalists because he had not been a U.S. citizen for the constitutionally required nine years. With the government in Philadelphia, the Senate seemed to recognize the "delicacy of the situation in which they were questioning the action of the Pennsylvania legislature in selecting Gallatin" and that doing so behind closed doors would not be politically prudent.[23] The implication is that the success of this public debate may have changed some minds by showing how it could work to the advantage of the Senate.

The problem with this attribution is that the decision to open the Senate doors for the Gallatin debate preceded the voting on the general open-door resolution by only five working days, during which little if any of the debate—public or otherwise—on the Gallatin case took place.[24] The eight days of the work on the Gallatin controversy, when the *Annals of Congress* for the first time records actual debate by individual senators, began after the final votes on the general open-door resolution on February 20, 1794. Gallatin was removed from the Senate on February 28 by a fourteen-to-twelve vote along regional and partisan lines, dividing the proadministration Federalist North from the increasingly antiadministration Republican South. After the Gallatin debate, the Senate's presiding officer, Vice President John Adams, wrote to his wife Abigail that "a great impression had been made upon the public by the learning, eloquence, and reasoning of some of the senators."[25] Perhaps, but just as likely is that the few who came to listen were impressed as well by the rather ordinary factionalism displayed by the Senate's voting.[26] The Senate wasn't so different from the House after all. The open-door resolution stipulated that the change in practice take place after the current session's conclusion and after galleries could be constructed. A problem of funding prevented construction during the months between the first and second sessions of the Third Congress. Construction of a gallery took place between the end of the Third Congress and the beginning of the Fourth. The doors of the Senate finally opened on December 9, 1795.

Personnel

Just as it did not take long for the Senate to shed most of its trappings of prestige and distinction, the early years of the upper house quickly showed it would not be a permanent aristocracy or, as framers such as Madison sought, an anchor of stability. The instability in the early membership of both houses of Congress and the rise of the congressional career has been thoroughly documented, and, as is well known, few representatives or senators in the first decades of the new government sought to or were able to make a career of Congress.

On May 14, 1789, the Senate of the First Congress divided its membership into three classes to carry into effect the provisions of Article I, section 3 for staggered terms. This means that two-thirds of the first senators did not have an automatic opportunity to serve six years, but abbreviated terms do not explain the relatively truncated tenure of these senators. Of the twenty-nine senators elected or appointed to the First Congress, only four (14%) lost reelection.[27] By contrast, twenty-five retired, resigned, or died, but unlike modern senators these twenty-five did not leave the Senate after long careers. The average tenure for the whole group is 4.86 years.[28] Eleven of the twenty-nine resigned (with none of the eleven finishing a second term). Many members did not seem to enjoy their time in New York and Philadelphia, and many sought or took the best opportunity to get back home. Even Robert Morris, who was a native of Philadelphia, retired after one term.

Duty rather than career is the appropriate term for early Senate service, and as the number of resignations shows, even duty had its limits. Several resigned to accept other state or, less frequently, federal offices. Senator Charles Carroll of Maryland, a signer of the Declaration of Independence, resigned after about four years of total service when he was forced to choose between being a U.S. senator and a state senator. He was holding both jobs, and Maryland passed a law to forbid such arrangements; Carroll chose to go home and stay in state politics. His Maryland colleague, John Henry, served a whole term and was reelected, but resigned halfway through his second term when he was elected governor of Maryland. William Samuel Johnson, a Connecticut delegate to the Constitutional Convention, was serving as the first president of Columbia College in New York City when he was selected to be one of Connecticut's first senators. He drew a six-year term, but to retain his Columbia post, he promised to resign when the legislature moved to Philadelphia at the end of the First Congress, and he did so. His state colleague, Oliver Ellsworth, served for two years and was reelected, but resigned near the end of his term to become Chief Justice of the U.S. Supreme Court. As part of the periodically chaotic South Carolina delegation (in sixteen years it had nine senators, who sat in the First through Eighth Congresses), Pierce Butler served and resigned from the Senate twice, once in 1796 to return to the state legislature and once in 1804 to contend, unsuccessfully, for a House seat. Anti-Federalists who had called for shorter Senate terms, mandatory rotation, and the right of state recall need not have feared: the Senate was experiencing a high level of rotation and engaging in a regular practice of self-initiated recall.

Although the membership of the First Congress is in certain respects unique, this pattern did not end soon. The average career for members elected during the first six Congresses was almost exactly the same: 5.38 years for the House and 5.45 years for the Senate. These figures are even a bit inflated because they include noncontinuous service. For those members elected during the first six Congresses, 43.7 percent of the senators resigned compared to 16.8 percent of representatives (31.7% of representatives did not seek reelection or retired at the end of their term, compared to 16.5% of senators). Another way of comparing the chambers is through the growth in average cumulative service (that is, how long the average member had served by the end of a particular Congress). From the First through Twelfth Congresses, the two houses tracked each other quite closely (fig. 7.1). The average representative from the Twelfth Congress (1811–13) had served 5.6 years and the average senator a remarkable 5.2 years.[29] By the end of that Congress, therefore, House members as a whole had a bit more experience than senators. The average number of senators per state over the course of the Tenth Congress, for example, was 2.47. With the typical senator not even filling out a full six years, a permanent Senate aristocracy was not in the making; and with House members serving the same number of years as senators, there was no bicameral difference in terms of stability or knowledge.[30]

As the data indicate, the establishment of a permanent seat of government in the District of Columbia did not alleviate the instability of the legislature. In fact, as we can see in James Sterling Young's description of Washington and its first decades, it may have exacerbated the situation. Early Washington, the capital ex nihilo, was a rural backwater village rather than a city like Philadelphia. It was not a pleasant place; most members lived in groups in boarding houses, and few tried to bring their families. The results were predictable. In fact, some legislators acted preemptively. Seven senators, or 22 percent of the chamber, resigned in an eleven-month period from just before the end of the first session of the Sixth Congress, when Congress said goodbye to Philadelphia, until February 1801 after it had just reconvened for the second session in Washington, D.C. The New York Senate delegation saw three resignations and five different senators in a three-year period from the end of 1798 to the beginning of 1802. One of them, DeWitt Clinton, who used his position

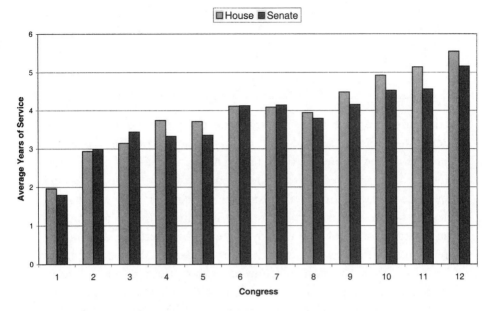

FIG. 7.1. Cumulative Career Service, 1st–12th Congresses. Career data from ICPSR, McKibbin 1997.

in the New York senate to help procure his U.S. Senate seat in 1802, wrote the governor of New York less than two years later to let him know that he could not "think of retaining my present situation beyond the next session." Another six months away from New York would be "insupportable" for reasons of family and finance. Clinton happily resigned to become mayor of New York City.[31]

Things did not improve for some time. As Young notes, from "1797 to 1829 (5th through 20th Congresses) more senators resigned than failed to be reelected by their state legislatures. On average 17.9 percent of the Senate membership resigned every two years, almost six times the biennial turnover in the modern Senate due to resignation. Among representatives, an average of 5.8 percent resigned in each Congress, about twice the percentage of resignations in the modern House." The vast majority of the House and Senate members who resigned (of which Young counted 229) did not leave public life: 69 percent went on to other public jobs outside Washington, almost half within one year of their resignations.[32] Eventually, but not for many decades, senators and representatives would develop the "congressional career" of long tenures in one or both chambers. Even with the establishment of the congressional career, the average tenure of Senate and House members would stay remarkably similar to each other.

SEPARATION OF POWERS: EXECUTIVE RELATIONS

If the early Senate was neither "permanent" nor an "aristocracy," was it, as some of the framers seemed to think, an executive council? Would the Senate form an essential bridge between the executive and legislative powers, or as anti-Federalists anticipated, a secretive cabal that would dominate the president? At the same time that senators were working out the issues of prestige and procedure, and assuming a less exalted status in the emerging order of national government, they were also forging the precedents for their relationship with the presidency. Although there had been talk at the Constitutional Convention about the Senate as an executive council, nothing in the Constitution, as it was finally written, created such an arrangement. The Constitution gave the Senate, and not the House, a share of two powers that straddled the executive and the legislature. The Senate's boundary powers were its role in executive and judicial branch appointments and its role in the process of making treaties. Read literally, the Constitution does not mandate a council-like relationship, but a literal reading ignores the expectations, however imprecise, of many of the framers. A close relationship between the Senate and president was something hoped for by many Federalists and feared by many anti-Federalists. Again, neither group would get what it expected. Instead, a rather strict separation of powers quickly alienated the Senate from the president, and most of the power fell on the president's side of the divide.

As we have seen, the delegates of the Constitutional Convention initially gave control of appointments and treaties to the Senate. Although tilting more toward the president by the end of the convention, the delegates left enough ambiguity in the Constitution's final language to raise questions and disagreements about the locus of authority in these matters. Were these literally shared powers? Was the president clearly the source of initiative in each, with the Senate as a check on unrestrained power? Or was the Senate a full partner, with the executive's role largely one of efficiency in selection of nominees and the actual negotiation of treaties? The argument in favor of presidential power in these areas pointed first to the fact that both powers were listed in Article II, which defines the presidency and its powers, rather than in Article I as a special power of the Senate. The Senate, from this perspective, was a check on the president's power. Others saw these as truly shared powers, especially the making of treaties, which were the supreme law of the land; the Senate's legislative approval, in this view, was the paramount aspect of treaties.

Potential disagreements notwithstanding, President Washington and the first Senate anticipated a close working relationship in both areas. Early in the First Congress, the Senate appointed a special committee on the nature of communications between the president and the Senate in the matters of appointments and treaties. When the committee visited the president in August 1789, Washington stated his preference for written communications on nominations and oral consultations on treaties. Nominations were simple and direct submissions of names for positions, and Washington felt senators should be free to discuss the qualifications of the nominees without the presence of the president; likewise there was no need for the president to witness this discussion. Treaties, on the other hand, because of their more complicated nature, often would require direct discussion. As we shall see, both the president and the Senate envisioned consultation during the whole process of treaty making, from the decision to initiate negotiations, to the instructions given to the negotiators, to the final treaty provisions. Washington, in his notes from the conferences with the members of the Senate committee, foresaw the appropriation of a chamber "for the joint business of the President and the Senate," and the Senate committee in its report echoed the president's views: "That whenever the Government shall have buildings of it's [sic] own, an Executive Chamber will no doubt be provided, where the Senate will generally attend the President: the place may depend on the nature of the business." The president also indicated the need for flexibility; some situations might be best handled by written communications, some by direct consultation.[33]

Yet, even in this relatively amicable early encounter between the two institutions, there was an assertion of presidential independence, however subtle from a modern perspective. Washington concluded from the spare language of Article II that "[t]he Senate when these powers are exercised, is evidently a Council only to the President, however its concurrence may be to his Acts—It seems incident to this relation between them that not only the *time*, but the *place* and manner of consultation should be with the President." The president urged the Senate to "accommodate their rules to the uncertainty of the particular mode and place that may be preferred, providing for the reception of either oral or written propositions, and for giving their consent and advice in either the presence or absence of the President, *leaving him free* [emphasis added] to use the mode and place that may be found most eligible and accordant with other business, which may be before him at the time."[34] The Senate concurred and promptly wrote a rule to govern communications with the president in person, a rule that likewise saw the relationship as direct and consultative: "That when the President of the United States shall meet the Senate in the Senate Chamber, the President of the Senate shall have a chair on the floor, be considered as the head of the Senate, and his chair shall be assigned to the President of the United States. That when the Senate shall be convened by the President of the United States to any other place, the President of the Senate and Senators shall attend at the place appointed."[35]

Appointments

Washington's early distinction between preferred forms of communication for nominations and treaties is logical but may have been prompted in part by the Senate's first rejection of a presidential appointment. On August 5, 1789, the Senate ended its consideration of a long list of appointments of collectors, naval officers, and surveyors for every state in the union by rejecting only one on the list, Washington's nomination for the Naval Officer of the Port of Savannah, one Benjamin Fishbourn. The president was miffed by the rejection and immediately submitted a new nomination with a curt request that in the future the Senate consider "whether on occasions when the propriety of nominations appear questionable to you, it would not be expedient to communicate that circumstance to me, and thereby avail yourselves of the information which led me to make them, and which I would with pleasure lay before you."[36] The next day the Senate committee on presidential communications first met with the president to discuss protocol. The president, as we have seen, concluded that written communications were in most cases sufficient for nominations. At that first meeting, the president elucidated his thinking on appointments: "It could be no pleasing thing, I conceive, for the President, on the one hand, to be present and hear the propriety of his nominations questioned, nor for the Senators, on the other hand, to be under the smallest restraint from his presence from the fullest and freest inquiry into the character of the person nominated . . . as the President has a right to nominate without assigning his reasons, so has the Senate a right to dissent without giving theirs."[37]

Whether out of logic, spite, or both, President Washington immediately made appointments into a presidential prerogative. He extended this power to encompass the decisions about where to post ambassadors and what rank to give them.[38] The president would initiate; the Senate could approve or disapprove, but there would be no formal consultation. In fact, it did not take long for any sense of a consultative relationship to be completely extinguished. This separation of powers in practice would be reasserted and reinforced by less imposing chief executives, including Madison, who reminded the Senate that the "appointment of a committee of the Senate to confer immediately with the executive himself appears to lose sight of the co-ordinate relation between the Executive and the Senate, which the Constitution has established, and which ought therefore to be maintained."[39] The precedent set by Washington would stick, but another evolved quickly, one that would force the president to consult more informally with senators and also would alter the nature of the Senate's idealized role in the appointment process.

The Senate was selected by the Constitutional Convention to handle appointments because of the longer tenure and greater knowledge of its members. The Senate would find, however, that its putatively superior qualifications for deliberating on appointments would compete directly with what would become one of the most parochial traditions in Congress: senatorial courtesy. Senatorial courtesy—the practice that a presidential nomination is not confirmed unless approved by the senators of the president's party from the home state of the nominee—is one of the Senate's most entrenched and cherished norms, and it got off to an early start, however nebulous. Benjamin Fishbourn, the rejected nominee, "apparently was not acceptable to the Senators from Georgia."[40] This tantalizing hint of senatorial courtesy in the making has a rather slim foundation of corroboration as far as contemporaneous evidence.[41] Nevertheless, Washington began to adjust to the reality that consultation with the appropriate senators *and* representatives facilitated the appointment process. Most evidence points to the active involvement of both in the informal suggestion or approval of nominees. In fact, as Roy Swanstrom argues, what really evolves during the Washington and Adams administrations is "congressional courtesy" rather than "senatorial courtesy."[42]

This early practice was a blend of a sincere quest for information about potential nominees—for what president could be possessed of the names, abilities, and reputations necessary to fill all offices?—with a process of political jobbery and ideological approval. It was, in fact, the habit of the early Senate to rely on senators from the state of the nominee to give an account of the person's abilities and character if these were not generally known.[43] The more formalized practice of senatorial courtesy would take some years to mature, but its roots and contrast with the idealized form of Senate participation were planted at the outset.[44]

The other half of the power to appoint is the power to remove, and the constitutional uncertainty of this power proved to be more durable; after all, it is what led to the impeachment of Andrew Johnson in 1868. That extraordinary episode notwithstanding, the general acceptance of the president's power of removal was established during the First Congress with the passage of the bill to establish the Department of Foreign Affairs (later changed to the Department of State). In part because the Constitution said nothing about removals, the bill addressed this issue by explicitly granting the president the power to remove the Secretary of Foreign Affairs, and the five days of floor debate in the House of Representatives over the bill were solely about the proper locus of the removal power. This was the first important congressional debate about constitutional powers, and opinions ranged widely on what the Constitution implied about removals.[45] A few even believed that impeachment was the only constitutional method. Led by Madison, however, the majority in the House favored presidential authority. In fact, Madison and his allies tried to excise the provision that made removal of the Secretary of Foreign Affairs an exclusive presidential power because they did not want any implication that Congress could alter the removal power by legislation or other actions. Many in the Senate felt otherwise, including Maclay, who spoke in favor of impeachment. Maclay's fragmented description of the Senate debate puts more emphasis on concerns about presidential power than the rights of the Senate per se, though he quotes Senator William Grayson, who felt that giving the power to the president meant that "consolidation is the object of the New Government, and the first attempt will be to destroy the Senate, as they are the Representatives of the State legislatures." The showdown in the Senate produced a ten-to-ten vote, with Vice President Adams, no doubt eagerly, breaking the tie in favor of presidential independence.[46]

Although the vote was confined to a law creating a single office, the precedent was set. The debate had been about the power of appointment and removal in general, and everyone knew he was voting on the principle. As we noted earlier, the removal power remained controversial, and fights between the Senate and president for control of that power affected administrations from John Quincy Adams's to Andrew Johnson's, and even Franklin Roosevelt's. Such tussles, however, show that the Senate (excepting the highly political Tenure of Office Act) had been reduced to fighting increasingly arcane battles over special cases—the general authority of the president was safe and repeatedly upheld.

During the same period of the initial expansion of presidential power under Washington, the Senate's constitutionally mandated role in removals through the process of impeachment was showing itself to be a paper tiger. Feared by anti-Federalists as another violation of the separation of powers, the Senate's role as the court of impeachments quickly proved to be the least important special power of the upper house. The decision to recognize the president's right of removal diminished the potential importance of impeachments. The political separation of the Senate and the president in the making of appointments had alleviated concerns about the Senate sitting in judgment on its own appointments. More importantly, impeachments were far less necessary or frequent than some had imagined. The House considered—let alone sent on to the Senate—very few articles of impeachment. The Senate, in turn, used its power sparingly. In two of the three early and important precedent-setting cases, those of Senator William Blount in 1798–99 and Supreme Court Justice Samuel Chase in 1805, the Senate did not convict. By their own actions, the House and Senate set impeachment aside as an extreme measure to be resorted to rarely and under extraordinary circumstances.[47]

In the area of appointments and removals, once again, the Senate practice diverged from republican hopes and anti-Federalist fears. The president had secured the right of initiative in appointments and, at least temporarily, gained the power of removal. The Senate would not be an executive council nor would it dominate the presidency in this area. Though the Senate still had the power of consent, at first it shared with the House its influence through "advice" on appointments. Eventually, senatorial courtesy would come into its own. In this way, the only truly significant power that would adhere to the Senate in this initial parsing of boundary powers would be, ironically, the most parochial.

The Treaty Power

A similarly rapid separation of powers characterized the development of the treaty-making process. The Constitution's phrasing of the treaty power implied a process by which the president and Senate together "make" treaties.[48] Very quickly the Senate and the president discovered that each was not comfortable with a close consultative relationship on treaties, and they established an early and respectful distance that has only increased since. Again, neither side started with this in mind, as President Washington and the first Senate anticipated a close working relationship. The president and most senators assumed that consultation applied to the entire process of treaty making—on the form and content of negotiations as well as on the final product. Initial expectations on both sides were, therefore, tending strongly toward the council arrangement. This inclination was in part mandated by a practical consideration that initially mixed the treaty power with the appointment power—treaties often had to be negotiated by special agents of the government appointed for that purpose. Several of Washington's most important treaties were negotiated by ad hoc appointees who had been approved by the Senate. In these cases the appointment process necessitated some discussion of what the negotiations would be about.

These expectations were revised by the time Washington first visited the Senate in person to discuss a treaty, in this case, an agreement with the Creek Indians.[49] As one measure of the extent to which both sides took Senate involvement seriously, Washington's visit was to discuss the potential terms to be reached through negotiations. The president was seeking the Senate's advice in forming the instructions for the commissioners sent to negotiate on behalf of the U.S. government. As has been noted by many other scholars, this meeting was the first and last of its kind. Besides the lifeless minutes of the *Senate Executive Journal*, the diary of Senator William Maclay provides the only insight into the events on August 22, 1789. Though Maclay's famous temper and self-involvement might prejudice his account, there is no reason to doubt its overall accuracy. Despite the vice president's efforts to facilitate, the Senate was in no hurry to give its approval. A motion was made to commit the matter, which resulted in Washington losing his temper and concluding that "this defeats every purpose of my coming here." The altercation was smoothed over with an agreement that the president would return that Monday, which would give the Senate a chance to consider matters. He did return, and the business was finished with the Senate giving approval to the purpose of the negotiations.[50] That was, however, the last time Washington or any other president appeared before the Senate to consult on a treaty or any other issue pertaining to a power shared with the Senate.

Washington continued on occasion to seek through written communications counsel from the Senate on the advisability and goals of specific negotiations. For example, in August of 1790, Washington sought the Senate's advice on three questions related to negotiations with the Cherokee Indians. The Senate provided written responses, which left certain issues to the president's discretion and included a commitment to ratify the resulting agreement.[51] The president, however, did not commit the whole matter for the Senate's consideration. At the president's discretion, and without Senate protest, other important matters in the Cherokee negotiations were not submitted to the Senate. In another case, concerning negotiations with the government of Algiers, Washington hypothetically asked the Senate whether it would approve certain dollar amounts that might be required as part of the possible agreements.[52] It should also be noted that the president, in more than one instance, kept both chambers of Congress apprised of ongoing negotiations.[53] Washington set another precedent with his 1793 Proclamation of Neutrality, which declared the United States to be neutral in the war between Great Britain and France. Washington's proclamation was not only a statement of foreign policy. By interpreting the country's obligations under the 1778 treaty with France, the president had asserted his right to do so without seeking advice and consent from the Senate (or for that matter, insofar as a declaration of neutrality certainly affected the war power vested in Congress, without involving the House). Practice was drifting toward greater executive initiative and independence.

Closer to the end of Washington's presidency, the bitter fight over the Jay Treaty completed what would become the basic architecture of the treaty process from that time forward. As early as February 1790, Washington had sought the Senate's advice on negotiations to solve increasing conflicts with Great Britain. By 1794, as matters between the two countries grew worse and the separation of powers had been sharpened in the matter of treaties, Washington received a more informal and unsolicited form of senatorial advice. A group of four proadministration senators— Oliver Ellsworth, Rufus King, George Cabot, and Caleb Strong—met and formulated a plan of action, which Ellsworth presented to the president. The plan's central component was the appointment of a special envoy to settle the host of disputes between Great Britain and the United States. Washington did not agree immediately to their plan but eventually concluded it was necessary to send such an emissary.

The first conflict with the Senate came with the appointment of U.S. Supreme Court Chief Justice John Jay to be "Envoy Extraordinary." Although there were objections to Jay, both personally and because of the conflict with his current job, the major dispute within the Senate was over a proposed request to see the "whole business with which the proposed Envoy is to be charged," in other words, the instructions.[54] The Senate defeated this resolution and, in effect, conceded that the content of negotiations was largely in the hands of the president. Washington had continued to consult with the group of influential proadministration senators who had helped to initiate the Jay mission, and they advised the president that it was unnecessary to submit instructions to the Senate. So, despite some precedents to the contrary, Washington decided not to send the Senate a copy of his instructions. The difficulty of the appointment notwithstanding, consultation was at the discretion of the president.

The other precedents set by the Jay Treaty followed its submission to the Senate in the spring of 1795 to be considered in a special session called by Washington for June 8. After some opening skirmishes, Senator Aaron Burr put forward a resolution to suspend consideration of the treaty and instruct the president to renegotiate seven particular aspects of the agreement.[55] The debate over this resolution freely mixed constitutional theory and partisan interests until the two were inseparable. Burr's motion was defeated on a twenty-to-ten vote, which would match the final vote on the treaty itself, an exact two-thirds majority. The final approval of the treaty contained the last important precedent. The Senate accepted the treaty with the condition that one article not be included (and that further negotiations proceed on the subject of that article). Washington, who was willing to drop the article in question, consulted his cabinet and concluded that, following British approval of the condition, he did not need to resubmit the treaty to the Senate. He did not, and the Senate did not object: "The first great treaty under the Constitution had been negotiated by the executive alone."[56] Once again, the initiative tilted in the president's direction.

Although the president would continue from time to time to consult the Senate as a whole (though not in person), the occasions were few and far between, and always at the president's discretion. In 1806, the Senate passed a resolution that requested the president to negotiate several specific grievances against Great Britain, as relations grew worse between the two nations. It passed, but many senators voted for it only because they thought it would bolster the president's position in any possible diplomacy. Jefferson did not seem to think of this as any sort of mandate. In 1815, Rufus King introduced a resolution to recommend and advise the president to pursue six specific goals in further negotiations with "his Britannic Majesty." By now, there was little support for this method of senatorial "advice." The 1815 effort, in fact, culminated with a report by the Senate Committee on Foreign Relations, which articulated the dominant constitutional interpretation of the separation of powers in foreign policy: "The President is the constitutional representative of the United States with regard to foreign nations. He manages our concerns with foreign nations and must necessarily be most competent to determine when, how, and upon what subjects negotiation may be urged with the greatest prospect of success."[57] The Foreign Relations report echoes John Marshall's 1800 pronouncement that "[t]he President is the sole organ of the nation in its external relations, and its sole representative with foreign nations."[58] It is no surprise that Justice Sutherland's opinion in *U.S. v. Curtiss-Wright Corporation* quotes both in support of its conclusion about the nearly exclusive nature of presidential power in this realm: "He *makes* treaties with the advice and consent of the Senate; but he alone negotiates. Into the field of negotiation the Senate cannot intrude."[59]

Unless, that is, the president initiates and controls the intrusion. Presidents from Jackson to at least Harding consulted with the Senate on proposed courses of action when they felt it prudent or expedient.[60] No president has felt constitutionally compelled to consult, and the Senate has never seriously contested this interpretation. The Senate would continue, of course, to play a major but post facto role in the success or failure of treaties through the power of advice and consent, and with it, the power to amend. But the precedent for the clear separation of powers, all to the advantage of the executive—or at least at the expense of special Senate powers—was set before the end of the first presidency.

During consideration of the bill to establish the department of Foreign Affairs, that first great congressional debate on presidential power, Representative James Jackson argued that the Constitution had with treaties and appointments "blended" the power of the Senate and the president. "It may be wrong," Jackson continued, "that the great powers of Government should be blended in this manner; but we cannot separate them; the error is adopted in the constitution, and can only be eradicated by weeding it out of that instrument," through the process of amendment.[61] Although Jackson would stay in the House only one term, even by the end of his two years it was perhaps becoming evident to him (and certainly to others) that certain provisions of the Constitution were quite susceptible to a different and efficient kind of "amendment" by precedent and practice.

The Vice Presidency and the Senate

We learned in chapter 5 that the creation of the vice presidency was as much about providing the Senate with a presiding officer as it was about presidential elections and succession. Likewise, we have seen that the vice president's position in the Senate was the subject of some criticism by delegates at the Constitutional Convention and during the process of ratification. Here, according to critics, was another violation of the separation of powers, this time with the Senate's independence endangered. For a while, the first vice president, John Adams, seemed to be doing his best to prove the skeptics right. Adams took the job of president of the Senate quite seriously, much to the chagrin of some senators, such as William Maclay, to whose diary, once again, scholars are compelled to turn for most details on Adams's performance. (Maclay quickly came to despise Adams and so his account is especially suspect in its characterizations of the vice president.)[62] Although Adams, as is often noted, thought the vice presidency to be "the most insignificant office that ever the invention of man contrived or his imagination conceived," he was the most active and important president of the Senate ever. Nonetheless, that might not be saying very much, and he and Senator Maclay had different perceptions of how active he was.[63]

As with everything else, the exact role of the vice president in the Senate was uncertain, and Adams expressed as much to the senators.[64] One thing was clear, however; the Constitution made the vice president the presiding officer of the Senate. It was, in fact, his only governmental function.[65] So it should come as no surprise that Adams was a relatively vigorous presiding officer, and, at least for the First Congress, he was a notable presence in the Senate. He used his power to rule on aspects of procedure, to take active part in the debates, to cast deciding votes in the event of ties, and in a few instances to shape the agenda and lobby for votes.[66] The Senate began with only twenty members (growing to twenty-six by the end of the First Congress), and so Adams's influence was magnified by the small numbers. He cast twenty-nine tie-breaking votes, the most of any vice president. Although a few nineteenth-century successors would match or exceed his per-year average over two terms, Adams cast twenty of his twenty-nine during the First Congress.[67] Some of these votes affected very important issues, including, as we have seen, the final decision to give the president power to remove executive branch officers. Given that Adams was a staunch Federalist and close to Washington (though he seems to have participated little in executive decision making), his potential influence on the proceedings of the first Senate could have been a cause for concern. The president seemed to have a powerful agent in the legislature.

Adams's influence and engagement appear to have waned, however, over the course of his eight years as vice president.[68] Senators, for reasons of partisanship and institutional prerogative, came to assert the independence of the Senate and to see the vice president increasingly as an intruder—though he had nowhere else to go—whose Senate functions were to be circumscribed. Thomas Jefferson, when elected to be Adams's vice president, believed that office's only constitutionally sanctioned function was as "a member of a Legislative body."[69] Given Jefferson's political alienation from Adams and his exclusion from the administration, though, no one was concerned any longer about a presidential agent in the Senate. For much of his term as vice president, Jefferson was active as head of the Senate and "occupied the chair daily."[70] In typical Jeffersonian fashion, this was not an idle exercise of constitutional duties. He devoted no small part of his four years in "the most insignificant office" to setting down on paper the rules and procedures of the U.S. Senate—which resulted in his famous manual—when he wasn't preparing his party for the next presidential election. Vice President Aaron Burr was seen as an effective presiding officer when present, but he had no influence in the administration. Whatever future the vice president might have in executive politics, his presence and purpose in the Senate was, after Adams, a limited and sometimes unwelcome one. Vice presidents would continue to preside on a regular basis for many years to come, but Senate rules and the emergence of party leadership, however informal, relegated the president of the Senate to a largely symbolic role. Once again political practice had quickly clarified an ambiguity in the Constitution by reinforcing the separation of powers.

SENATE AND HOUSE:
LEGISLATION AND THE BICAMERAL RELATIONSHIP

As the Senate was working out its relationship with the executive, it was also determining its role with the House in the legislative process. As we shall see, the two were related. Characterizations of the early Senate as the less active chamber and as a council of revision are deeply rooted in political science.[71] Despite some refinements and subtleties, modern treatments echo these early assessments and often lean heavily on the council of revision theme.[72] Many characterizations of the early Senate's legislative activity, however, oversimplify what turns out to be a more complex and interesting reality. We do not argue that the Senate was as active as the House or that the Senate was not in some respects reactive, but that such a conception, extended too far, distorts the reality of an institution in formation that was following its constitutional duties.

This dominant impression is partly based on a repetition of a select number of quotations about the early Senate's putatively leisurely schedule and early adjournments, and references to Senate members going to watch the action in the House. Quantitative evidence supports this conclusion as well. As Sarah Binder notes, "a single perfect measure of the level of demands on Congress over time does not exist." Nevertheless, for bicameral comparisons, the major and imperfect surrogate for workload has been legislative initiative (broadly defined). By counting the "number of public bills originating in and passed by each chamber," Binder concludes that "House workload clearly outpaced the Senate's for the first 14 Congresses (1789-1817)." In a similar fashion, Elaine Swift's analysis of legislative initiation for selected sessions from early Congresses shows a 3.41 to 1 ratio in favor of the House, which is still a 3 to 1 ratio when revenue bills (which she does not define) are excluded. Her conclusion from this data is that the Senate "fulfilled" the hopes of the framers by being less active than the House.[73]

The image of the early Senate as the reactive chamber obscures important patterns that emerge from a sharper focus. The quantitative comparisons of House and Senate workloads are at some level irrefutable evidence of differences in bicameral activity, but they are insufficient for reaching broad conclusions about workload and the collective psychology or ethos of each chamber implied by such differences. The Senate may have initiated less legislation but that does not mean it was not working hard, nor does it mean that the Senate felt itself to be fundamentally different, except in the ways the Constitution prescribed.

The image of hyperactive senators and a hyperactive Senate keeping pace with the House is in any event a relatively contemporary one, coincidental with the rise of professional staff. One obvious point is that in a Congress devoid of staff, the number of legislators in each chamber mattered. The First Congress started with a House to Senate membership ratio of 2.5 to 1, which increased unsteadily to 3.34 to 1 by the Fifth Congress. Swift's data on per capita workload show that somewhere between the Second and Fifth Congresses the Senate had surpassed the House in the number of public bills originated per member. (The exact trend is unknown because Swift skips from the Second Congress, second session to the Fifth Congress, third session.) Despite its small numbers, the Senate was, by this measure, outpacing the House somewhere near the end of Washington's presidency or the beginning of Adams's.

More to the point, the aggregate quantitative analysis makes no distinctions among types of legislation. The basis for a more refined assessment is offered by Lane Lancaster in his 1928 article on Senate initiative in legislation.[74] Without calling it such, Lancaster makes what amounts to a division of labor argument. He begins by acknowledging that the House was, for the first ten Congresses, the more active initiator: Of 895 public acts passed, just over 22 percent were started in the Senate. He compares this record to that of the Senate of his era—during the 68th Congress—when the Senate initiated 38 percent. While Lancaster cites that difference to show how much the Senate's activity increased, one could look at the same change from quite another perspective. The 73 percent increase is significant, but it still leaves the Senate of the 68th Congress well short of parity with the House. That aside, Lancaster argues that aggregate statistics fail to discriminate among areas of public policy and their importance. Analysis of the subject and the nature of the legislation yields a different story. Lancaster finds four areas where the Senate did take the initiative consistently and for a long time: "1. Courts and judicial procedure. 2. The organization of state and territorial governments. 3. Foreign affairs. 4. Finance, coinage and banking." While the last of these—

finance and banking—might not fit, the others seem to form a pattern that reflects the formal and informal divisions of labor created by the Constitution. The judiciary and foreign affairs clearly fell under the prevailing sense of the Senate's division of responsibilities. Though nothing about appointments or treaties prevented the House from taking the first step in the areas of courts and foreign affairs, it appears that both the House and Senate saw this as a job for the latter. The organization of state and territorial governments is a perfect blend of matters involving foreign policy (especially as conceived at that time) and the Senate's embodiment of state equality. Given the rapid growth of the country during this time, in terms of territory gained as well as states admitted, this was not a small undertaking. This division of labor was apparent from the beginning, when in the first Congress the House took up the formidable task of the revenue bill while the Senate drafted what would become the vital Judiciary Act of 1789.

The revenue bill points to another factor in bicameral workload comparisons that has been underrated and that was dealt with only implicitly in Lancaster's analysis. The constitutionally mandated requirement that the House originate all revenue bills seems to have been significant in shaping the degree of initiative each chamber took. From the start, the chambers adopted a broad interpretation of the revenue clause; that is, with the House originated not only pure revenue-raising legislation but also most "supply bills," later known as appropriations bills. Though there were some disagreements, the broad definition flowed from the fact that the founders "frequently used 'money bills' and 'revenue bills' as synonymous, and in contemporary usage, both in England and in America, 'money bills' often included bills for the spending as well as for the raising of money."[75] At the Constitutional Convention, the clause first appeared as follows: "All Bills for raising and appropriating money and for fixing the salaries." The leaner final phrasing has been interpreted as either an implicit embrace of the broad definition or a deliberate exclusion and restriction.

Whatever the original intent, the Senate itself upheld a fairly broad definition. As Haynes notes, "the Senate was not five months old when it denied to itself the power to originate a bill for imposing an increased duty of tonnage."[76] A committee chaired by Senator Butler was appointed on June 17, 1789 to work on a bill "to arrange and bring forward a system to regulate the trade and intercourse between the United States and the territory of other powers in North America and the West Indies." The committee reported the following on August 5: "That it will be expedient to pass a law for imposing an increased duty of tonnage ... but such a law being of the nature of a revenue law, your committee conceive that the originating a bill for that purpose, is, by the constitution, exclusively placed in the House of Representatives."[77]

The Senate approved this report. Beyond this, the record of the First Congress provides only a few hints about Senate thinking on such matters. On a bill regarding the effect of a funding law on Rhode Island, Senator Maclay notes in his diary that "I voted against this and gave as a reason that as it respected the Revenue, altho' not raising Yet it should be left to the other house."[78] Senator William Patterson's notes on the State Debt Assumption Bill debate record a colloquy among Senators Richard Henry Lee, Ellsworth, and Carroll over whether it qualified as a "money bill." Lee argued that it was, while Carroll and Ellsworth demurred.[79] It could be that some, like Maclay and Lee, used a broad definition of the restriction in a politically motivated fashion. If they didn't like the way the Senate was tending on a revenue-related issue, the revenue clause restriction could be invoked as another objection.

Mixed motives and debates notwithstanding, the Senate took the revenue clause seriously and, with these few exceptions, broadly defined it.[80] Given that a significant aspect of getting the new nation up and running involved several types of "money bills" (tariffs, appropriations, etc.), it is not surprising that the House initiated many such bills. Conversely, it is not an indicator of Senate aristocratic sloth that they sometimes found themselves waiting for the House to finish its work on such bills before they could begin theirs. When the House did finish, the Senate took an active role in extensive revisions and amendments. Senator Maclay's diary is replete with details on the debates over, for example, the impost bill, with senators showing considerable interest in the minutiae of these tariffs and the exact duties to be imposed on myriad goods.[81]

The final major deficiency in the standard assessments of bicameral activity in the early Congresses is that they all overlook the unique duties given to the Senate by the Constitution. Appointments and treaties were a significant part of the early Senate's workload. The first Senate, which did much of its work on the floor, devoted some time and effort, as we have seen, to determining its proper role and method of operation in the consideration of appointments and treaties. These were, by the letter and intent of the Constitution, fundamental duties of the Senate. They also constituted a sizeable and often unrecognized portion of the Senate's workload.

The only continuous and reliable source of information about Senate executive business is the *Senate Executive Journal* (SEJ). Kept separately from the *Senate Journal* (SJ), which records regular legislative business, the SEJ chronicles action on appointments, treaties, and some presidential messages to the Senate. The SEJ is typically devoid of detail save for the full reproduction of presidential messages and papers submitted to the Senate. Otherwise, it records parliamentary actions taken by the Senate (motions, votes, decisions) but not the debate. The perfunctory entries of the SEJ make it impossible, therefore, to judge how much time was actually spent on these items of business. Nearly all entries fall into three categories. Many are presidential messages announcing nominations for appointments (officers, judges, ambassadors, port collectors, etc.). Some such messages are one or two names long; some contain dozens of names. The next kind of entry, often coming on the day following the nomination message from the president, records the Senate's action on the nominations. The final category is entries concerning foreign relations involving treaties, also sometimes divided between presidential messages and Senate action. The closest one comes to an indication of time consumed in debate are the following phrases that appear intermittently: "The Senate proceeded to consider"; "The Senate resumed the consideration of"; "ORDERED, That the farther consideration hereof be postponed"; "and after debate." With rare but notable exceptions, SEJ entries occur on the same day as SJ entries. That is, the Senate did both kinds of work on the same days. The principal exception is the grand debate over the Jay Treaty that took place in a special session of the Senate in the Fourth Congress.

As one measure of the extent of Senate executive business, we compared the number of entries in the SJ and SEJ for each of the first five Congresses (fig. 7.2). The number of SEJ entries as a percentage of SJ entries varies from 25.5 percent in the First Congress to 60 percent in the Fifth, with a distinct upward trend in the proportion of SEJ entries and an average of 41 percent across the five Congresses. The Fourth Congress, for example, was extraordinary for the level of activity devoted to treaties (fifty-four days, with sixteen of those during the special session devoted to the Jay Treaty). The Fifth Congress, the first under Adams, saw an unprecedented number of days featuring action on presidential appointments. Though one cannot accurately compare the actual amount of work or effort devoted to legislative and executive business, the overall data show that executive business was a consistent and frequent aspect of Senate action. This also shows that the level of executive business did not subside following the First Congress and President Washington's efforts to constitute the first executive branch and judiciary.

The number and variety of appointments—though perhaps small by modern standards—was at that time unprecedented for legislative consideration. The data show that the early SEJ is filled with communications from the president nominating judges, envoys, ambassadors, military officers, and department officers. What is not known is how much time the Senate spent in debate or deliberation on nominations. If nothing else, the Senate was doing much of its work on the floor, and so presidential messages (as far as the record shows) were read aloud to the senators. It does appear, however, that the Senate deliberated over the nominations, relied on testaments from senators of the nominee's state, and occasionally formed committees to inquire further into particular cases. The president even called the Senate back for a special one-day session (March 4, 1791) to consider a long list of nominations.

Treaties, while fewer in number than appointments, seemed to occupy more time. In an era before the use of executive agreements, treaties were a regular part of diplomacy, and again, the United States was a new nation reaching agreements with not only other nation-states but also Indian tribes. From 1789 to 1793, the Senate ratified, rejected, or made changes to at least six treaties with Indian tribes.[82] The treaties with Algiers and Spain, the Jay Treaty, and the Creek Treaty of 1796 all involved significant Senate deliberations over the course of several years, with the president seeking advice and consent at various stages of each set of negotiations. The Senate appears to have deliberated at length over most of the early treaties. Moreover, as we have seen, some of the action on treaties involved considerations that would seem novel in the modern Senate, including several instances of presidential consultations about the form and content of prospective negotiations and treaties. The quality and durability of international agreements was one argument for having scrapped the Confederation Congress, so the Senate no doubt took this responsibility quite seriously.

Little time probably was spent on some items, especially many appointments. Our point is that the aggregate of all appointment and for-

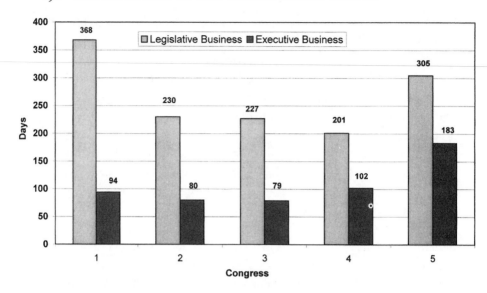

FIG. 7.2. Legislative and Executive Business in the Senate, Congresses 1–5.
Source: *Senate Journal* and *Senate Executive Journal*.

eign policy action was significant and contrasts, again, with the measures
of workload that rely almost exclusively on legislative initiative. There is
no way to assign a "bill equivalency" value to some unit of executive
business, but clearly any measure of workload that fails to account for the
Senate's activities in this area is inadequate. Given the general level of
Senate executive action, it is fair at least to say that bicameral workload
balance in the earliest Congresses is more even than typically portrayed.
In fact, given that the Senate, by some legislative workload measures
(such as per capita bill introduction), had caught up to the House by the
Fifth Congress, it is credible to argue that the early Senate was, in some
ways, more burdened than the House.

That the early Senate would take such duties seriously and be compelled to devote considerable time and energy to them is quite natural. It
certainly is no indication of a haughty pseudo aristocracy at work. If
anything, the Senate's efforts are the sign of a legislature performing the
tasks assigned to it. Moreover, it is somewhat ironic to conclude, as others
have, that the Senate was reactive and, in this way, aping the House of
Lords, through the use of incomplete workload measures that ignore the
burdens of the constitutional duties that were, in reality, the true distinctions between it and the House.

The importance and temper of some of the legislation the early Senate handled also prevents any easy interpretation of that body's role as a check on the House's more precipitous behavior. The early Senate did little to, in the reputed words of George Washington, "cool the coffee." The Judiciary Act and the national bank legislation, both initiated by the Senate, were aggressive and far-reaching laws, which did as much as anything to expand the power and reach of the federal government. During the Adams presidency, amid the fervor created by the quasi war with France, the Senate initiated and passed the most draconian of the acts concerning aliens and likewise was the source of the Sedition Act, both of 1798. The House embraced the Senate versions of these measures and added minor amendments to mitigate some of the harsher features of the Senate's work.[83] As the more Federalist of the two chambers, it is no surprise that the alien and sedition laws originated in the Senate under Adams. Just a few years later under Jefferson, when the Senate was thoroughly Republican, it initiated the first Embargo Act, one of the most draconian national measures of the nineteenth century. As the Senate came under the sway of partisan politics, its power could be used for any cause.

Like most of the anti-Federalist fears, concern about Senate dominance was quickly put to rest. While thoroughly contradicting the anti-Federalist worry of a Senate that would dominate the House, the early Senate's record is hardly that of a revisory House of Lords. While the House was certainly more active, the Senate initiated legislation whenever it wanted and was allowed to do so, and never behaved as though it was simply waiting for the House, except in the constitutionally mandated cases of money bills. Unlike the House, the Senate had to consider treaties and nominations, and while these duties might not explain most of the difference in legislative output, they were part of the division of labor, and took the time and energy of what we must remember was a small group of men. As Swanstrom concludes, "Experience from the very beginning did, indeed, prove that in legislative matters the two Houses were coordinate Chambers."[84]

FOR THE STATES OR FOR THE NATION?
RECALL AND INSTRUCTION

We have seen that the Senate's putatively Lords-like distinctions disappeared and its special powers were diminished. What about the more private Federalist fear that the Senate would be a parochial instrument of state legislatures and the relatively quiet anti-Federalist hope that the Senate would be just that? On this question, the evidence is less decisive; after all, the tension in that dualism was not fully resolved until the Seventeenth Amendment mandated direct elections. Furthermore, it is often a fine distinction between legislative behavior that is parochial and that which is not. Nevertheless, the fate and effect of recall and instruction—the two attempts to bolster the Senate-state relationship through extraconstitutional means—illustrate the degree to which the senators were beholden to the bodies that elected them or were able to assert their independence.[85] Here was the earliest contest between the Senate in its role as a national republican institution and its federal role as the repository of states rights. Recall, even as a concept, disappeared quickly, and though instruction would never become a significant problem for the early Senate, nothing better reflected the contradictory nature of the Senate: Was it the core of national republicanism—the great anchor—or was it simply the mouthpiece of state legislative interests?

The doctrine of instruction—originally the right of citizens to petition their representatives on how to vote on particular issues—enjoyed widespread acceptance in theory if not practice in the postrevolutionary states of America and was seen by some as an essential facet of liberty. In state constitutions, it was an aspect of the free speech rights of assembly and petition. The declaration of rights in North Carolina's 1776 constitution declared "[t]hat the people have a right to assemble together, to consult for their common good, to instruct their Representatives, and to apply to the Legislature, for redress of grievances."[86] Instruction was from the start a somewhat ambiguous concept. It did not mandate that representatives obey; it primarily protected the right of petition. This was a powerful enough current that several states debated or included the right of instruction in their lists of amendments to be added to the new national constitution. In this form, instruction applied equally to the House and Senate.

Even during the process of ratification, a closer connection between instruction and the Senate was taking shape. The combination of the precedent of the Confederation Congress and the structure of the new Senate implied a more direct and mandatory relationship between instruction and representation. The connection between the Senate and the state legislatures was hard to deny, however much it was the imperfect fusion of theory and compromise at the Constitutional Convention. State legislatures chose senators, and each state was given an equal number of two. Equality implied the representation of states as corporate entities, and the decision in favor of two senators was motivated in part by the concern that every state be assured of having at least one senator present at all times. This close association magnified the parallels between the Senate and the Congress of the Confederation. Representatives to the Confederation Congress were delegates from their state governments. That they could be instructed on how to vote in Congress was implicit in the structure of the system. (Imagine a national government thinking it could not "instruct" its delegate to the United Nations.)

Recall, though bearing a logical relationship to instruction, did not apply to state governments and was not rooted in state constitutionalism. Most state representatives were subject to annual election. Under such circumstances, recall was an unnecessary precaution. No state constitution provided for recall of its elected representatives. Instead recall—think, again, of a nation recalling its ambassador—applied to the confederation. The Articles of Confederation contained the right of recall. States could at any time recall any of their representatives and substitute another (a power that was never exercised). At the Constitutional Convention the proposal for recall made a quick and quiet exit. Its only mention was in the Virginia plan, and it was to apply to the democratic branch, the House, not the Senate. During ratification, the anti-Federalists, who did their best to establish that the Senate should be a continuation of the Confederation Congress, argued that recall therefore should apply to the Senate just as it had to Congress. Melancton Smith noted at the New York ratification convention: "[A]s the senators are the representatives of the state legislatures, it is reasonable and proper that they should be under their control. When a state sends an agent commissioned to transact any business, or perform any service, it certainly ought to have a power to recall."[87] Several states debated or included amendments with the right of recall applied to senators, though the concept would quickly disappear when the new Congress labored over the first set of amendments to the Constitution.[88]

Although anti-Federalists worried generally about the power of the national government and its distance from the people and states, as we have seen, they worried particularly about the Senate with its long terms. During the ratification conventions, at least two prominent Federalists referred to instruction as a way to reassure those worried about the independence of senators. In Massachusetts, Rufus King argued that state legislatures "can and will instruct" their senators. New York's John Jay presumed that state legislatures would instruct senators and "that there will be a constant correspondence supported between the senators and the state executives."[89] While they may not have believed in this practice, given the constitution of the Senate they were not being deceptive in their assumptions. Yet such notions contradicted the republican spirit of the Constitution, and at the Constitutional Convention instruction and recall were nowhere mentioned in regard to the Senate. Indeed, nothing could be more anathema to the Senate as conceived by the convention majority. Antithetical as they were to many framers' notions of republicanism, instruction and recall harmonized with the principles and interests of those who anticipated the new national government with grave concern and skepticism. In one of the ironies attached to the Senate, the legislative body designed in republican theory to be alien to anything like instructions became, in the Senate's compromised form, the most logical target for a vigorous doctrine of instruction.

The closest instruction ever came to being constitutionally sanctioned was with the consideration in August 1789 of an addition to the proposed first amendments to the Constitution. The draft list of amendments submitted to the House for debate did not include the right of instruction, which had been in the amendments proposed by several states. Representative Thomas Tucker from South Carolina moved to include among the rights of citizens the "right to instruct their representatives," parallel to the provisions in state constitutions. The debate over the amendment revealed the ambiguity of instruction. Some proponents viewed it mostly as a way to encourage active participation by the population and to require elected representatives to pay some attention to that participation. Opponents saw any expression of a right of instruction as a threat to the deliberative process. The instruction amendment was defeated decisively by a vote of ten to forty-one in the House and two to fourteen in the Senate.[90] Neither chamber would be the object of a constitutional right of instruction.

This defeat did not kill the doctrine of instruction. Some state legislatures proceeded to "instruct" anyway. In December of the same year, 1789, the first direct use of instruction in the new government, as we have seen, was from the Virginia state legislature to its senators (followed by North Carolina, South Carolina, Maryland, and New York), telling them to make every effort to open up the Senate's deliberations to the public. According to the secondary literature, this was the only significant use of instruction in the first years of Congress. Senator Maclay's diary makes several brief references to other instances during the First Congress.[91] The lower house of the Pennsylvania legislature passed three resolutions expressing a "hope" that their senators would oppose parts of the Duties and Distilled Spirits Act, but the state senate did not support these resolutions. The highly controversial bill on the assumption of state debts prompted state instructions from South Carolina and Massachusetts; Maclay was disappointed that instructions from his state legislature were apparently thwarted. He himself was supportive of instructions but recognized the danger of a slavish application of the principle. He expressed more than once his view that instructions should be applied in a uniform manner; that is, all states should instruct on an issue before the Senate takes final action. The state legislature of North Carolina seems to have been among the most active in issuing instructions. In turn, that state's first senators, Benjamin Hawkins and Samuel Johnston, maintained a regular correspondence with the state government, particularly the governor, apprising him of their efforts and justifying their votes.[92]

Although instructions about open sessions were a matter for the Senate only, many at the time thought that instruction still applied, though less strictly, to the House. There thus arose the practice of state legislatures "instructing" their senators and "requesting" their representatives to support or resist a measure.[93] This distinction mirrored the ambivalent nature of instruction: as an order and as a petition. As the direct agents of senatorial elections, state legislatures could command their senators but not representatives, who were selected by the people directly. This also reflected a deeper political reality. State legislatures, unlike most citizens in legislative districts, could overcome the collective action problems necessary to make instructions seem obligatory because of the effective threat of a sanction for disobedience, namely, a high probability the senator would not be reelected.[94]

In practice, instruction seems to have been infrequent, and the effect of it was limited. Federalists, mostly from the North, largely eschewed instructions. Republicans, mostly from the South, practiced it more regularly but with mixed effects. One of the other notable instances of widespread use of instruction on a single issue came in the aftermath of the

1800 elections, when several state legislatures instructed their federal representatives to support an amendment to prevent another electoral deadlock such as that between Jefferson and Burr. Yet instruction's heyday would not come for many years. With the rise of Republican power, some Federalist state legislatures in the North found themselves willing to use instruction. Some senatorial resignations followed disagreements over instructions, which in these relatively rare instances made the practice work as the functional equivalent of recall. (As we have seen, many senators from the early Congresses seemed ready to resign and go home anyway.) One victim was John Quincy Adams in 1808. Adams suffered the wrath of the Federalist Massachusetts legislature when he dared to support Jefferson's embargo. The legislature sent Adams instructions to the contrary and proceeded to elect another senator six months before the end of Adams's term. Adams resigned. Other senators who ignored instructions were occasionally not reelected or, because of their long terms, outlasted the legislature that instructed them.

With its limited impact, instruction did not so much become a symbol of state influence on senators. Rather, instruction came to reflect the role of party in Senate politics. Faction and party played a strong role in "normalizing" the Senate and making it a coequal legislative institution. The most frequent use of instruction grew out of the rise and fall of partisan majorities in state legislatures and their relationship with their senators in Washington. If on some important partisan issue, for example, a state legislature controlled by one party wanted to put pressure on a senator elected by an earlier state legislature controlled by a different party, they might instruct the senator on how to vote. State interests, as such, did not exist; partisan interests did, and they, for most part, dictated the ebb and flow of instructions. This was particularly true in the 1830s, the zenith of instruction, especially with the battle between Whigs and Democrats over Jackson, the bank, and censure. Later, with the sharpening of party sectionalism over the issue of slavery and the consequences of the Civil War, instruction wasted away in theory and practice. As with other aspects of the Senate's role, where one stood ideologically on instruction was mostly a function of where one sat politically. Senators would not be minions of their states, but the rise of party politics meant they would not be insulated from the pulling and hauling of ordinary politics.

FACTIONS, PARTIES, AND THE SENATE

As with everything else in American politics at the time, one cannot separate the shaping of the Senate from the rapid rise of factional and then partisan politics. The emergence of the national political divisions that led to the first two-party system in American politics needs no rehearsal here; likewise, the dispute over when real parties, as opposed to sectional alignments or mere factions, finally emerged, need not detain us.[95] For our purposes, what is important is when and how the Senate became integrated into the pattern of national political divisions that formed during this era, whatever label one chooses to attach to those disagreements. Such issues as the Hamiltonian fiscal program and the French Revolution quickly divided senators from each other, and sometimes the Senate clashed with the House as the factional imbalances became apparent. The roll-call voting studies of party formation in the early Congress show the rapid emergence of factional and then party-like voting blocs during Washington's two-term presidency.[96] This happened in nearly the same way and at the same time in the House and the Senate. From the start the Senate was not insulated from the sometimes incendiary passions that quickly engulfed American political life.

Criticism of the early Senate could hardly be separated from this nascent factional split. The complaints about Senate secrecy and special powers came primarily from the emerging antiadministration faction. As Joseph Lynch has shown, constitutional arguments and factional politics were interwoven from the start.[97] That is, politicians' views of the proper interpretation of the Constitution's institutional designs and distribution of powers tended to flow from their political position on the issue at hand. The criticisms increased in the Third Congress when the Senate, which was still solidly proadministration or Federalist, faced a House with an antiadministration, proto-Republican majority. This helped to produce the decision in favor of open sessions and the removal of Albert Gallatin from the Senate. Yet procedural reform would not assuage critics whose animosity was based on other things. In a 1794 letter to Madison, Jefferson recommended shortening the senatorial term and "complet[ing] the experiment whether they [the senators] do more harm than good."[98]

Party politics and nature of the Senate came together in the defining controversy of the era. In June 1795 the Senate took up the Jay Treaty for consideration in a special session called by President Washington. "The outpouring of popular feeling over the Jay Treaty, as has long been understood, was more directly responsible than anything else for the full emergence of political parties in America, and of clearly recognized Federalist and Republican points of view on all political questions."[99] We have seen already that the consideration of the treaty in the Senate and the House set important precedents for the separation of powers and bicameral relationship. By accelerating the integration of the Senate into national partisan politics, the Jay Treaty fight also helped to make the Senate, for better or worse, more like the House.

Perhaps in part because few were willing to directly attack George Washington for the contents of the treaty, John Jay took much of the blame, but so did the Senate. Many Republicans were inherently opposed to negotiations with England, let alone actually reaching a treaty, and so their opposition was not necessarily dependent on the actual terms of the treaty. Based upon rumors he had heard about the progress of Jay's mission, James Monroe wrote from Paris to express his anxiety that a strong and favorable agreement had been reached.[100] The five-month gap between the first news of the completion of negotiations and the presentation of the agreement to the Senate fueled speculation and rumors about the treaty. With the text and terms of the treaty a secret even after Washington received the papers in March, the opposition drew the conclusion that the adherence to secrecy meant the terms of the treaty were unfavorable to the United States. The same Senate that had voted the year before to open its doors to the public was still deliberating in closed sessions because galleries had not been built. The Senate exacerbated the suspicion surrounding the treaty by choosing to keep deliberations confidential and not publishing the text of the treaty while they debated its merits. (Senate rules, the vote for open sessions notwithstanding, still provided for going into secret executive sessions on a motion and required a majority vote to do so.) All this made the situation ripe for an attack on the Senate as an institution. The antiadministration newspaper *Aurora* rhetorically asked: "How does *the secrecy* of the Senate, in relation to the Treaty, comport with THE SOVEREIGNTY of the people? . . . The Constitution of the United States gives to the President and Senate the power of making Treaties; but it communicates no power to hatch those things *in darkness*. This practice is borrowed *from Kings and their Ministers*, and seems to imply a disposition to assimilate our Government, if not in theory, at least *in practice*, to

Monarchy."[101] In short, the proadministration, pro-British Senate was giving away American rights behind closed doors. Despite the vituperations, the Senate continued its closeted debates and approved the treaty, albeit by the exact two-thirds required by the Constitution.

The year ended with a number of calls to alter the Senate by constitutional amendment. The farthest any of these got was the passage by strong majorities in the Virginia legislature of a resolution, which in the usual fashion, "instructed" its senators and "requested" its representatives to do their utmost to secure passage of a series of amendments, including three concerning the Senate: that any treaty touching on Article I, section 8 powers of Congress be adopted by both houses; that the power to try impeachments be removed from the Senate; and that the Senate term be reduced to three years. No other legislature passed anything like the Virginia resolution; indeed some, including Pennsylvania, counterattacked their southern neighbor's premature assault on the young Constitution.[102] For a variety of reasons, by the spring of 1796, when the House finally received the treaty to consider appropriations for its implementation, public opinion had turned in favor of the treaty.[103] The new Republican majority in the House, despite a forceful attempt to assert its role in the treaty-making process, was eroded and the treaty appropriations passed fifty-one to forty-eight.

With the waning of the "British Treaty" controversy in the summer of 1796, attacks on the Senate likewise subsided. Control of the government as a whole by people of the right political persuasion was now the issue, rather than the right balance of powers among institutions. The 1796 elections were a major test of the emerging party system. Adams and the Federalists won that contest, but the Republicans had shown considerable strength. The same Jefferson who had led the charge on the Jay Treaty and had excoriated the Senate was now president of that body. Because, as we have seen, he was not welcome in the circles of presidential power, he had plenty of time to spend contemplating the nature of Senate behavior and codifying its rules of procedure. This was one way to bide his time until, with the complete triumph of his party in 1800, Jefferson would find that "the Senate could adjust itself nicely to the new Republican era."[104]

In fact, despite six-year terms and staggered elections, the Senate almost immediately mirrored the House in the balance between factional or partisan majorities and minorities (fig. 7.3). Because of the uncertainties surrounding early factional or partisan attachments, there are disagree-

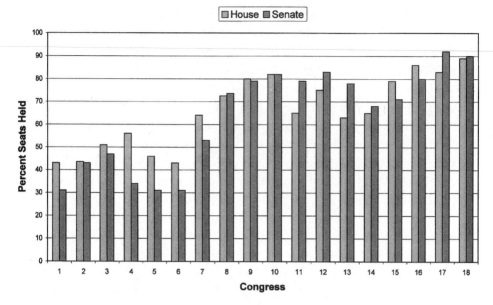

FIG. 7.3. "Republican" Congressional Seats, 1789–1824. Factional/partisan iden-
tification data from Martis 1988. "Republican" incorporates Martis's "Antiadministration" category for the First–Third Congresses. pearson = .909

ments about how to categorize members in the first few Congresses.
Nevertheless, the Third and Fourth Congresses are the only probable
cases in the first decades of the House and Senate having clashing partisan
majorities, and the ratios are consistently close throughout. This shows
the extent to which the Senate came to be integrated into the ebb and flow
of national politics. The triumph of party politics also undermined the
effect of six-year terms. Insofar as partisanship was the measure and major
predictor of congressional behavior, the longer term of the Senate would
have less of an impact on the formation of public policy.

The Senate, much like the House, quickly came to be dominated by
factional or partisan behaviors. The more pronounced this behavior became, the more it undermined the idealistic and contradictory visions of
the Senate as either a detached and independent second chamber or as a
parochial mouthpiece of state interests. The Senate, instead, would fully
reflect the complex interplay of state, regional, and partisan interests that
quickly became the substance of national politics.

THE SENATE ARRIVES IN WASHINGTON

In their attacks on the proposed constitution, many anti-Federalists con-
flated their concerns about the Senate with the provision for the creation
of a capital district. The district inevitably would become, in their view, a
corrupt citadel, and senators, due to their long terms and supposedly
permanent sessions, would be at the heart of that fortress. During the
New York debates, Gilbert Livingston painted a florid and inelegant
portrait for his fellow delegates of a federal "Eden," with senators en-
sconced on "hallowed ground" beyond the reach of state laws and "sur-
rounded, as they will be, by an impenetrable wail [sic—presumably *wall*]
of adamant and gold, the wealth of the whole country flowing into it."[105]
Livingston's awkward metaphor aside, he was not alone in his sentiments.
The proposed federal district, though very much part of the politics
of state accommodation and compromise, became for many a symbol
of consolidation of governmental power, influence, and wealth. Patrick
Henry asked his fellow Virginians whether or not their senators, with
their long terms, would "fix themselves in the federal town, and become
citizens of that town more than of our state?" They would, he thought,
"become inhabitants of that place," "vote themselves handsome pay," and
thereby be capable of "worrying the House of Representatives into a
compliance with any measure."[106]

By the time the senators and the rest of the government arrived in
Washington, this fear was as ludicrous as the new capital itself. One of the
wonderful and indisputable aspects of Young's *The Washington Community* is his description of the backwater Acropolis that was early Washington, D.C.[107] New York Senator Gouverneur Morris's sarcastic assessment that all the district required was "houses, cellars, kitchens, well
informed men, amiable women, and other little trifles of this kind to make
our city perfect" was probably widely shared.[108] Even after the completion
of nearly three administrations, the creation of the national capital did not
produce the expected boom town. The failure of the national district to
become the fortress of Leviathan could be seen as both the cause and the
effect of the Senate's failure to become the engine of consolidation and
aristocracy that some anti-Federalists had feared, but the Senate's more
humble status was already assured by the time the Sixth Congress arrived
in Washington.

It is often noted that the Senate's early years bore out the expectations of the founders. We have shown in many ways how this is an over-simplified and often inaccurate characterization, but it also is a somewhat odd claim, given the hopes and fears of Federalists and their opponents. Within a few years it was clear that the Senate was not as powerful as desired by many Federalists and feared by many anti-Federalists.

The Senate's rapid evolution was part and parcel of the signal features of the Federalist era in American politics. A turbulent confluence of events helped to forge the Senate, in much of its constitutional place and behavior, into the shape and substance with which we are familiar today. The Jay Treaty process, from the time Washington received Jay's text of the agreement in late 1794 to the end of the struggle with the House over appropriations and the 1796 elections, was part of a three-year chain of events that shaped and symbolized the relatively rapid resolution of many of the Senate's constitutional ambiguities. The vote in February 1794 to open the Senate was followed by the Senate's 1795 debate on the Jay Treaty and the precedents that set for the separation of powers as well as its effects on partisanship. The actual opening of the Senate at the beginning of the Fourth Congress in December 1795 was followed a few months later by the Senate's acceptance of pay equity with the House and the House treaty appropriations controversy that summer. Finally, the elections of 1796 evinced the growing organization and influence of parties in the election of the executive and both chambers of Congress. Before the end of its first decade of existence, the Senate had acquired many of its basic and enduring characteristics. Evolutionary and episodic alterations would come, but much was determined early on. As Washington, one who was ever mindful of proper form and precedent, put it: "Many things, which appear of little consequence in themselves, and at the beginning, may have great and durable consequences from their having been established at the commencement of a new general government."[109]

EIGHT

From Invention to Evolution
The Irony of the Senate

> The fact is that it is possible in your thought to make almost anything you please out of the Senate. It is a body variously compounded, made many-sided by containing many elements, and a critic may concentrate his attention upon one element at a time if he chooses, make the most of what is good and put the rest out of sight, or make more than the most of what is bad and ignore everything that does not chime with his thesis of evil. The Senate has, in fact, many contrasted characteristics, shows many faces, lends itself easily to no confident generalization.
>
> WOODROW WILSON

The United States Senate, as we have seen, was the product of a complicated mixture of forces: precedent and invention, theoretical models old and new, ideology and interest, careful planning and contingency, logrolling and deliberation, coercion and compromise. Institutional precedents, for example, were regularly cited; the state governments offered models to be imitated or avoided in a national republic. These precedents did not point in the same direction, though, and they had to compete with the residual appeal of the existing constitution of the Confederation. Similarly, framers drew on theoretical models, but even the same source could be used to support contending positions. Interests had a strong presence at the birth of the Senate, but, again, the interests brought to bear were numerous and, in the medium of deliberation, fluid. All the while, framers had to be mindful of what public opinion would accept. We are not arguing that the Senate was simply a hodgepodge. Modifying the diverse influences were liberal and republican principles, and the Senate was repeatedly the focus of efforts to balance the complicated liberal-republican equation of government. On the other hand, the liberal and republican principles did not determine entirely the resulting form.

Although the Constitutional Convention's eventual resolution of the disputes and uncertainties has been enduringly consequential for the character of the Senate, the framing itself must be understood as another beginning. As with the other institutions of national government, the Senate and its place within the political order were reshaped by the precedents and practices of its first years. Thereafter, more or less dramatic changes—the rise and evolution of political parties, and the amendment of its constitutional design, for example—have influenced the character and importance of this body. As the words of Woodrow Wilson also indicate, the multifaceted nature and complexity of the Senate did not go away. Our conclusion does not summarize two hundred years of political and constitutional evolution. Instead, it reviews some important and ironic features of the Senate's design and development.

THEORY'S HORSE AND THE CONVENTION'S CAMEL

The first irony is that the institution conceived as the essential and most thorough provision for prudence and strictly national character emerged from the convention as a clumsy hybrid, particularly burdened with a strong attachment to state interests. It may be an exaggeration to present the other institutions as thoroughbreds, but it does not stretch the truth to suggest that the framers' Senate was a committee's version of a horse. A camel was, perhaps, the best that could be hoped for under the circumstances, and indeed, camels are well designed for certain purposes. Even so, we cannot draw on the idea of a sober, wise, thoroughly national body to describe the actual Senate then or now. James Madison's idea of a senate—a small body of experienced, learned, and nationally minded legislators, free from the narrowing influences of particular, interested constituencies—failed to carry the convention. If the Senate retains features, such as the longer term and the gradual rotation, that were designed to foster those qualities and responsibility, it has others that complicate and collide with them. Election by state legislature and, presently, direct election by citizens have necessarily wedded the Senate to diverse and particular constituencies. Leaving aside the crucial question of whether those most favored by these modes of election tend to have the qualities that match the Senate's distinctive responsibility, these modes have certainly infected its deliberations with particular, local interests and the various and narrowing calculations of electioneering.

Yet, had the convention followed Madison's ideas, could the result have been as he had conceived it? Perhaps Madison was trying to fill too perfectly a gap between the liberal principle of separated and checked powers for the sake of individual liberty, and the more republican principle of legislative prudence for the sake of wise and systematic policy. He certainly tried to split the difference. Accepting that separation and checks were necessary conditions of liberty, Madison wanted to give prudence significant influence over compromise, law, and policy. He could rely on the work of liberal theory that had reduced the demands government would place on prudent deliberation, and he did not try to make deliberation sovereign in the government as a whole.

Was it possible, nevertheless, to establish a single institution with practical wisdom, foresight, and the common good as its sovereign principles? Assuming that a fitting design could be contrived, what would sustain that institution and its promised good effects? Madison, writing as Publius, acknowledges the difficulties of generating support for a deliberative Senate. Against the specific charge that the upper house will facilitate aristocratic usurpation of democratic control, he uses the House of Lords and other examples to argue that a popular House of Representatives will always be strong enough to defeat any such attempt. In fact, the upper house must be guarded against the popular chamber. His form of protection, however, is of doubtful practicality. "Against the force of the immediate representatives of the people, nothing will be able to maintain even the constitutional authority of the senate, but such a display of enlightened policy, and attachment to the public good, as will divide with that branch of the legislature, the affections and support of the people themselves."[1]

The ambitious and popular House will be particularly menacing to the independent deliberation of the Senate. More generally, the House and the presidency cannot be relied on to support the authority and character of a Senate responsible for refining their impulses with greater wisdom, steadiness, and system. These institutions were expected to be ambitiously grasping of power, jealous of their particular bailiwicks, and whether by design or not, more responsive to constituencies and susceptible to the lures of popularity.

In any case, to maintain that authority and influence, the republican Senate must rely, oddly enough, on popular support. In the absence of any inclination or habit of deference or respect, popular support must be based, as Publius clearly suggests, on appeals to utility or, more precisely, on the actual good effects of policies and the intentions inferred from those effects. Yet who is the audience for such appeals to general and long-term effects? How can that audience be reached? Montesquieu predicted, and our history has in various ways confirmed, that there is some tendency for society to divide into parties favoring either the legislative or the executive powers. It is hard to imagine, however, any significant portion of the population forming a party of steady support for the Senate and prudent deliberation. The framers' liberal constitutionalism was designed to protect a diversity of particular interests, and it takes for granted a general preference for one's own interests to the exclusion of broader considerations of justice and utility. In fact, Publius does not count on a particularly senatorial party. He seems, instead, to be suggesting that latent in each of us is a partisan for general and long-term goods, and this more deliberate sense can be brought into competition with our narrow partisanship. The good effects of the Senate's prudence could, in other words, divide the affections and loyalty of each citizen, the factious partisanship attaching itself to the House and the more enlarged interest to the Senate. A capacity to discern the more remote effects of policies and to reflect on their source would ground a citizen's indirect support for the Senate's deliberation and prevent the clash of diverse particular interests from making compromise completely sovereign.

Yet how exactly could the Senate, to gain popular support, establish a record of its distinctively good effects and judgment? How could it direct popular gratitude for often remote and long-term good effects exclusively to itself? The Senate is not like the judiciary and, particularly, the Supreme Court, which can act without the leave of other institutions and can patiently wait for cooler heads to discern the wisdom of its decisions. The Senate must build popular support from actions that necessarily involve the concurrence of at least one other branch. Although it could gain some credit, as the president can, from blocking an unjust or unwise policy, the Senate was designed to have a regular and positive influence on policy. Popular trust would need to be raised on that foundation. Its distinctive responsibility and contributions would tend, however, to be obscured within the negotiation and agreement of the three legislative institutions. Most of the good effects, moreover, would be palpable only over time. Is it reasonable to expect a citizenry to then notice the difference from what might have been and attribute responsibility for the better outcome to the Senate? More likely, credit for a result would be distributed among the institutions and even the citizenry itself. The Senate could readily fail to carve out a peculiar affection that would sustain its authority and deliberative character in confrontations with the House and presidency. Far more than Publius admits, even the theoretical and ideal Senate is left quite susceptible to the debilitating influences of democracy and popularity.

THE SENATE AND DEMOCRACY

For the real Senate, the forces of democracy and popular politics were not long in coming. Another irony of the Senate's invention is that its fundamental purpose as the anchor of the republic was compromised not only at its moment of creation by decisions made at the Constitutional Convention but also by its awkward place in history. What the founders perhaps could perceive only dimly was that their moment of republican creation was perilously close to the age of mass democracy—that is, broad popular participation and authority based on the idea that all political power flows directly from the people, not indirectly through some vague conception of popular sovereignty. Government, as Lincoln would put it, "of the people, by the people, for the people." Nearly from the start, the Senate of the founders' republican ideals was at odds with this ineluctable tide. Just as the Constitution began forming the new republic, free of the vestiges of mixed government, the forces of national democracy were already knocking at the door. The framers' attempt at national republicanism seems to have been a brief and largely theoretical epoch squeezed between monarchy and democracy. Moreover, as Jack Rakove points out, the process of ratification was a precursor of democracy at work on a national level and became a spur to forces of national democracy, and an indicator of how much and how quickly things were changing.[2] The Senate stood somewhat awkwardly at this historical threshold. It was certainly different from the House, which strolled into the democratic era as if it were made for it. The presidency likewise made the adjustment to popular politics, despite some difficulties, even though it was not made for democracy. On the other hand, the Supreme Court had little trouble playing its part as the explicitly undemocratic institution. Only the Senate was left betwixt and between.

Another irony of the Senate's invention is that, regardless of their intentions, Madison and others who sought a republican senate did not get what they came to the Convention to create, the advent of mass democracy notwithstanding. Instead, the Senate became a product of and permanently attached to the other set of forces the advocates of a strong and independent Senate sought to mitigate if not destroy: the influence of state loyalties and interests on national government. An institution meant to overcome or temper the effects of the pulling and hauling of self-interested politicians, the Senate itself was transformed by those very forces more than any other institution created in Philadelphia that summer. The Senate became the linchpin of the compromise over representation. State equality put the Senate at the center of one of the principal innovations of the convention: strong or centralized federalism.[3] In that process of compromise, the Senate, the most classical and in some ways backwards-looking institution, instead was inextricably linked to one of the most modern of the convention's creations.

THE IRONY OF THE SENATE'S EVOLUTION

From the perspective of the twenty-first century, we see considerable irony in the contrast between the Madisonian republican vision and the Senate's evolution. The Senate exhibits a remarkable degree of continuity but has also experienced some important changes, especially in particular compositional and institutional features, when compared with the House. Specifically, congressional history has seen a diminution in many of the compositional differences between the two chambers and an early creation of and entrenched stability in specific nonconstitutional institutional differences.

Three key provisions in the Constitution were to provide the basis for the Senate's compositional difference from the House: the mode of appointment, term length, and staggered terms. Each was a dike against irregular tides of public opinion. In general, however, these provisions failed to insulate the Senate, even before the change to popular election. As we have seen, with the rise of the first party system, the Senate was subject to the same partisan political forces as the House. Even though fewer seats were up for change, the Senate tended to mirror the House in partisan composition. Early on, the effect was magnified by rapid turnover—many senators did not finish their terms, so seats were open nearly as often as House seats in some cases. Partisan divisions and congressional careers moved, for the most part, in bicameral harmony.[4] Evidence suggests that nineteenth-century senators, though appointed by state legislatures, were increasingly subject to democratic pressures, especially as the doctrine of instruction by state legislatures died away and the public canvass, an early form of campaigning by senate candidates, took hold.[5] Finally, if the age and citizenship requirements ever mattered at all, it is especially difficult to see their influence in the modern era.

Not every aspect of this compositional convergence was evolutionary, however. The most dramatic and seemingly abrupt change, of course, was the Seventeenth Amendment, which produced the direct popular election of the Senate. The rapid ratification of the Seventeenth Amendment in eleven months from May 1912 to April 1913 belies the long struggle to get the amendment through Congress.[6] The Seventeenth Amendment remains the only fundamental change in the constitutional structure of the national governmental institutions and the only aspect of institutional design to become the object of a popular movement for governmental reform, with the exception of the less successful terms limits movement. This completed a process of democratization and eliminated one aspect of the Senate's links to states as corporate entities. The Seventeenth Amendment resolved one of the tensions created in the heat of the summer of 1787. Gone was the direct partiality of selection by state legislatures that Madison never liked, but in its place was popular election, something that many warned would make the Senate no different from the House. The consequences of a directly elected Senate were fairly subtle[7] not only because of the ways in which many senators were elected de facto, prior to the amendment, but also because national politics probably did little to make the distinction between selection by state legislatures and direct elections very interesting. In the early twentieth century prior to the New Deal, the federal government's activities and the nature of campaigns did not engender any revolution in the kind of representation citizens might expect.

The democratization of the Senate began the electoral convergence of the House and Senate. Yet the Senate was still different. In the slow-paced world of early twentieth-century politics, the six-year term and staggered elections could still make a difference in a senator's perspective and the relative composition of the two bodies. More importantly, there were still two senators per state, and in a period of growing disparities between large and small states, equal representation would continue to have significant consequences, including the overrepresentation of rural states. From the late 1950s through the early 1970s, with the interrelated forces that decreased the influence and importance of parties in elections while creating the personalized electoral politics of today, the convergence took on its contemporary characteristics.[8] The somewhat different political factors at work in modern House and Senate elections have made the bodies more alike in composition and even have inverted, to some extent, the intentions of the constitutional architects, with the House becoming more electorally secure and stable than the Senate.[9] This result has had, as well, an impact on the effect of election by districts versus states. Both large- and small-state senators are vulnerable and seem to act much like their House counterparts in the lavish attention and resources they devote to constituent service, seemingly regardless of the size of the state. The convergence of electoral forces does not prove, however, that senators and representatives act alike. It is suggestive rather than conclusive.

This political convergence contrasts with the separate paths taken by the House and Senate concerning rules of procedure.[10] Throughout the nineteenth century, the House and Senate developed along parallel lines in several important areas. With the House leading the way in most cases, the two chambers underwent the familiar process of institutionalization. Both incorporated the two-party system into their basic structures as committee systems and leadership systems formalized gradually.[11] However, House and Senate rules of procedure (and the norms they enforced) diverged from the beginning and became more different and entrenched as the decades unfolded. The rapidly increasing size of the House motivated those who sought to control the institution and put it to effective use to seek changes in the rules that would facilitate control by the majority party. The House adopted the use of the previous question—a parliamentary motion for ending debate to vote on the question—and had a one-hour general debate limit. In short, the majority would have its say and sooner rather than later. With some exceptions, the House continued on this course of enhanced majority control through the nineteenth century.

During this same early period, the smaller Senate took its rules of procedure in a different direction. The previous question existed in the original Senate rules, but in practice it was not used to limit debate and was dropped in an 1806 revision. Although a few attempts were made to subject the Senate to a greater degree of majority control, by the late nineteenth century, the idea of the Senate as an institution to protect the rights of the political minority (in this case mostly understood as the minority party) was deeply rooted in Senate culture.

As if to symbolize the contrast between the paths of convergence and divergence, not long after the ratification of the Seventeenth Amendment, the Senate adopted its first version of a rule for cloture—a parliamentary mechanism to limit debate on a particular question.[12] The cloture rule provided, for the first time in the Senate's history, a mechanism, albeit an elaborate one, for closing debate on a legislative question.[13] This, the single most important change in the Senate rules and the only successful attempt to limit debate, ironically had the effect of entrenching the power of Senate minorities and even individual senators. Like the unintended consequences of many reforms, what seemed at first like a limitation on debate evolved into the most effective way to obstruct the Senate's business. As legislative individualism rose in the 1960s and 1970s at the same time that the legislative agenda expanded dramatically, the ability to filibuster in the Senate became an increasingly powerful tool that produced spin-offs such as the "hold."[14] The combination of Senate rules that have long protected minority interests and relatively recent changes in norms about the exploitation of those rules has created an all too frequent requirement of a sixty-vote majority to pass a resolution of any importance. The undemocratic idiosyncrasies of the Senate are especially evident when the need for a supermajority is linked to the representational bias resulting from each state having two senators.

In the 1970s, with the full flowering of the modern individualized Congress, some scholars argued that the House and Senate had converged. The modern era of new political technologies, national media, and money had made representatives and senators into basically the same kind of political actor, subject to the same political forces. Just as senators seemed increasingly sensitive about elections and parochial about their states, more House members were becoming national figures. Both bodies were now populated by career politicians who were issue entrepreneurs. Ross Baker would later argue that the convergence idea was a bad description because of the fundamental differences that remained.[15] The culture and behavior of the Senate were fundamentally different because of the distinctions produced by the contrasting size and rules of each chamber. Our argument is that the convergence-divergence debate is a false distinction because electoral convergence and institutional divergence (or, more precisely, persistence of difference) are two sides of the same coin—the two have worked together to produce the modern Senate. The modern Senate is defined by the combination of election-sensitive issue entrepreneurs (not unlike in the House) with a set of institutional norms and rules that allow and even encourage the exploitation of individual and minority interests (quite unlike the House). In this way the final irony of the Senate's development is that it has become the ultimate perversion of the Madisonian intention: a Senate with greatly reduced electoral independence coupled with the enshrined ability to use the institution for purely individual (as opposed to collective) purposes—to be potentially exploited, moreover, by entrepreneurs elected for six years and often from relatively small states.

This view of the Senate's evolution suggests that the Senate still embodies some of the central tensions and contradictions of American democracy, a few of which were built into the Senate from the start, and that it continues to pose problems for the theory and practice of American democracy. Indeed, in this era of public disenchantment with politics and political institutions, the purpose and utility of the Senate have been the subject of some confusion and renewed debate.

At other times in its history, the Senate has been either applauded as the bastion of good sense and deliberation or condemned as the black hole of progress and responsive government, and popular election did not end disputes over the Senate's power and prerogatives. Politics and principle have mixed rather freely in such disputes—like those over the president and the Court. Partisanship and ideology frequently cloud our judgment of constitutional issues, including our feelings toward our political institutions. For example, arguments about the proper power and prerogatives of the executive have been tinged by partisanship as early as Washington's presidency. Partisan positions on the virtues of postwar presidential power have flip-flopped back and forth between the two parties with some regularity. Democrats and liberals who lauded presidential action in the 1960s abhorred Reagan's version in the 1980s. Republicans who defended Reagan's use of power in the 1980s decried Clinton's less far-reaching efforts in the 1990s. The Supreme Court is likewise often the victim of partisan attacks on its power. It is as natural to be all for presidential energy and prerogative when one's own man is in the White House as it is to be all for judicial activism when the activism is going in the right direction. The Senate has been the subject of similar controversies.

For example, with the clouds of divided government dissipated following the election of Bill Clinton in 1992, the consequences of bicameralism and the singular characteristics of the Senate were having their day in the sun. Though hardly the only cause of Clinton's troubles, the Senate became the roadblock for several important administration initiatives and Democratic proposals. As a result, the 103rd Congress featured the highest level in decades of animosity directed toward the Senate by members of the House and political commentators, who came, once again, to see the Senate as more of an obstruction to, than an essential component of, good government.[16] The legislative consequences of the Senate and bicameralism became, if anything, more apparent with the historic Republican takeover of Congress after the 1994 elections. This time, however, many of the liberals who decried Senate obstruction in the 103rd were breathing a sigh of relief as the Senate, in most cases, took a more leisurely approach to the Republican agenda, particularly the Contract With America (and many conservatives experienced the converse of these sentiments). One day the Senate is commended (and the founders' foresight extolled) for stopping a putatively dangerous piece of legislation passed by the House; the next the Senate is excoriated for allowing a single senator to filibuster an important bill or presidential appointment on behalf of a personal cause. What began as journalistic and tentative academic commentary on the apparently increasing impact of Senate rules on congressional action evolved into a more general explanation for the nature of contemporary policy making. The Senate had become a "supermajority institution," a choke point in the legislative process, comparable to the presidential veto.[17] The unfairness of a de facto three-fifths majority requirement has been linked as well to the over-representation of small states.[18]

As the twenty-first century gets under way, the Senate remains controversial, albeit in a sporadic fashion that does not augur any danger of being targeted by a popular movement. If not terribly controversial when measured against other problems of government, the Senate certainly fits awkwardly in the scheme of contemporary democracy. Madison would hardly be alone in his dismay at a Senate characterized by supermajority procedures and the glaring inequalities produced by equal representation. We have seen that Madison fought desperately to prevent equal representation in the Senate, but he and other founders also did not favor supermajority requirements for ordinary legislative business. He certainly would not agree with the senators and scholars who defend the filibuster as an important means of defending minority rights and interests.[19] These arguments are regularly presented as an extension of the original argument for the Senate's equal representation of states as a defense for the smaller states against national majorities.[20] In still another irony, one of the central features of a prudent Senate, small size, which was intended to promote collective deliberation, instead helped to foster and protect rules that benefit, primarily, the political interests of individual senators.

The framers' solution to the problem of minority rights and interests was surely not to distribute a veto authority to individual legislators. The various provisions for improving the justice and wisdom of the government's decisions were designed to foster a *generalizing* disposition that would elevate deliberation from particular to common goods. The Senate's influence on deliberation and policy, its action and inaction, were to reflect practical knowledge directed by a national sense and personal responsibility for the reputation of the body as a whole. These characteristics would help protect minority interests by promoting policies that served "the permanent and aggregate interests" of the nation rather than the passions and interests of any particular part.

In fact, the passions and interests of those particular parts—the states—have been well represented in the Senate. As we have seen, the most important crisis of adaptation the Senate faced was the contradiction between the original form of Senate selection and the advance of democracy. The Seventeenth Amendment completed the most significant change in the Senate's history, and the democratization of the Senate was perhaps an inevitable adjustment. Popular election, however, was also a partial deviation from the original purpose—the corporate representation of states. The previously tight relationship between a senator and his state government was now attenuated. The state did not choose its senators; senators were elected by people within a particular state. Yet the resolution of one democratic contradiction paved the way for another that would begin to emerge as the century progressed.

The advent of direct Senate elections, along with other aspects of democratization—including women's suffrage a few years later—and nationalization of policy in many areas, undermined, at least in theory, some of the justification for equal representation of states in the Senate. One consequence of settlement of the West and industrialization was a growth in the population gap between large and small states. As Frances Lee and Bruce Oppenheimer have shown, the minimum percentage of the nation's population able to elect a Senate majority declined steadily from an already low 26 percent in the 1860s to 17 percent in the 1970s (the high point was 33 percent in the 1810s), and more sophisticated measures show that the disparity in representation continues to grow.[21] By the 1970s, though, a revolution in American voting rights had taken place. One of the most important constitutional principles of this century is that of political equality, especially in regard to the power of a person's vote. A series of Supreme Court decisions under Chief Justice Earl Warren created the principle of "one person, one vote" that produced redrawn electoral maps around the country. The most sweeping changes came at the state level, with the biggest impact on state senates, many of which were composed of districts of significantly unequal populations. Such disparities were declared unconstitutional, and nearly all states had to change the apportionment schemes for one or both of their legislative chambers.[22] In other words, the U.S. Senate was unconstitutional except for the fact that it was in the Constitution.

By this time, and the apportionment decisions were part of this process, federalism was nearly dead as anything but an uncontroversial division of labor between an increasingly sovereign national government and increasingly subordinate state governments. At the same time that the Court was radically changing state legislatures, congressional action on civil rights, including strong voting rights legislation, would be among the last blows to substantive federalism. Thus, two important changes converged in time. The original justification for the Senate as a defense of federalism was badly eroded, and the principle of one person, one vote implicitly called into question its mode of representation. What justifies, in the first decade of the twenty-first century, the ability of 16.3 percent of Americans (in the twenty-five least populous states) to elect half of the Senate, leaving the other fifty senators to be elected by 83.7 percent of the nation's population in the most populous states? Why should a single Wyoming citizen's vote in a senate election have the same power as nearly seventy in California, for example? (The Alabama state senate districts at issue in one of the landmark Supreme Court decisions from the 1960s varied by *only* forty-one to one.) Several senators represent fewer citizens than reside in the average House district. Even in the late nineteenth and early twentieth centuries, a few social scientists had questioned the justice of this disproportion in its earlier versions, and such critiques continue to be produced as the Senate is well into its third century.[23] That this disparity, however measured, goes unquestioned beyond a few op-eds, articles, and books speaks to the reverence for (or path dependent immutability of) American institutions that makes this contradiction nearly invisible to most Americans.

The relationship between minority empowerment and Senate apportionment is evident in the powers shared by the presidency and the Senate. This area of power also indicates the lack of any inherently superior deliberative qualities in the modern Senate. Only from a deeply historical perspective does this division of labor between president and Senate make any sense. The original justifications for placing the boundary powers in the Senate were lost partly before the Constitution was even completed and partly during Washington's presidency, and the rationale has eroded ever since. No one aside from sitting senators argues that equal representation and Senate rules improve deliberation on appointments and treaties; the best that can be argued is that they might not do any real harm. Such factors as secrecy, relative experience, and knowledge of character no longer have any significant bicameral distinction. One is left searching for positive reasons for the Senate's exclusive power to give advice and consent on judicial appointments and treaties. It could be argued that this division of labor avoids the inefficiency of involving both houses. Yet why not give these powers to the more representative and efficient house? Indeed, the supermajority requirement of two-thirds for treaty approvals only magnifies the overrepresentation of small states. Judicial appointments remain the bastion of senatorial courtesy, which has allowed senators of the president's party to have individual veto power over judicial nominees to their state. Individual holds on nominations are not uncommon and have led to protracted vacancies in many diplomatic and judicial posts.

Our point is not to call into question the legitimacy of the Senate. This book is about the invention of the Senate, not its contemporary status. Drawing attention to the ironies of the Senate's invention and evolution, we seek to show how some of the consequences of the creation of the Senate remain central to fundamental questions of modern democracy. The contrasts between the foundations and the contemporary reality of this crucial institution might be mostly of historical interest—simply an interpretation of the disjunctures between an institution's conception, creation, and evolution. These contrasts, however, can also shed light on some current criticisms of the national government and bring us closer to an accurate diagnosis of our political ills. Numerous scholars and political observers have argued, for example, that the constitutional separation of powers does not produce the sort of legislative deliberation needed in a national government; members of Congress tend to respond to the more immediate and particular desires of their constituencies, and congressional majorities, fashioned out of compromises and logrolling, cannot effectively address the nation's common and long-term interests.[24] These defects are similar to those anticipated by Madison and for which he designed a senate as the remedy. Indeed, the contemporary critics agree in part; the remedy must be an institutionalized force that is free from the influence of particular interests or constituencies and able to redirect responsibility and deliberation toward the general interests and needs of the nation. The contemporary Senate, however, is often viewed as part of the malady and not as a cure, and the critics turn instead to an enhanced presidential government and to the development of disciplined, programmatic, and responsible political parties. Each of these proposals suffers from inherent defects as well as a low probability of ever producing the desired results with any consistency.

Of course, it could be equally vain to recommend that we undo the Constitutional Convention's compromises and institute Madison's small and independent national senate. The Constitution makes this all but impossible, and democratic sensibilities will rebel at the mere suggestion. With such political realities in mind, one might be tempted to conclude that the Senate still serves the country well. Bicameralism is easily justified, and the Senate might constitute a serviceable second chamber, even if we would never construct such an institution in quite the same way. And yet, while it may occasionally appear to fulfill some of the same functions of Madison's Senate, the modern U.S. Senate does so largely by different means and for different ends. A Senate that bears little resemblance either to the one Madison sought or to one we might now devise may be worthy of reconsideration as we contemplate the government that will take us through the twenty-first century. But that is the dilemma. Although today we would never design the Senate as it was given to us in 1787, in Madison's view we never designed the Senate as it should have been, and that was perhaps our only opportunity to do so. Such a Senate may be, in the republican ideal, something we need but never have had, and, indeed, can never attain.

Notes

ONE. THE REPUBLICAN INSTITUTION

1. Madison 1969–1985, 10:209.

2. Hamilton, Madison, and Jay 1961, 51: 349. Subsequent references will be to *Federalist*.

3. For discussions of unicameralism, relative power within bicameral legislatures, and modern senates in the world, see Lijphart 1999; Tsebelis and Money 1997; Patterson and Mughan 1999; Longley and Olson 1991.

4. Bryce 1995, 1:103.

5. Matthews 1960, 5.

6. Swift 1996, 1.

7. Barbara Sinclair, "Coequal Partner: The U.S. Senate," in Patterson and Mughan 1999, 33.

8. Kerr 1895; Rogers 1926; Haynes 1938; Swanstrom 1985; Baker 1988; Baker 1995; Tsebelis and Money 1997.

9. For supporting discussions, see Lee and Oppenheimer 1999; Tsebelis and Money 1997. For an example of an emphasis on functional justifications, see Longley and Oleszek 1989, 14–17. See Pierson 2000 for a general critique of functionalism as an explanation for institutional origins.

10. Among others, see Rossiter 1966; Bailyn 1967; Wood 1972; McDonald 1985. The Senate holds an understandably large place in Paul Eidelberg's 1968 account of the "mixed" character of the Constitution, but he focuses on only two elements of the Senate in his contrast with the House: the method of apportionment and the length of term.

11. Main 1967; Adams 1980.

12. Swift 1996. Moreover, as we shall see, her "House of Lords" analogy is flawed both as an account of the theoretical influences on the framers and as an explanation of the design of their Senate. A very good account of the Constitutional Convention's adoption of equal representation of states in the Senate is offered by Lee and Oppenheimer 1999, 16–43, but in keeping with the goal of their project, they make no attempt to cover other aspects of the Senate's invention.

13. An excellent review of general approaches to the convention's politics is available in Jillson 1988, 1–17.

14. Wolfe 1977; Nelson 1987; Rakove 1987b; Jillson 1988; Onuf 1989; Rakove 1996.

15. By institutional theory, we refer to what is commonly called the "new

institutionalism." See Peters 1999 and Steinmo, Thelen, and Longstreth 1992 for discussions.

16. Peters 1999, 150; Steinmo, Thelen, and Longstreth 1992, 14–15.

TWO. SOURCES AND MODELS

1. Kramnick 1982 and Shalhope 1972 are two comprehensive reviews of the literature. For excellent critiques, see Rahe 1992 and Pangle 1988.

2. Swift 1996; Wood 1972; Eidelberg 1968.

3. *Federalist* 63: 426. Publius lists Sparta, Carthage, and Rome as the only examples of long-lived republics, which quality he attributes here to each having a senate. Venice, presented as a pure, hereditary, and despotic aristocracy, is dismissed as any sort of model (250–51, 335). See Rahe 1992, 254–55, 742–45.

4. Cicero 1928, *De legibus,* 3.1–3, 11, 18; Aristotle 1984, 1140b8–25, 1141a20, 1141b13–14, 1141b25, 1142b27–35.

5. Cicero 1928, *De legibus,* 1.12–13, 15–16. Virtue generally, or "reason completely developed," is the fulfillment of human nature and, therefore, the proper aim of political life. See Nicgorski 1991, 241–43.

6. Cicero 1928, *De legibus,* 1.6, 12, 14–15, 23; 2.5–6; 3.12; *De republica,* 1.6, 3. See Wood 1988, 160, 169, 171.

7. Cicero 1928, *De officiis,* 1.25. See also *De republica,* 2.22–34.

8. Cicero 1928, *De legibus,* 1.17, 3.1–3, 5, 7, 10, 12–14, 17, 24–25, 28, 38.

9. Mansfield 1989, 76; Walbank 1972, 149–50.

10. Polybius 1923, 6.4, .7, .9–10. See Mansfield 1989, 78, and von Fritz 1954, 84–89. The good forms are similar insofar as they are moderate, but they promote the common good in different ways: through reason (kingship), justice and prudence (aristocracy), and reverent and dutiful attention to gods, customs, and laws (democracy).

11. Polybius 1923, 6.11, .15.

12. Polybius 1923, 6.18, .51, .57. In times of prosperity and security, the vain and ambitious, including the nobility, will seek above all the notoriety of public office and wealth.

13. Polybius 1923, 6.44.

14. Polybius 1923, 6.9, .44–45, .51, .57–58. Cf. Wood 1988, 154; Walbank 1972, 134, 143–44; and von Fritz 1954, 86, 339. The predominance of a senatorial institution distinguishes Sparta from the inferior constitutions: Athens, Thebes, and Crete. Indeed, the Athenian constitution was a "ship without a commander." See also 6.4, .6, .9, .51.

15. Polybius 1923, 6.10, .14. Specifically, the consuls in most cases directed the administration of government and had command over the armed forces in wartime. The people controlled the distribution of honors and punishments, "the

only bonds by which . . . human society in general [is] held together." The people also had final say over the enactment of laws, the ratification of treaties, and, "what is most important of all," the decision to go to war. Von Fritz 1954, 159–60, 182, 183, 196, sees Polybius's indirectness as more odd than purposeful.

16. Polybius 1923, 6.15, and von Fritz 1954, 158. Cf. Walbank 1972, 149, 153. Polybius earlier called this consular war power "*almost* uncontrolled" (6.12, emphasis added).

17. Polybius 1923, 6.14, .16, .17, and von Fritz 1954, 172–73.

18. Polybius 1923, 6.58. See also 6.51 on the senate's "wisdom." At the beginning of book 6, Polybius mentions one of these qualities, high-mindedness (*megalopsychia*), as the distinguishing quality of the perfect human being, and he draws an analogy between the measure of a perfect human being and the measure of a good constitution (6.2).

19. Polybius 1923, 6.56; Cicero 1928, *De legibus*, 2.7, 10; Wood 1988, 171–73.

20. Locke 1980, sec. 3. See Grant 1987, 52–98. All references to the *Second Treatise* use section divisions found in most editions.

21. Locke 1980, sec. 123. See Mansfield 1989, 184–85, and Manent 1995, 46.

22. Locke 1980, secs. 4, 124. See also Locke 1983, 26, 35, 44, 47, 49, and Pangle 1988, 253–54.

23. Locke 1980, sec. 129. Locke locates the old virtues, at least the political ones, in a past "golden age" that has been overcome by ordinary human vice (secs. 111, 162–64). The new virtues of the "rational and industrious" (sec. 34) are, essentially, private virtues. See Pangle 1988, 141–71.

24. Pangle and Ahrensdorf 1999, 144–61.

25. Locke 1980, secs. 95, 134, and Manent 1995, 39–52.

26. Locke 1980, secs. 6–13, 21, 87–88, 132–33, 136–38, 143–44, 149, 207.

27. Grant 1987, 75.

28. Locke mentions oligarchy and a mixed form, but the purpose of a mixed form is not explained and oligarchy is presented as merely rule by some few (1980, secs. 132–33).

29. Locke 1980, sec. 151. A senate is introduced only as one possible form of legislature (secs. 94, 139), and a house of hereditary nobility sharing the legislative power arises in an example of a constitution (sec. 213).

30. Locke 1980, secs. 145–47, 153. The federative power is not an executive power as such, but Locke argues that it is usually, and generally should be, given to the executive. See Vile 1998, 66–67. For a full account of Locke's complicated understanding of executive power, see Mansfield 1989, 181–211.

31. Locke 1980, sec. 156, 158, 160. Locke's separation of powers does not, then, divide simply between legislating and executing only in their narrow meanings. It also distinguishes between security through law and security through effective responses to emergencies, regardless of the law (Mansfield 1989, 204–5).

32. Locke 1980, secs. 159, 161–62, 164, 210. See secs. 154–55 for a similar relationship between the executive's discretion and "prudence," on the one hand, and the threat of a popular check on the other.

33. More generally, the principle of consent establishes the ultimate sovereignty of the people, and this sovereignty acts as a continuous check on government through the threat of legitimate revolution. See Locke 1980, secs. 164, 168, 209, 225–26, 230, 242, and Pangle 1988, 257.

34. On Montesquieu's influence, see Vile 1998, 133–35, 142–44.

35. This argument generally follows Pangle 1973.

36. Those arguments are discussed in chapter 3.

37. Montesquieu 1989, 2.2, 8.5. References to the *Spirit of the Laws* follow the standard division into books and chapters.

38. Montesquieu 1989, 3.3, 3.4, 4.5, 5.2–3, 8.

39. Montesquieu 1989, 2.2–3, 8.2.

40. This mix does not require a combination of the two "principles" or "springs" of democracy and aristocracy. Montesquieu, apparently, doubts that the principles of the three constitutions can be mixed. See Montesquieu 1989, 8.21, and Vile 1998, 91.

41. Montesquieu 1989, 3.4, 4.8, 5.8. Montesquieu claims to be following the "judicious Polybius," but he also seems to be changing the emphasis.

42. Montesquieu 1989, 5.8.

43. Montesquieu 1989, 11.13, 17.

44. Montesquieu 1989, 11.1–3.

45. Montesquieu 1989, 4.7, 6.1–2, 8.16, 20, 20.1.

46. Montesquieu 1989, 11.6. See Vile 1998, 101. See also Montesquieu's provisions for controlling standing armies as a potentially dangerous arm of the executive (11.6, pp. 164–65). Montesquieu argues for a hereditary executive to preclude competition between democrats and nobles for control of the executive power, which risks a ruinous unification of the legislative and executive powers.

47. Montesquieu 1989, 11.4–6, and Pangle 1973, 5, 89–92, 114–15, 123–26, 203–4. On the importance of a separated judicial power, see Vile 1998, 96–99, and Pangle 1973, 132–33.

48. Montesquieu 1989, bks. 20–23.

49. Montesquieu 1989, 11.6, p. 159.

50. Montesquieu 1989, 11.6, p. 160; 19.27, p. 326.

51. Montesquieu 1989, 11.6, p. 160; 11.16, and Pangle 1973, 124–25.

52. Montesquieu 1989, 11.6, p. 161, 163; 11.8.

53. Manent 1995, 57–58.

54. Montesquieu 1989, 11.6, p. 160–61. There is also a threat to the balance between the legislative and executive powers from the tendency of individuals "to have more affection for one of these powers than for the other" (19.27, p. 325–26).

55. Montesquieu 1989, 11.6, p. 164. The differences between this and Polybius's

summary of the Roman constitution are telling. In times of peace, Montesquieu's republic will be stable, and emergencies will not require a virtuous senate.

56. Manent 1995, 62.

57. *Federalist,* 47: 324; 51: 349.

58. Other thinkers influenced the framers' political and constitutional principles, but they did not offer clear institutional models. *Cato's Letters,* for instance; see Rossiter 1953, 141; Rahe 1992, 552–53; Zuckert 1994, 20, 22, 160, 175. Although these letters express concerns about the prudence of democratic government (lets. 22, 24, 38, 115, 134) and argue that only a "very small part of mankind have capacities large enough to judge the whole of things" and pursue "prudent measures" (lets. 89, 97), they do not offer any specific institutional means or form (let. 105). Similarly, Algernon Sidney's *Discourses Concerning Government* was "hardly ever appealed to as an authority on [government's] proper structure" (Sidney 1990, xxvii).

59. Shklar 1959, 686–88.

60. Harrington 1992, 11–16, 33–34. See Pocock 1975, 387–88, and Blitzer 1960, 114–15.

61. Harrington 1992, 20, 137–38. See Fink 1945, 63–64, 71–73.

62. Harrington 1992, 11, 18. See Blitzer 1960, 137–38, and Fink 1945, 58–59.

63. Harrington 1992, 23–25. See Pocock 1975, 404–14; MacPherson 1962, 172–73; Blitzer 1960, 151–52.

64. *Federalist,* 10: 57. See Fink 1945, 59–60.

65. Beer 1993, 108, 113–14, 233, and Fink 1945, 55–57. The mix is "a matter of talent and functional utility, not of balancing powers" (Shklar 1959, 688).

66. Pocock 1975, 389–90, 393–95.

67. Beer 1993, 99–100. Cf. Blitzer 1960, 144–45.

68. Harrington 1992, 18, 20–22. See Pocock 1975, 393–95; Blitzer 1960, 148–49; and Fink 1945, 61.

69. Harrington 1992, 22–23.

70. Harrington 1992, 23. This is unlike, in some ways, the appeals to "necessity" that seem to sustain the constitutions of Machiavelli, Hobbes, Locke, and Montesquieu. See Mansfield 1989, 184–85.

71. Beer 1993, 115–16; Pocock 1975, 394–95; Blitzer 1960, 151–52.

72. Harrington 1992, 23, 137–38, 142.

73. Harrington 1992, 95–97, 118. For a more detailed summary, see Blitzer 1960, 220–23.

74. Harrington 1992, 37–38, 145–47. Harrington allows that different circumstances might argue for different term lengths.

75. Harrington 1992, 23–24, 146–47.

76. Harrington 1992, 24, 143, 149–50, 166. For the point about debate, faction, and representation, see Blitzer 1960, 243–44. Harrington expects a natural shame to support an oath not to debate (149–50) but also doubts the adequacy of this

provision (167). One administrative council has the authority to try anyone accused of introducing debate into the lower assembly. See Fink 1945, 76.

77. *Federalist*, 62: 419.

78. Harrington 1992, 123–24, 130.

79. For Hume's influence on Madison and Hamilton in particular, see Adair 1974, Werner 1972, and Stourzh 1970. For Harrington's influence on Hume, see Smith 1971, 146–48.

80. Hume 1985, 514, 516, 528–29.

81. Hume 1985, 515–17, 522–23.

82. Hume 1985, 516, 522, 524. Hume argues that large republics in particular allow for this sort of progressive refinement in elections.

83. Hume 1985, 515, 524. Most administrative offices are filled at the local level.

84. Hume 1985, 216–17, 224. The senators elect from among themselves the principal executive officers. The senate also has significant judicial authority not only from the power of appointment but especially from its authority to hear appeals in criminal cases.

85. Swift 1993 is a good example of the former, and Wood 1972 is the leading example of the latter. Both of these arguments will be addressed in the following chapters.

THREE. AMERICAN SENATES IN THEORY AND PRACTICE, 1776–1787

1. Main 1967, 188–215.

2. Wood 1972. His arguments are addressed in detail below.

3. Paine 1945, 1:4–5, 22–23, 29, 37.

4. Paine 1945, 1:4, 6–9. On contemporaneous views similar to Paine's, see Main 1967, 202–3; Wood 1972, 222–26; and Adams 1980, 259–64.

5. Thorpe 1909, 5:3083–88, 3091–92. For Paine's influence on the Pennsylvania constitution, see Vile 1998, 138–39, 150, and Wood 1972, 230.

6. Thorpe 1909, 2:778, 780–81, and Vile 1998, 147–48. Five postrevolutionary state constitutions (GA, MD, MA, NH, NC) stated their adherence to the principle of separated powers (Thorpe 1909, 2:778; 3:1687, 1893; 4:2457; 5:2787; 6:3813).

7. Vile 1998, 131–32, 149–50, 155. See also Spurlin 1940, 152 n. 21.

8. Main 1967, 94–96, and Vile 1998, 139–48, 154–55.

9. Vile 1998, 149–50; Wood 1972, 230–31. Wood provides solid evidence that the framers of the Pennsylvania constitution explicitly rejected a mixed form (230–31), but in his view, the only available alternative is a democracy centered in a unicameral legislature (197, 200, 204, 206–9, 225, 237). Any provision for stability and greater practical knowledge is associated with mixed government as a

fundamentally different paradigm and form (209–10, 214, 216, 234–35, 238–39). In Wood's view then, a senate is a reliable indicator of a mixed constitution (246).

10. Its executive, for example, could recommend measures but was given no powers to review, let alone to veto, legislation (Thorpe 1909, 2:778, 781, 784). Governors in most state constitutions were denied a veto, which was a legislative power. In the Georgia constitution, the governor was even forbidden to preside over the executive council when it was reviewing legislation. This council, when reviewing, was acting something like a second legislative house, but its review could result in advice only.

11. Thorpe 1909, 5:3091–92.

12. Thorpe 1909, 5:3084.

13. Most notably Wood 1972 and Swift 1996.

14. Jefferson 1984, 244–45, 290–91; Harrold 1970.

15. Main 1967, 197–202, 205, 235–36.

16. Main 1967, 208, and McDonald 1985, 87. New York was notable for the governor's comparatively robust veto power.

17. The upper house in New Hampshire's interim 1776 constitution was selected by the lower house. South Carolina adopted the same form but moved to popular election for both houses in 1778. See Thorpe 1909, 4.2452, 2458–61; 6:3243, 3250–51.

18. Main 1967, 114.

19. Thorpe 1909, 3:1692–94, and Main 1967, 102, 236. Maryland's upper house, as well as South Carolina's, New Jersey's, and Virginia's, could not initiate or amend money bills.

20. Main 1967, 197, and chaps. 4–6. See also Vile 1998, 149.

21. Vile 1998, 158–61, and McDonald 1985, 155–57, 173–79.

22. Quoted in Vile 1998, 161. See also Jefferson 1984, 243. On Harrington's and Montesquieu's prominence as authorities during the founding era, see Smith 1971 and Spurlin 1940.

23. See Main 1967, 205–7; Wood 1972, 203; Adams 1979b, 4:65, 69–72; and Vile 1998, 164. Wood's opinion that the *Thoughts* was "the most influential work guiding the framers of the new republics" (568) is especially important. This work is, he argues, an example of mixed constitutionalism (208–9). In fact, the *Thoughts* is a deliberately contrived alternative to both mixed constitutionalism and civic republicanism.

24. See chapter 2. Both sides of many disputes over the right form for a republican government claimed Montesquieu as their authority. See Pangle 1988, 89–90.

25. Adams 1983, 402–3

26. Adams 1983, 402–3.

27. Adams 1983, 408–9. On Adams's early skepticism concerning virtue as a

practicable foundation for government, see Lerner 1987, 27. In particular, a 1776 letter to Mercy Warren (see Adams 1979b, 4:123–25) describes in terms quite close to Montesquieu's the rigorous virtue of ancient republics. Yet it also argues that the "[w]ant . . . of virtue" makes this form impracticable. Cf. McDonald 1985, 71–72, and McCoy 1980, 69–72, who seems to overlook the distinction between public and private virtues in the *Thoughts*.

28. Adams 1983, 403–4. Cf. Wood 1972, 208–9, and Bailyn 1967, 290–91. On Harrington's influence on Adams and the *Thoughts*, see Smith 1971, 187–88, 194.

29. Adams 1983, 403–4. Adams allows for, and even assumes, some limiting qualifications for voters and candidates, but he does not specify any.

30. Adams 1983, 405–6.

31. Adams 1983, 405–6. See Bailyn 1967, 296–97, 299–300.

32. Adams 1983, 405–6.

33. Braxton 1983, 330–33.

34. Braxton 1983, 333–35. Braxton begins by using one of Adams's authorities, Montesquieu, against him: highly democratic republics like Adams's must be founded upon a rigorous civic virtue, for which Adams fails to make provisions. His accusation that Adams confounds public and private virtue seems to overlook the development of Adams's argument and his eventual reliance upon institutional structures to support a liberal republic. Cf. Pangle 1988, 288 n. 13.

35. Braxton 1983, 335–36, 337.

36. Braxton 1983, 337.

37. Braxton 1983, 337 (emphasis added).

38. Jefferson 1984, 244–45. The 1776 Virginia constitution was apparently influenced by Adams's *Thoughts* (see Adams 1979b, 4:70).

39. Jefferson 1984, 755–56, 339. In a letter to Madison concerning the constitutional plan emerging from the Philadelphia convention, he notes that direct popular elections will not tend to produce a body competent in national and foreign affairs (912–14). See Harrold 1970, 284–85, 289–90.

40. Jefferson 1984, 756. See Adams 1980, 265–66. Property qualifications for office should be distinguished from property qualifications for electors, which were intended to exclude from political life those entirely dependent upon another for their sustenance and, therefore, devoid of the wherewithal for the independent exercise of judgment. See also McDonald 1985, 26–27, 74–75, 153. Adams's 1779 draft of a constitution for Massachusetts included property qualifications; see Adams 1979b, 4:66.

41. See Wood 1972, 220–21.

42. For example, Swift 1996.

43. Seven states included strong assertions of property rights in their constitutions (McDonald 1985, 152).

44. Main 1967, 214–15; Wood 1972, 209–10, 214, 216, 234–35.

45. Parsons 1983, 481–83, 487–89, 492. The aim of a "FREE republican consti-

tution" should be the "security of [the individual's] person and property"; it should rule by law only and be organized by the principle of separation of powers. On the liberalism of the *Essex Result*, see Schmitt and Webking 1979, 205–7. The *Result* borrows from Adams's *Thoughts*, and Adams declared that it was "in general agreeable to the Principles" of the *Thoughts*; see Adams 1979b, 4:71.

46. Parsons 1983, 484–86.

47. Parsons 1983, 489–90, 492–96, 504–5, 507–8, 517–18. The commitment of the *Result* to the principle of separation of powers is evident, for example, in its repeated stress on the independence of the executive, armed with a veto, and the complete independence, in elections, of one branch from the others.

48. Parsons 1983, 496–98, 510.

49. Parsons 1983, 500.

50. Parsons 1983, 490–91, 511–12, 518–19. Nonetheless, all officers are to be paid so that no one "must injure his estate by serving the public." On property and leisure as qualifications for office, see Wood 1992, 77–92, and Adams 1980, 161–62, 225–26.

51. Qualifying service is confined to serving the previous year in the senate, the house, or the governor's privy council. The privy council, a refining check on the governor, would be elected from the senate by the lower house (518).

52. Parsons 1983, 502–4, 512, 518.

53. See the discussion of Locke in chapter 2.

54. Parsons 1983, 492–93, 510, 512. The *Result* expresses Montesquieu's concern that "all orders of men" be attached to the benefits of this government (514).

55. Parsons 1983, 511–12, 515–16.

56. Parsons 1983, 512–13, 515, 518.

57. Any attempt to summarize even the first volume of this work is fraught with perils; it is long and assiduously repetitive. On the style and the arguments, see Adams 1979a, 3:503; Ellis 1993, 147–48; and Kurtz 1968, 611–12. As in the *Thoughts*, Adams opposes unicameralism, but the degree to which the *Defense* agrees with or contradicts the earlier work has been argued every which way. Lerner 1987, 29, is persuasive about Adams's consistent skepticism about motives and virtues. Also convincing, though, is Appleby's argument (1992, 196) that Adams "drastically changed his concept of balanced government" from one founded on institutions or powers to one founded on social and economic class. See also Wood 1972, 578. Throughout the *Defense*, Adams argues against a rather general unicameralism (1:3–7). Consequently, he is not compelled to develop, in any one place, a detailed and methodical account of the moral and practical principles that constitute his alternative, and he uses widely divergent counter examples.

58. Adams 1979a, 1:183; 3:164, 216–17, 292, 349–50, 366–67, 404.

59. Adams 1979a, 1:1–2, 256–59, 322, 342; 2:387–88; 3:224–25, 293–94.

60. Adams 1979a, 1:342; 3:159–60.

61. Adams 1979a, 1:87, 102–3, 121–24, 128, 325, 362. To protect the executive from being "invaded" by the "necessarily sovereign and supreme" legislature, it must be given a veto to "defend itself."

62. Adams 1979a, 1:127–28, 372–82.

63. Adams 1979a, 1:xiii–xiv, 93, 109, 113–14, 362; 3:254–57, 262, 385–86, 414–15, 436, 440–41. Adams acknowledges that American circumstances and principles (e.g., the lack of "artificial inequalities," liberal principles of equality, separation of church and state) tend to mitigate class distinctions and enmity. He even asserts that "there are different orders of *offices,* but none of *men;* out of office all men are the same species, and of one blood; there is no greater nor lesser nobility."

64. Adams 1979a, 1:99, 109–16; 3:207, 360, 362, 457. Cf. 3:457–59.

65. Adams 1979a, 1:v, 103, 116, 129–32, 369; 3:216, 218, 232, 238–39, 349. Adams acknowledges a natural "moral sense" (3:363) but argues that it is not a reliable basis for a political order. Neither was the "habituation" to virtue in ancient republics (1:322).

66. Adams 1979a, 1.x–xi, 35, 44, 53–55, 68, 71, 94, 116–21, 362.

67. Most of Adams's arguments for a strict and effectual separation of the executive power are to the end of a properly balanced constitution, and only mixed governments can secure a separation (Adams 1979a, 3:421, 425). See his discussion of the lack of balance in the Roman constitution, which led to "altercations and wars" requiring heroic virtues in its senators (1:169–87, 218–23, 336–38, 344, 348, 356–58, 361). Adams criticizes Hume's "Perfect Commonwealth" for lacking adequate separation and, consequently, laying the groundwork for oligarchic government (1:60, 370–371).

68. Adams 1979a, 1:iii–x, 70, 94–95, 259–60, 362; 3:273, 296, 365, 371–73, 376–77.

69. Adams 1979a, 1:70, 96, 134–38, 158–61, 168–69, 182–83, 260; 3:275–76, 296, 307, 377, 435.

70. Adams 1979a, 1:iii–x, 31, 70; 3:328.

71. Adams 1979a, 3:305, 446. These virtues are assumed in the face of his skeptical assessment of ancient republican virtues, virtues that in any case are rare (2:386–88, 484–96; 3:224–25).

72. Matthews 1995, 171–72, 198–99; Banning 1995, 135–37; McDonald 1985, 134–35; McCoy 1980, 129–32; and Martineau 1838, 193–94.

73. Madison 1969–1985, 8:350–52.

74. Madison 1969–1985, 8:353–54. Cf. Wood 1972, 221–22. He does refer to the Maryland model, which placed property restrictions on senators. On Madison's abandoning the dualistic understanding of social and political classes or parties, and on his use of Scottish thought in developing these ideas, see Branson 1979, 243–49.

75. Madison 1969–1985, 6:144–47, 270–74, 286–87, 488–94; 7:90 n. 8, 249–50;

9:25–26, 83, 140–41, 294–95. On these circumstances and experiences generally, see McDonald 1985, 166–73, and Banning 1995, 45–57, 66–73, 98–107. Madison's experiences seem to have been confirmed by his study of ancient and modern confederations (Madison 1969–1985, 9:4–22).

76. Rakove 1996, 41, and Banning 1995, 137.

77. Madison 1969–1985, 9:348.

78. Madison 1969–1985, 9:348–49.

79. Madison 1969–1985, 9:349–50.

80. Madison 1969–1985, 9:353–54.

81. Madison 1969–1985, 9:355.

82. Madison 1969–1985, 9:356–57.

83. Madison 1969–1985, 9:355. Matthews 1995, 85, argues correctly that Madison was not a pluralist and that competing factions open some necessary space for prudent deliberation. He understates the importance of a well-designed senate in filling that space (81–82, 178, 181–83, 203–4) and overstates the degree to which prudent results can be attained through "mechanical" means (22–23).

84. Madison 1969–1985, 9:357.

85. Madison 1969–1985, 9:355.

86. Madison 1969–1985, 9:355–56.

87. Madison 1969–1985, 9:355. The tendency of popular elections to exclude these necessary types from office is exacerbated by the generally bad motives of most successful candidates for office (9:354).

88. Madison 1969–1985, 9:317–22 (let. to Jefferson), 368–71 (let. to E. Randolph), 382–87 (let. to Washington).

89. He raises his concern about property again after the convention, but in "observations" on Jefferson's draft of a constitution for Virginia (Madison 1969–1985, 11:288–89).

90. Madison 1969–1985, 9:318, 370, 383–84. Madison defended this remarkable proposition during and after the Philadelphia convention; in no other way could the national government effectively defend its powers against state ambitions.

91. Madison 1969–1985, 9:369–70, 383–85.

92. Madison 1969–1985, 10:15–17. The plan is broken into resolutions, and particular resolutions will be cited below. We follow the editors of Madison's papers on the authorship of the Virginia Plan: "JM never claimed to be the author of this plan, but his guiding influence in the Virginia caucus, which drafted the resolutions, is beyond dispute" (Madison 1969–1995, 10:12). For a fine overview of the plan and Madison's thinking, see Banning 1995, 111–37. Banning does not note some specific places where the senate is particularly important (127, 135), but he does see its overall importance in securing the crucial quality of impartiality (137).

93. Madison 1969–1985, 10:16. Main 1967, 217–18, sees this mode of election as

odd, but he overlooks its precursors. Swift 1996, 26–27, tries to interpret the mode as a substitute for hereditary nobility and, therefore, as support for her thesis that the framers sought an American House of Lords. In general, she overlooks earlier arguments proposing a similar form.

94. Rakove 1996, 78.

95. Madison 1969–1985, 10:15–16. The executive would also be selected by the entire legislature. Instead of using a long term to ensure institutional independence, the plan limits the executive to one term (Madison 1969–1985, 10:16).

96. Of course, nothing in the Virginia Plan precludes requiring each state to nominate at least one person who is not a state resident.

97. Eidelberg 1968, 48.

98. Madison 1969–1985, 11:286. In this case, concerning a constitution for Virginia, he suggests either statewide elections or, because it favors "merit," electors as in Maryland.

99. Eidelberg 1968, 50–51, 81. Swift 1993, 216, dismisses the provision for pay as an "only token" concession.

FOUR. THE CONSTITUTIONAL CONVENTION

1. Farrand 1966, *The Records of the Federal Convention of 1787*, 1:321. Subsequent references to Farrand 1966 will be cited parenthetically in the text and notes as *Records,* with volume and page number.

2. *Records,* 1:568–69. Madison's motion lost on a vote of nine to two in probably the only vote in which Virginia and Delaware together formed the minority (1:570).

3. Rakove 1996, 78.

4. Although no one, including Madison had a chance to justify the particular stipulations of the fifth resolution regarding state nominations, it seems fairly clear that the nominations by state legislatures were to prevent the sort of electioneering and corruption that would occur if the selection was to be strictly a House decision. (Those seeking a Senate seat could lobby that specific body, and members of the House would tend to prefer one of their own.) Nominations by the state legislatures would mitigate this problem. Aspirants to the Senate would not have any particular body to lobby. House members would not have any particular advantage; they could seek the nomination of their state legislatures, but that would not guarantee actual election by the House. In other words, there is a clear rationale for state nominations that has nothing to do with proportionality or federalism.

5. He states this three times, in letters to Thomas Jefferson (March 19, 1787), Edmund Randolph (April 8, 1787), and George Washington (April 16, 1787). See Madison 1969–1985, 9:318–19, 371, 383.

6. The search for comments was done in three ways: a direct reading of Madison's notes (*Records*); a cross check with Benton's (1986) topical arrangement of Madison's notes; an electronic search of Madison's notes in the *American Reference Library* CD-ROM, which contains the text of *Journal of the Federal Convention*, ed. E. H. Scott (Chicago: Albert, Scott & Co., 1893).

7. Comments ranged from brief allusions to one characteristic or goal, to lengthy commentaries that referred to three or four. Most of the comments are clear and direct in reference. Others, of course, are open to interpretation. The main categories that potentially overlapped were "check on democracy" and "stability." Speakers sometimes were specifically referring to stability as a virtue in policymaking; others seemed to be referring to stability as a check on democracy's tendency to rapid change or as part of the general bicameral check (see, e.g., John Dickinson's remarks in *Records*, 1:86). We tried to judge on the basis of the full commentary and context. Also, we classified stability as a purpose or end rather than a characteristic because that is the way most of the speakers used the term—stability as an end in itself. The following speakers' comments were excluded from the tally for being too vague or indirect to classify, or for being too directly related to state representation: Madison (*Records*, 1:50, 490), Ellsworth (1:484), General Pinckney (1:429), Davie (1:542). Butler's somewhat indirect reference to size (1:51) was included because of the context provided by Pierce's notes (1:57–59), which clarify Butler's concern about the size of the Senate. Dickinson's comments that a large Senate was fine (1:150, 153) were not included, in part because he was the only delegate to express this opinion but more importantly because he did not seem to be expressing his ideal as much as commenting that size was not so important.

8. *Federalist*, 55: 342.

9. Wilson's district proposal is rejected on June 7 by a one-to-ten vote, with only Wilson's Pennsylvania voting for it (*Records*, 1:149).

10. Collier 1971, 262.

11. Given the eventual crisis over this issue, many scholars assume that the small-state delegates knew what they were aiming for from the beginning. However probable, it is still an assumption that can lead to errors. For example, in his account Irving Brant claims that Dickinson's comments on June 7 about the need for a Lords-like upper house was him "jockeying for state equality" (Brant 1950, 46). Why then would Dickinson, during the same debate, dismiss concerns about the size of the Senate (*Records*, 1:150)?

12. In a footnote that may have been added much later, Madison outlines the dilemma and forces at work on the issue of Senate selection: "It must be kept in view that the largest States particularly Pennsylvania & Virginia always considered the choice of the 2d. Branch by the State Legislatures as opposed to a proportional Representation to which they were attached as a fundamental prin-

ciple of just Government. The smaller States who had opposite views, were reenforced by the members from the large States most anxious to secure the importance of the State Governments" (*Records,* 1:408).

13. Kelly, Harbison, and Belz 1983, 97.

14. See also Luther Martin's postconvention assessment of the same issue (*Records,* 3:187). On the general question of state size and politics during the founding, see Zagarri 1987.

15. See comments of Lansing, Patterson, Martin, and Sherman (*Records,* 1:249–52, 340–43). These four are the only delegates during the convention to speak in favor of a single-chamber legislature.

16. Yates's notes record that Madison invoked the north-south division on June 29, not June 30 (*Records,* 1:476).

17. Rakove 1996, 75.

18. Georgia, with only Houston (no) and Baldwin (yes) present, divided. The other Georgians, Pierce and Few had left for Congress in New York. On Baldwin's vote, see Luther Martin's assessment (*Records,* 3:188). Scholars have debated the significance of this. Some credit Baldwin with saving the convention. One problem is that Baldwin and Georgia switched back to opposing the compromise on the July 16 final vote on the representation question.

19. CT, NJ, MD, DE, NC (5); PA, VA, SC (3); MA, NY, GA (3). This in some ways presages the compromise vote, with North Carolina the lone large state voting yes and Massachusetts divided on the issue (*Records,* 1:547). This vote could also imply that the money bills compromise was not meaningless, at least to North Carolina, or that North Carolina had, by this time, been persuaded of the inevitability of the compromise. As we shall see it is the votes of the key delegates that matter, and here the evidence is somewhat mixed.

20. Rakove 1987b, 426–27; Lee and Oppenheimer 1999, 39. Madison may have stated this directly. Lansing's notes on Madison's speech during the July 5 debate on the report of the compromise committee, while paralleling Madison's account of his own speech that day, are a bit more blunt. According to Lansing, Madison lamented that "All the Concessions are on one Side" (Hutson 1987b, 150).

21. See, for example, Oliver Ellsworth's remarks on the subject (*Records,* 1:492).

22. Though somewhat vague about causes, Farrand 1913 tends to emphasize the small state versus large state conflict and the need to save the convention. Likewise, Roche 1961 spends little time on the actual compromise but clearly fits it within his framework of pragmatic compromise politics. For other accounts that focus on the small versus large state compromise, see Rossiter 1966, Bowen 1966, Collier and Collier 1986, and William Peters 1987.

23. Because the three-fifths rule was part of the package offered by the compromise committee, it has been seen by some to be an important part of the Great

Compromise. Although neither points to direct vote changes (on the Great Compromise) as a result of the three-fifths decision, both Jillson 1981 and Rakove 1996, 75, argue that it had the effect of enervating the large-state coalition and deflating further resistance to equal representation after the July 16 vote.

The logic is, of course, that the slave states accepted equal representation in the Senate in return for the enhancement of their representation in the House. Others do not see a connection. As Farrand argues, "the so-called 'three-fifths rule,' has very generally been referred to as a compromise and as one of the important compromises of the convention. This is certainly not the case" (Farrand 1913, 107). Farrand emphasizes that the rule was adopted by the Confederation Congress for tax purposes and familiar to all the delegates. The first vote at the convention for three-fifths was on June 11, and it passed nine to two. It was upheld by a six-to-two-to-two vote on July 12 as part of the voting on the compromise committee report. In the heated and often quite blunt debates during this period, the only reference to a connection or bargain between three-fifths in the House and equal representation in the Senate came from Pennsylvania's Gouverneur Morris. He accused the South of seeking domination and said that he would be "obliged to vote for ye. vicious principle of equality in the 2d. branch in order to provide some defence for the N. States agst. it" (*Records*, 1:604). Pennsylvania's vote did not change; among the northern states only Massachusetts was divided, and not apparently for that reason. If it was part of a deal, why did only North Carolina change its vote?

24. In this view, the ordinance is given significant credit for "resolving the thorny question of the disposition of the western lands that had emerged as a source of contention in Philadelphia. Given final form in Congress on July 11, with the help of four southern delegates who left the convention and traveled to New York so Congress would have a quorum, the ordinance was at once reported to the Philadelphia assemblage, where it appears to have assisted in settling the North-South conflict over the composition of the legislature" (Kelly, Harbison, and Belz 1983, 99). For the historical detective work on this question, see Lynd 1966 and Jillson and Anderson 1978. The argument is that the settlement of the western land question helped ease the fears of northern states by limiting the number of western states, at least above the Ohio River; whereas the southern states implicitly got the opportunity to expand their social institutions and influence westward with easier terms of state admission. But, except for Massachusetts dividing, there was no arguable impact on northern state voting (after all, they didn't compromise). As for the South, if the ordinance was agreeable, why did only North Carolina (and perhaps only Williamson) change its (his) mind? Georgia voted against the compromise though two of its delegates left during the crisis to help Congress finish the ordinance. This theory also seems at odds with the debate on July 14. Gerry, who was probably the most consistent voice and vote for compromise, interrupted the flow of the debate to express his anxieties about

new western states and to propose a direct limit on the number of representatives from such future states. His motion was generally disapproved (only King seconds), yet Gerry persisted in his role as chief compromiser. So it is not obvious how the ordinance was a source of comfort to Massachusetts. Moreover, that day's debate made no reference to the ordinance. The issue in general seems to have had no effect.

25. Big but poor, North Carolina, it is argued, was more concerned about taxes than other states. It wanted all the representation it could get, including three-fifths of its slaves. Yet it didn't want the taxes that went with that representation. One way to maximize the potential for squaring this circle was the money bill compromise, which would leave the power of taxation in the hands of the larger states, such as North Carolina. In turn, North Carolina was eager to see the new stronger union succeed, and the state wanted help with its Indian problem (Barbash 1987, 113, 251). See the delegation's September 18 letter to Governor Caswell (*Records*, 3:83–84).

26. Some have noted that the departures of certain delegates influenced the way events played out during this crucial period, especially from July 2 onward. The Georgia case, for example, was discussed earlier. Another change took place when the disgruntled New Yorkers, Lansing and Yates, departed for home. While the departure of the New York delegation on July 10 certainly made life more difficult for the small-state coalition, none of the other comings and goings of the delegates in this period seem crucial. In fact, as we show, the main shortcoming of this and other explanations for the compromise are their somewhat tenuous connection to the crucial changes in voting that produced the vote on July 16. The only other possibly relevant departure was that of William Blount from North Carolina, and it is a possible explanation for the North Carolina switch. Blount left, as did a few other delegates, to help Congress achieve a quorum and complete the North West Ordinance. He did so the day after the July 2 deadlock vote, the last clear vote by North Carolina against compromise. Assuming Blount was a firm vote against equal representation, one could deduce that his absence tipped the scales in favor of compromise. This view is, however, at odds with Blount's July 10 letter, in which he assures Governor Caswell that his absence is no cause for concern because the North Carolina delegation was "Generally unanimous" (*Records*, 3:57). Perhaps Blount was lying or at least exaggerating, but this, in absence of other evidence doesn't amount to much. Likewise and later, Alexander Martin writes on August 20 to the governor to assure him that the state delegation has "generally been unanimous on all great questions." (3:72–73).

27. Hutson 1987a.

28. Jillson and Anderson 1978, 544.

29. In fact, Gerry was, again prior to the crisis, the first delegate to suggest the prohibition of senatorial origination of money bills as desirable in and of itself, "as

the people ought to hold the purse strings" (*Records*, 1:233). On July 2, in calling for a compromise committee, Gerry made among the most impassioned remarks about the need to compromise or risk "war and confusion" (1:519). See the remarks by Gerry on July 6 (1:545), and Gerry and Strong during the July 14 debate, the day before the Great Compromise vote (2:5–7). These also show that to the end Gerry preferred proportional representation in the Senate but felt that even a modified version (Pinckney's scheme) would not be acceptable to the small states. During the ratification debate in Massachusetts, Gerry asserted that the money bills concession was crucial to the compromise and that he would never have agreed to Senate equality without it (3:263–7). Likewise, Strong tells the Massachusetts convention that "the Convention would have broke up" if it had not agreed to Senate equality (3:261–62).

30. A few chroniclers of the convention mention size as a concern but discuss only Davie's specific remarks about size. None attributes his vote to this concern (let alone Williamson's). See, for example, Barbash 1987, 108–9, and Collier and Collier 1986, 112–13, 124.

31. Williamson later defends proportional representation by analogy to states and counties within states (*Records*, 1:180).

32. Without substantiation, William Peters 1987, 127, asserts that North Carolina was "swayed by William R. Davie . . . who had served on the compromise committee."

FIVE. COMPLETING THE COMPROMISED SENATE

1. It is worth noting that on June 21, Dickinson preferred three years and suggested one-third rotation for the House as a way to alleviate the wholesale turnover that could result (*Records*, 1:360–61). Many small- and large-state delegates alike were interested in some form of insulation even for the lower house.

2. Williamson's language ("to receive a compensation for the devotion of their time to public service") eliminated the word "fixt," which no one seemed to like and which was one sticking point in the existing resolution.

3. The closest the convention got to consideration of separate property qualifications for the Senate was on June 26, in the middle of the debate on pay, when Mason rose not "to make any motion, but to hint an idea which seemed to be proper for consideration. One important object in constituting a Senate was to secure the rights of property . . . He suggested therefore the propriety of annexing to the office a qualification of property." Following his comments, the convention immediately resumed consideration of pay and other issues (*Records*, 1:428).

4. Main 1967, 204–5, 207.

5. The delegates' concern about the influence of strangers on legislative counsels extended to their fellow citizens. The August 8 vote to raise the House citizenship requirement from three to seven years was immediately followed by a

debate over whether to require seven years of residence within the state as an eligibility requirement. As Rutledge put it, "An emigrant from N. England to S.C. or Georgia would know little of its affairs and could not be supposed to acquire a thorough knowledge in less time." Read "reminded him that we were now forming a *National* Government and such a regulation would correspond little with the idea that we were one people." Though any specific period of residence was defeated, the debate evinced that the concerns about strangers was not limited solely to foreigners and again was not by any means a concern exclusive to the Senate (*Records*, 2:217–19).

6. These two issues surface again briefly on August 9 in debate on the dilution of the money bills restriction. Yet neither the number of senators per state nor per capita voting is ever threatened (*Records*, 2:232–34). As is indicated in Charles Pinckney's remarks after the convention, delegates with experience in the Confederation Congress wished to avoid the difficulties caused by state voting (3:252).

7. This analysis parallels Swift's (1996, 39) idea of a "watchdog on a long leash." Swift argues that after the apportionment compromise, many small-state delegates joined with the large states to ensure that the Senate, though tied to the states through state selection and equal representation, retain some independence through long terms, national pay, and rotation. We think the per capita voting decision is one of the strongest indicators of this.

8. Some see the diminution of the Senate's role as part of a general withdrawal by such delegates, particularly Madison, of support for strong national power after the apportionment compromise. For example, see Lynch 1999, 8–30.

9. The most thorough account of the evolution of the executive at the convention is provided by Thach 1922, 76–139. See also Jillson 1988, 101–20, 170–75.

10. Farrand 1913, 168.

11. It should be noted, however, that some of the opposition to popular election of the president stemmed from concerns about the decisive influence of the large states on the outcome (although the methods of aggregation or apportionment were not specified during much of the debate on tentative proposals for direct or indirect popular election). See comments by Hugh Williamson (*Records*, 2:32) and Oliver Ellsworth (2:111).

12. McDonald 1994, 176.

13. Dickinson "was in favor of giving the eventual election to the Legislature, instead of the Senate. It was too much influence to be superadded to that body" (*Records*, 2:513).

14. See Goldstein 1982, 4–5, for a discussion of the peculiar and weak nature of the justifications for the vice presidency.

15. Warren 1967, 327; Ferling 1974, 61.

16. Farrand 1913, 165. The method of presidential selection proved unsatisfactory, but the deal on appointments and treaties stuck.

17. See also Ferling 1974 on the appointment power at the convention.

18. Warren 1967, 179.

19. Warren 1967, 641–42.

20. On the evolution of the executive council during the convention see Warren 1967, 643–49; *Records*, 1:21, 65–66, 96–104, 138–40; 2:73–80, 284, 328–29, 342–43, 367, 537–39, 541–42.

21. Warren 1967, 276.

22. Bestor 1979 and Rakove 1984 provide thorough analyses of the evolution of the treaty power at the convention.

23. On the varied motives of the antiwestern, eastern elite, see Jensen 1981, 171, and Morris 1987, 229, 231.

24. On the issue of the West and the fight in Congress over Jay's instructions, see Morris 1987, 220–44; Jillson and Wilson 1994, 268–73; and Bestor 1979, 60–68.

25. *Records*, 2:543, 548; 3:307.

26. Just as the successful creation of an independent executive allowed the convention to modify the Senate's power in the area of treaties and appointments, the creation of the judiciary allowed the delegates likewise to diminish a potential Senate power and simplify what had been a cumbersome procedure under the Articles of Confederation (of which it was also the longest section). The Committee on Detail, with its instructions to give the national legislature all the powers given to Congress, took several powers (including, as we have seen, the power of appointment and treaties) that the Articles enumerated and gave them to the Senate alone. One of these was the power to resolve interstate disputes over jurisdiction or territory. This procedure was copied from the Articles into the committee's draft constitution and became, likewise, its longest section. This section came before the convention on August 24, and the delegates quickly voted eight to two to eliminate this provision because the national judiciary was empowered to handle any such disagreements (*Records*, 2:131, 183–85, 400–401).

27. The crucial aspect of the war power, though barely alluded to at the convention, would, of course, become the president's use of force prior to or in the absence of a declaration of war. See Lofgren 1972; Warmuth and Firmage 1989; Adler 1989; Reveley 1981.

28. Ferling 1974; Strauss and Sunstein 1992; Levy 1997.

29. Rakove 1984, 248.

30. Tansill 1924; Bestor 1979; Rakove 1984.

31. The only subsequent change to the substance of the proposed constitution came just before its final approval on September 17 when the convention agreed unanimously to lower the ratio of representation in the House from a maximum of one representative for every 40,000 persons to one for every 30,000 (*Records*, 2:644).

SIX. UNFOUNDED HOPES AND FEARS

1. Swanstrom 1985, 18–27; Haynes 1938, 30–38; Main 1967, 224–29; Main 1974, 136–39.

2. As Riker 1996, 48, notes, both Main 1974 and Storing 1981 list consolidation as the primary anti-Federalist theme (with liberty taking second place in part because some of the concerns about liberty are derivative from the threat of consolidation). Riker's quantitative analysis of the published materials from September 1787 through March 1788 ranks liberty ahead of consolidation, though, as Riker notes, "Because neither they nor I can read the minds of eighteenth-century men, I do not—indeed cannot—dispute their assertion that in the minds of the Antifederal pamphleteers consolidation was the primary evil of the Constitution." See Main 1974, 120–42; Lynch 1999, 31–49. For examples of anti-Federalist discussions of consolidation, see Bailyn 1993, 1:537–41, 732–36, 783–88, 818–19, 906.

3. Main 1967, 224.

4. Storing 1981, 1:48.

5. Main 1967, 224; Kurland and Lerner 1987, 355–57. For two of the only examples of direct objections to national bicameralism, see *The Documentary History of the Ratification of the Constitution* (subsequently referred to as *DHRC*), 13:332, and Bailyn 1993, 2:269. Both objections emphasize the dangers of division in obscuring responsibility.

6. For histories of the forces at work within each state, see the essays in Gillespie and Lienesch 1989. Among the few anti-Federalists to object to equal representation are Centinel 1 (*DHRC*, 13:335), Brutus 3 (*DHRC*, 14:121), and Cato 5 (*DHRC*, 14:183–84).

7. *DHRC*, 17:66.

8. Swanstrom 1985 also makes this point.

9. This list is based on extensive use of the following primary sources: *DHRC*, especially volumes 13–15; *The Debates In the Several State Conventions on the Adoption of the Federal Constitution* (subsequently referred to as *Debates*); Storing 1981; Bailyn 1993.

10. *DHRC*, 14:187–88.

11. Among others, see *Debates*, 2:287, 508–9; 3:58, 61, 221, 354, 493–94; 4:119, 124, 245, 265; *DHRC*, 13:548, Bailyn 1993, 1:99, 542–47.

12. *Debates*, 3:58.

13. *DHRC*, 14:123.

14. *DHRC*, 14:298–99.

15. *DHRC*, 13:350; *Debates*, 2:477; 3:501–2; 4:119; Bailyn 1993, 1:99.

16. *DHRC*, 18:24–30.

17. *Debates*, 3:356–58, 4:119–23, 279–80; *DHRC*, 13:553–54.

18. *Debates,* 4:123, 142.

19. *Debates,* 3:493.

20. See Mason's objections to the Constitution (*DHRC,* 13:349) and Samuel Spencer's comments in the North Carolina convention (*Debates,* 4:116–17, 124).

21. *DHRC,* 13:561; see also Melton 1998, 47–55.

22. *Debates,* 3:486; see also *Debates,* 3:487, 490; 4:26, 42–43; Storing 1981, 2:66–67.

23. *DHRC,* 17:68, 69.

24. *DHRC,* 13:335. See also Bailyn 1993, 1:546–47.

25. *DHRC,* 13:391.

26. *DHRC,* 13:324.

27. *Debates,* 3:493–94.

28. Swanstrom 1985, 20, and Malbin 1987, 199. Both Rufus King and John Jay suggested during their respective ratification conventions that senators would receive instructions from their states (see *Debates,* 2:47, 283).

29. Swanstrom 1985, 21; Bailyn 1993, 2:521, 589; *Debates,* 2:202. On the interpretation of the slavery clauses, see Knupfer 1991, 333.

30. Wood 1972, 560–62; Swift 1996, 13, 52; Ellenbogen 1996, 265. This general view has been echoed in popular publications (see Dole 1989).

31. Knupfer 1991.

32. *Debates,* 3:94–95.

33. *Debates,* 2:306.

34. *Debates,* 2:319–20.

35. *Debates,* 4:257, 325, 329.

36. *Debates,* 2:91–92.

37. *Debates,* 4:40–41.

38. *DHRC,* 13:341.

39. *DHRC,* 13:264; *Debates,* 2:200.

40. Bailyn 1993, 1:135.

41. *Debates,* 4:38–40, 129, 132–34; Bailyn 1993, 1:294–95; *DHRC,* 16:164–68.

42. Davidson and Oleszek 1998, 23; Banning 1995, 170–72; Baker 1995, 37–38; Harris 1993, 13–16; Beer 1993, 302–5; Kurland and Lerner 1987, 356–57; Wood 1969, 557–59; Main 1967, 223–24; Diamond 1959, 59–60.

43. *Federalist,* 1961, 62: 418.

44. Rakove 1996, 395 n. 20.

45. The strongest statements concerning the good effects of this mode of appointment come in essay no. 64. John Jay's assertions—that state legislators will pick those "most distinguished by their abilities and virtues" and that those selected will "best understand our national interests" (433)—highlight how little, and with what little enthusiasm, the two main authors discuss this feature. See also *Federalist,* 27: 172.

46. Eidelberg 1968, 49, argues that a senator's long term will protect his deliberative independence and national character from state influence because the views of his state's legislature will regularly shift as a consequence of more frequent elections. Yet whoever sits in that state legislature would be concerned with a relatively stable set of state interests. See Banning 1995, 152–55, 166.

47. Kramnick 1987, 42–43; Ceaser 1979, 41–87. Publius may have paid less attention to the selection of the Senate because it was far less controversial than the equality of representation, its powers, and its connection to the executive branch; see Storing 1981, 1:48–52.

48. In general, Publius argues, state and local matters would be a "slender allurement to ambition": *Federalist*, 17: 105–8; 28: 176, 179–80; 31: 198; 45: 309–11; 46: 317–19. His general dismissal of the charge helps explain why Publius does not counter it with the Senate's confederal design. See Banning 1995, 117–19, 146–47, 152–53; Beer 1993, 295–99; and Epstein 1984, 52–55.

49. Cf. Rahe 1992, 599.

50. A few scholars dismiss the Senate as essential to this enlargement of policy: Wills 1981 and Morgan 1986. On the other hand, see Matthews 1995, Beer 1993, Kramnick 1987, Epstein 1984.

51. Using a standard word count the texts of *Federalist* nos. 62 and 63 yielded 5,415 words, of which 638 were devoted to state selection and state equality.

52. Hume 1987, 43. Adair 1974 makes the connection between Madison and Hume but without extending it to the importance and design of a senate. See Eidelberg's excellent discussion of how size influences personal conduct and deliberation (1968, 85–86).

53. Swift, for example, argues that the framers' Senate was to be composed of "members of a high social and economic elite" whose function would be to defend their class's interests. To arrive at this conclusion, she must twist Madison's discussion of the need for "individuals of extended views and national pride" into "the upper rank representing its own kind" (1996, 190). His point is exactly opposed to that purpose. As elsewhere, Madison stresses the need for an institution that is "sufficiently neutral between the different interests and factions" (Madison 1969–1985, 9:355). In the convention, Madison compared Dickinson's class-based senate, "when the weight of a set of men depends entirely upon their personal characters," to a republican form that would gain influence with the public and politicians from its constitutional authority (*Records*, 1:152).

54. "Besides as [respect for character] has reference to public opinion, which is that of the majority, the Standard is fixed by those whose conduct is to be measured by it" (Madison 1969–1985, 9:355–56; 10:212–13).

55. See Hibbing and Theiss-Morse 1997, 61–80, and Stark 1995, 92–106.

56. Epstein 1984, 147–61. Taking this logic to its extreme, Publius argues that, regardless of the size of its population, a state that is uniform in its interests could be competently represented by one person (*Federalist*, 56: 381).

SEVEN. REALITY

1. Polsby 1968; Bogue et al. 1976.

2. Our view contrasts somewhat with that of Swift 1996. Swift argues that the Senate was the American equivalent of a House of Lords until 1809 when the Senate began to face a crisis of purpose and identity. Over the subsequent twenty years, the Senate became more attuned to public opinion, less attached to state legislatures (though the earlier attachment hardly seems Lords-like), and more active legislatively and complex internally. We think Swift's own evidence points to more of an evolution and not, as she terms it, a *reconstitutive* change: "a rapid, marked, and enduring shift in the fundamental dimensions of the institution" (5). Our point is that the most important ambiguities of the Senate's place and purpose were resolved around the end of the Washington presidency; things continued to develop from there.

3. Haynes 1938, 50–51; Swanstrom 1985, 57–60; William Maclay, "The Diary of William Maclay," in *Documentary History of the First Federal Congress of the United States of America, March 4, 1789–March 3, 1791* (subsequently referred to as *DHFFC*), 9:4–5, 16–17, 27–32, 35–40.

4. *Annals of Congress,* 1st Cong., 1st sess., 23–24, 221–22. Haynes 1938, 70–73; Swanstrom 1985, 61–62; "The Diary of William Maclay," in *DHFFC,* 9:12, 23–24.

5. Haynes 1938, 888–89; Swanstrom 1985, 62–67. On the 1789 compensation bill, see *Annals of Congress,* 1st Cong., 1st sess., 701–14; "The Diary of William Maclay," in *DHFFC,* 9:133–34, 138–41, 149.

6. McPherson 1946, 224; Rakove 1987a, 290; Swanstrom 1985, 238.

7. Rakove 1987a, 290–91.

8. Maclay was on the Senate select committee that drafted the first rules for the Senate, and he left among his papers a somewhat mysterious set of rules proposed for the Senate. One of the "rules" in his memo was that: "Inviolable Secrecy shall be observed with respect, to all Matt[ers trans]acted in the Senate, While the doors are shut, or as often as the same is enjoined from the Chair" (*DHFFC,* 9:404). The editors of the *Documentary History of the First Federal Congress,* correctly we think, read into this Maclay's "support for keeping the Senate doors open whenever possible" (405), while Swanstrom 1985, 68, takes it to be an indication of Maclay's initial support for the policy of secrecy. See Maclay's record of his speech in the Senate on this subject (*DHFFC,* 9:389).

9. Swanstrom 1985, 238. The argument about accommodation sounds like a rationalization, but it is true that the tight Senate chamber in New York precluded many guests. This does not explain, of course, why things could not have been different from the start once the government moved to Philadelphia. As it turned out, the second-floor courtroom that was converted into the Senate's home in Philadelphia was also quite small.

10. In a July 26, 1789, letter, President Washington speculates as to the reason: "Why they keep their doors shut, when acting in a Legislative capacity, I am unable to inform you; unless it is because they think there is too much speaking to the Gallery in the other House, and business is thereby retarded" (Washington 1989, 324). Maclay also saw this as the only potentially valid reason to not have an audience (*DHFFC*, 9:389).

11. Kerr 1895, 39. The first rules of the Senate can be found in the *Senate Journal*, April 16, 1789, 13.

12. McPherson 1946, 227.

13. Grotta 1971, 667–71.

14. From the Virginia resolution, quoted in McPherson 1946, 228.

15. The supposition is based on a June 2, 1790, letter from David Stuart to George Washington (*DHFFC*, 9:255). It is somewhat surprising, however, that Maclay mentions the introduction of the motion in his April 29 entry but then says nothing of the vote in his April 30 entry (*DHFFC*, 9:255–56). See also *Senate Journal*, April 29 and 30, 1790, 135–36.

16. Ernst 1968, 196 (note).

17. Bowling 2000, 32.

18. Letter to James Madison, February 8, 1794 (Monroe 1898, 1:280).

19. Swanstrom 1985, 239, 241.

20. *Senate Journal*, February 25, 1791, 287; March 26, 1792, 415; January 3, 1793, 467–68; February 4, 1793, 478.

21. The only account we have found to supplement the spare Senate records of the voting is a March 3, 1794, letter from Monroe to Jefferson. Monroe writes that when the motion to postpone the matter to the next session won by only one vote, fourteen to thirteen, Senator Bradley of Vermont "finding he co'd. carry it, moved to reconsider, w'ch. gained us immediately three others, & upon the final vote the opposition was reduced to 8 or 9 only" (Monroe 1898, 1:284).

22. McPherson 1946, 238; Swanstrom 1985, 246.

23. Baker 1988, 25.

24. Prior to the victory of the general open-door resolution, February 17 is the only day during which the *Senate Journal* records any resumption and consideration of the committee report on Gallatin. It is uncertain whether the Senate's doors were yet open, and probably little progress was made, as the Senate did other regular business and held an executive session that same day.

25. Adams quoted in Ernst 1968, 195.

26. The senators seem to have been keenly aware of their factionalism. Senator James Monroe, in a March 3 letter to Jefferson, reported that "Upon this occasion Mr. H. [Senator Hawkins] of N.C. left us wch. prevented a division" and that Morris of Pennsylvania was forced to vote on the matter, after intimating that he would take no part, when it was discovered that Langdon of New Hampshire "was with us" (Monroe 1898, 1:282–83).

27. This is using a generous definition of *lost*, given the often incomplete data available on the careers of the early senators. For example, Senator Few served his four-year stint, was not reelected, but came back to run in 1795 and lost. Though there was no evidence that he actively sought reelection in 1792, we count it as a loss.

28. Class 1: 3.9 years; Class 2: 4 years; Class 3: 7.25 years.

29. By contrast, for example, the cumulative service for the average senator of the 50th Congress (1887–89) was just over 8 years and 11.5 years for the 100th Congress (1987–89).

30. All statistics calculated using data from Inter-university Consortium for Political and Social Research and Carroll McKibbin 1997.

31. Bobbe 1933, 99–100; Cornog 1998, 49–50.

32. Young 1966, 57, 263.

33. Washington 1989, 400–403.

34. Washington 1989, 408–9.

35. *Senate Executive Journal,* August 21, 1789, 19. The anticipation of a close relationship and the distress over his uncertainty about protocol are evident in the first recorded remarks Vice President Adams made to the Senate (*DHFFC,* 9:5–6).

36. Washington 1989, 391–93. See also "The Diary of William Maclay," in *DHFFC,* 9:121.

37. Washington 1989, 401.

38. Haynes 1938, 726–27; Swanstrom 1985, 98.

39. *Senate Executive Journal,* July 6, 1813, 382.

40. Haynes 1938, 54.

41. The editors of Washington's papers (Washington 1989, 393) cite a letter published in a Savannah newspaper, supposedly written by someone in New York at the time of the Fishbourn episode. The letter specifically blames the personal and unjustified opposition to Fishbourn by Georgia senators Few and Gunn. For skeptics, see Hart 1948, 123–25, Swanstrom 1985, 103.

42. Swanstrom 1985, 111. White 1961, 82–87, offers many examples of the involvement of both houses and of consultations by Washington and Adams with state delegations. See also Hunt 1896 and 1897; Swanstrom 1985, 99–101; Rakove 1987a: 289–90.

43. For example, see Maclay in *DHFFC,* 9:283.

44. On the development of senatorial courtesy in the nineteenth century and its association with patronage and senatorial privilege, see Haynes 1938, 723–52, and Kerr 1895, 104–35.

45. The debate consumed the House for five days in June. See *Annals of Congress,* 1st Cong., 1st sess., 473–608. White 1961, 20–25, provides a synopsis of the debates, as does Lynch 1999, 54–65.

46. "The Diary of William Maclay," in *DHFFC,* 9:109–16.

47. Swindler 1974; Hoffer and Hull 1984; Melton 1998.

48. This account parallels Kerr 1895, Hayden 1920, Tansill 1924, and Haynes 1938.

49. It should be noted that executive branch officials had visited the Senate on treaty matters at least three times prior to Washington's visit (Secretary of War Knox twice and Foreign Affairs Secretary Jay once). With the possible exception of Knox's second visit (which seemed to involve some consultation), these appear to be more analogous to modern situations where secretaries come to committee hearings to answer questions on a treaty, with the Senate, in this case, sitting in essence as a committee of the whole. See Hayden 1920, 4–8, and Tansill 1924, 462, on Jay's visit; Haynes 1938, 63, sketches all three.

50. "The Diary of William Maclay," in *DHFFC*, 9:128–32; *Senate Executive Journal*, August 22 and 24, 1789, 20–24; Hayden 1920, 28–29.

51. Haynes 1938, 68. See Tansill 1924, 466–68, for other examples.

52. *Senate Executive Journal*, May 8, 1792.

53. The treaty relating to Algiers is one example, as are the preliminary negotiations leading to the Jay Treaty.

54. Hayden 1920, 71.

55. Hayden 1920, 77–78, provides the text of the Burr resolution.

56. Hayden 1920, 80.

57. Quoted in Tansill 1924, 472.

58. Marshall was then a representative from Virginia (*Annals of Congress*, 6th Cong., 1st sess., 613).

59. *United States v. Curtiss-Wright Export Corp.*, 299 U.S. 304, 319 (1936).

60. For examples and accounts, see Tansill 1924, 472–77, and Haynes 1938, 586–90.

61. *Annals of Congress*, 1st Cong., 1st sess., 506.

62. Maclay disliked Adams particularly for what he saw as the vice president's predilection for aristocratic trappings if not actual monarchy. At one point in his diary, Maclay exclaims, "Oh Adams Adams what a Wretch art thou!" (*DHFFC*, 9:153).

63. Maclay makes numerous references to Adams interrupting senators and making daily speeches. Adams, conversely, expressed his frustration at not being able to contribute to the debate. See Haynes 1938, 208.

64. "The Diary of William Maclay," in *DHFFC*, 9:5–6.

65. This fact was a source of controversy in the First Congress when it came to deciding compensation for executive officers. When it was proposed, in parallel to the president, that the vice president receive an annual salary, Representative Alexander White argued for per diem pay for the vice president when presiding over the Senate (otherwise for what would he be paid?). Congress settled on an annual salary in part to keep someone of quality in line to succeed to the presi-

dency in the event of disability or death (*Annals of Congress*, 1st Cong., 1st sess., 657–58, 668–76).

66. Maclay's account of the first session of Congress is the main source of evidence for this. One of the best narratives of Adams's role as presiding officer of the Senate in the First Congress can be found in Smith 1962, 744–813.

67. Adams 1968, 144. Only John C. Calhoun, one of the few other two-term vice presidents, came close to that total with twenty-eight. Adam's per year average of 3.6 casting votes was exceeded by that of George Dallas's 4.75 from 1845–49, and nearly matched by Calhoun's 3.5 (1825–32), Richard Johnson's 3.5 (1837–41), and Schuyler Colfax's 3.25 (1869–73). Modern vice presidents have cast very few tie votes. For example, Lyndon Johnson–0, Spiro Agnew–2, Walter Mondale–1 (see Cronin 1982, 327).

68. Adams 1968, 154–55. Even so Adams continued to be a diligent presiding officer despite periods of tedium and his longing to go home. The close division in the Senate, especially when the Jay mission and treaty became the signal issue, obliged his reluctant attendance (Adams 1968, 166, 169, 170–71, 175–76).

69. Jefferson quoted in Warren 1967, 635 (note). This was hardly a unique or quickly outdated point of view. Eisenhower, for example, viewed the vice president as a legislative officer not subject to presidential control (see Cronin 1982, 329).

70. Cunningham 1987, 221.

71. See the examples and exceptions from the early literature cited by Lancaster 1928, 67–68. Kerr 1895, 92–96, and Haynes 1938, 999–1000, fit this tradition.

72. Swanstrom 1985, 82–92; Baker 1989, 299–313; Stewart 1992, 86; Swift 1996, 63–64; Binder 1997, 61–64.

73. Binder 1997, 218, 62; Swift 1996, 64.

74. Lancaster 1928.

75. Haynes 1938, 455.

76. Haynes 1938, 432.

77. *Senate Journal*, August 5, 1789.

78. "The Diary of William Maclay," in *DHFFC*, 9:193.

79. *DHFFC*, 9:495–96.

80. The early Senate appears not to have been deterred from originating legislation that reduced revenue (see Haynes 1938, 433; Kerr 1895, 71–72). The Senate also introduced a number of special appropriation bills; that is, while the House originated all general appropriations, the Senate originated some bills that appropriated money for particular purposes (Kerr 1895, 69).

81. "The Diary of William Maclay," in *DHFFC*, 9:51–60, 62–69, 72–74, 83–84.

82. Hayden 1920, 11–39.

83. Smith 1956, 50–62, 94–111.

84. Swanstrom 1985, 92.

85. This account of instruction and recall draws upon the following secondary sources: Anderson 1962; Haynes 1938, 1023–34; Eaton 1952; Swanstrom 1985, 154–74; Skeen 1991; Hemberger 1996, 307–15.

86. Thorpe 1909, 5:2788. For another example, see the 1780 constitution of Massachusetts (Thorpe 1909, 3:1892).

87. *Debates,* 2:311.

88. The New York and Rhode Island conventions approved proposed amendments that essentially replicated the provision of the Articles of Confederation. The subject was recorded as part of the debates in Massachusetts, Maryland, and Virginia.

89. *Debates,* 2:47, 283.

90. *Annals of Congress,* 1st Cong., 1st sess., 761–76; *Senate Journal,* September 3, 1789, 70. See also Hemberger 1996, 307–15, and Anderson 1962, 34–36, on the House debate.

91. "The Diary of William Maclay," in *DHFFC,* 9:199, 219, 225, 289, 360–61, 371, 388–89, 414.

92. Grant 1981.

93. Anderson provides some examples 1962, 45.

94. John Lansing, a staunch anti-Federalist at the New York ratification convention, said as much: "It is asked, Why not place the senators in the same situation as the representatives? or, Why not give the people a power of recall? Because, sir, this is impracticable, and contrary to the first principles of representative government. There is no regular way of collecting the people's sentiments. But a power in the state legislatures to recall their senators, is simple and easy, and will be attended with the highest advantages" (*Debates,* 2:294).

95. Elkins and McKitrick 1993; Sharp 1993. On the origins of American parties, see inter alia, Cunningham 1957; Chambers 1963; Cunningham 1965; Hofstadter 1969; Nichols 1967; Hoadley 1986; Aldrich 1995.

96. Two of the bicameral studies are Hoadley 1980 and Ryan 1971.

97. Lynch 1999.

98. Jefferson to Madison, May 15, 1794; quoted in Swanstrom 1985, 134.

99. Elkins and McKitrick 1993, 415; also Charles 1961, 122; Sharp 1993, 113; Combs 1970, ix.; Stewart 1969, 113.

100. Monroe to Edmund Randolph, December 12, 1795 (Monroe 1898, 2:154–61).

101. Quoted in Elkins and McKitrick 1993, 418. See also Carroll and Ashworth 1957, 237–51, and Combs 1970, 59–61.

102. Swanstrom 1985, 147–49.

103. Elkins and McKitrick 1993, 431–49.

104. Swanstrom 1985, 151.

105. *Debates,* 2:287.

106. *Debates*, 3:405. For another example, see Bailyn 1993, 1:708. Some anticipated this possibility with hope rather than trepidation. One reason Delaware was so eager to ratify the Constitution was its eagerness to offer some of its land for the federal district to bolster its political and economic power as a state (see Saladino 1989, 44).

107. Young 1966, 13–48.

108. Quoted in Dole 1989, 57.

109. Quoted in Haynes 1938, 40.

EIGHT. FROM INVENTION TO EVOLUTION

Epigraph: Wilson 1961, 112.

1. *Federalist*, 63: 431.

2. Rakove 1987a.

3. Zuckert 1986; Riker 1987.

4. Stewart 1992; Abramowitz and Segal 1992, 15.

5. Riker 1955.

6. Haynes 1906; Hall 1936, 369–442; Haynes 1938, 96–117; King and Ellis 1996; Wirls 1999.

7. Hall 1936; Crook and Hibbing 1997; Hoebeke 1995.

8. Sinclair 1989.

9. Abramowitz and Segal 1992; Stewart 1992; Westlye 1991; Krasno 1994.

10. See Binder 1997 for the most comprehensive bicameral account.

11. On the bicameral origins of standing committees, for example, see Gamm and Shepsle 1989; Smith and Deering 1990. See also Swift 1996.

12. For an account of the adoption of the cloture rule, see Haynes 1938, 402–5.

13. Under the original rule a petition signed by sixteen senators produced a nondebatable question on whether to close debate. An affirmative vote by two-thirds of those voting set an automatic limit on debate and shut off further amendments, except by unanimous consent.

14. Sinclair 1989; Binder and Smith 1997; Beth 1994.

15. Baker 1995.

16. Cutler 1993; Frank 1993; Mathias 1994; Lewis 1994; Geoghegan 1994. A private group called "Action, Not Gridlock!" was organized in early 1994 to give impetus to an antifilibuster campaign.

17. Binder and Smith 1997; Krehbiel 1996, 1998; Brady and Volden 1988.

18. Eskridge 1995; Lind 1998.

19. Binder and Smith 1997, 30–33, and Binder 1997, 36–38, make a similar argument.

20. White 1956; Reedy 1986; Harris 1993; Baker 1995. See Binder and Smith 1997 for a thorough and critical assessment.

21. Lee and Oppenheimer 1999: 10–11, 237–38.

22. *Reynolds v. Sims,* 377 U.S. 533 (1964).

23. Moffett 1895; Wooddy 1926. Recent critiques include Lazare 1996; Baker and Dinkin 1997; Lind 1998; Lee and Oppenheimer 1999. Wirls 1998 offers an analysis of how equal representation affects bicameral outcomes in voting.

24. Wilson 1961; Burns 1963; Huntington 1965; Cutler 1980; Fiorina 1980; Stark 1995; King 1997. Buchanan and Congleton 1998 argue for some generalizing influence to overcome the "capricious forces" of both particular and "rotating coalitional" interests" (xi–xii, 12, 19–20, 26, 95). See pp. 40, 48, for a description of an institution, without a particular constituency, that resembles Publius's senate rather closely.

References

Abramowitz, Alan I., and Jeffrey A. Segal. 1992. *Senate Elections.* Ann Arbor: University of Michigan Press.

Adair, Douglas. 1974. *Fame and the Founding Fathers.* Ed. T. Colbourn. New York: Norton.

Adams, Charles Francis. 1968. *The Life of John Adams.* New York: Haskell House.

Adams, John. 1979a. *A Defense of the Constitutions of Government of the United States of America.* Germany: Scientia Verlag Aalen.

———. 1979b. *Papers of John Adams.* Ed. Robert J. Taylor. Cambridge: Harvard University Press.

———. 1983. "Thoughts on Government." In *American Political Writings during the Founding Era: 1760–1805.* Ed. Charles S. Hyneman and Donald S. Lutz. Indianapolis: Liberty Press, 402–9.

Adams, Willi Paul. 1980. *The First American Constitutions.* Chapel Hill: University of North Carolina Press.

Adler, David Gray. 1989. "The President's War-Making Power." In *Inventing the American Presidency.* Ed. Thomas E. Cronin. Lawrence: University Press of Kansas, 119–53.

Aldrich, John H. 1995. *Why Parties?: The Origin and Transformation of Political Parties in America.* Chicago: University of Chicago Press.

American Reference Library (CD-ROM). 1998. Western Standard Publishing Company.

Anastaplo, George. 1989. *The Constitution of 1787.* Baltimore: Johns Hopkins University Press.

Anderson, Clinton Lee. 1962. "Right of State Legislatures to Instruct United States Senators." Master's thesis, University of North Carolina at Chapel Hill.

Annals of Congress, at http://memory.loc.gov/ammem/amlaw/lawhome.html.

Appleby, Joyce. 1992. *Liberalism and Republicanism in the Historical Imagination.* Cambridge: Harvard University Press.

Aristotle. 1984. *The Politics.* Chicago: University of Chicago Press.

Bailyn, Bernard. 1967. *The Ideological Origins of the American Revolution.* Cambridge: Harvard University Press.

———, ed. 1993. *The Debate on the Constitution: Federalist and Antifederalist Speeches, Articles, and Letters during the Struggle over Ratification.* 2 vols. New York: Library of America.

Baker, Lynn A., and Samuel H. Dinkin. 1997. "The Senate: An Institution Whose Time Has Gone?" *Journal of Law and Politics* 13:21–103.

Baker, Richard Allan. 1988. *The Senate of the United States: A Bicentennial History.* Malabar, FL: Robert E. Krieger Publishing.

———. 1989. "The Senate of the United States: Supreme Executive Council of the Nation, 1787–1800." *Prologue* 21:299–313.

Baker, Ross K. 1995. *House and Senate.* 2d ed. New York: W. W. Norton.

Banning, Lance. 1987. "The Practicable Sphere of a Republic: James Madison, the Constitutional Convention, and the Emergence of Revolutionary Federalism." In *Beyond Confederation: Origins of the Constitution and American National Identity.* Ed. Richard Beeman, Stephan Botein, and Edward C. Carter II. Chapel Hill: University of North Carolina Press, 162–87.

———. 1995. *The Sacred Fire Of Liberty: James Madison and the Founding of the Federal Republic.* Ithaca, NY: Cornell University Press.

Barbash, Fred. 1987. *The Founding.* New York: Simon and Schuster.

Barry, Richard. 1942. *Mr. Rutledge of South Carolina.* New York: Duell, Sloan, and Pearce.

Beard, Charles A. 1913. *An Economic Interpretation of the Constitution of the United States.* New York: Macmillan.

Beer, Samuel. 1993. *To Make a Nation: The Rediscovery of American Federalism.* Cambridge: Harvard University Press.

Bemis, Samuel Flagg. 1962. *Jay's Treaty; A Study In Commerce And Diplomacy.* 2d ed. New Haven: Yale University Press.

Benton, Wilbourn E., ed. 1986. *1787: Drafting the U.S. Constitution.* 2 vols. College Station: Texas A&M University Press.

Bestor, Arthur. 1974. "Separation of Powers in the Domain of Foreign Affairs: The Original Intent of the Constitution Historically Examined." *Seton Hall Law Review* 5:527–665.

———. 1979. "Respective Roles of Senate and President in the Making and Abrogation of Treaties—The Original Intent of the Framers of the Constitution Historically Examined." *Washington Law Review* 55:1–135.

Beth, Richard S. 1994. "Filibusters in the Senate, 1789–1993." Congressional Research Service.

Binder, Sarah A. 1997. *Minority Rights, Majority Rule: Partisanship and the Development of Congress.* New York: Cambridge University Press.

Binder, Sarah A., and Steven S. Smith. 1997. *Politics or Principle?: Filibustering in the United States Senate.* Washington, DC: Brookings Institution.

Biographical Directory of the United States Congress, 1774–1989. 1989. Bicentennial ed. Washington, DC: Government Printing Office. [Also available through the United States Senate at www.senate.gov/learning/bioguide.html.]

Blitzer, Charles. 1960. *An Immortal Commonwealth: The Political Thought of James Harrington.* New Haven: Yale University Press.

Bobbe, Dorothie. 1933. *DeWitt Clinton.* New York: Minton, Balch & Co.

Bogue, Allan G. et al. 1976. "Members of the House of Representatives and the

Processes of Modernization, 1789–1960." *Journal of American History* 63 (September): 275–302.

Bowen, Catherine Drinker. 1966. *Miracle at Philadelphia.* Boston: Little, Brown.

Bowling, Kenneth R. 1990. *Politics in the First Congress, 1789–1791.* New York: Garland.

———. 2000. "The Federal Government and the Republican Court Move to Philadelphia, November 1790–March 1791." In *Neither Separate nor Equal: Congress in the 1790s.* Ed. Kenneth R. Bowling and Donald R. Kennon. Athens: University of Ohio Press, 3–33.

Brady, David W., and Craig Volden. 1998. *Revolving Gridlock: Politics and Policy from Carter to Clinton.* Boulder, CO: Westview Press.

Branson, Roy. 1979. "James Madison and the Scottish Enlightenment." *Journal of the History of Ideas* 40:235–50.

Brant, Irving. 1950. *James Madison: Father of the Constitution, 1787–1800.* New York: Bobbs-Merrill.

Braxton, Carter. 1983. "Address." In *American Political Writings during the Founding Era: 1760–1805.* Ed. Charles S. Hyneman and Donald S. Lutz. 2 vols. Indianapolis, IN: Liberty Fund, 328–29.

Bryce, James. 1995. *The American Commonwealth.* Vol. 1. Indianapolis, IN: Liberty Fund.

Buchanan, James, and Gordon Tullock. 1962. *The Calculus of Consent.* Ann Arbor: University of Michigan Press.

Buchanan, James M., and Roger D. Congleton. 1998. *Politics by Principle, Not Interest: Toward a Nondiscriminatory Democracy.* New York: Cambridge University Press.

Burns, James MacGregor. 1963. *The Deadlock of Democracy.* New York: Prentice-Hall.

Carroll, John Alexander, and Mary Wells Ashworth. 1957. *George Washington: First in Peace.* New York: Charles Scribner's Sons.

Ceaser, James W. 1979. *Presidential Selection: Theory and Development.* Princeton: Princeton University Press.

Chambers, William Nisbet. 1963. *Political Parties In A New Nation: The American Experience, 1776–1809.* New York: Oxford University Press.

Charles, Joseph. 1961. *The Origins of the American Party System.* New York: Harper and Brothers.

Cicero. 1928. *De republica, De legibus.* Trans. C. W. Keyes. New York: Putnam's.

Collier, Christopher. 1971. *Roger Sherman's Connecticut: Yankee Politics and the American Revolution.* Middletown, CT: Wesleyan University Press.

Collier, Christopher, and James Lincoln Collier. 1986. *Decision in Philadelphia.* New York: Random House.

Combs, Jerald A. 1970. *The Jay Treaty: Political Battleground of the Founding Fathers.* Berkeley: University of California Press.

Cornog, Evan. 1998. *The Birth of Empire: DeWitt Clinton and the American Experience, 1769–1828.* New York: Oxford University Press.

Cronin, Thomas E. 1982. "Rethinking the Vice-Presidency." In *Rethinking the Presidency.* Ed. Thomas E. Cronin. Boston: Little, Brown, 324–48.

Crook, Sara Brandes, and John R. Hibbing. 1997. "A Not-so-distant Mirror: The Seventeenth Amendment and Congressional Change." *American Political Science Review* 91(December): 845–53.

Cunningham, Noble E., Jr. 1957. *The Jeffersonian Republicans: The Formation of Party Organization, 1789–1801.* Chapel Hill: University of North Carolina Press.

———. 1987. *In Pursuit of Reason: The Life of Thomas Jefferson.* Baton Rouge: University of Louisiana Press.

———, ed. 1965. *The Making of the American Party System 1789–1809.* Englewood Cliffs, NJ: Prentice-Hall.

Currie, David P. 1997. *The Constitution in Congress: The Federalist Period 1789–1801.* Chicago: University of Chicago Press.

Cutler, Lloyd. 1980. "To Form a Government." *Foreign Affairs* 59:126–43.

———. 1993. "The Way to Kill Senate Rule XXII." *Washington Post,* April 19.

Davidson, Roger H., and Walter T. Oleszek. 1998. *Congress and Its Members.* 6th ed. Washington, DC: Congressional Quarterly Press.

The Debates in the Several State Conventions on the Adoption of the Federal Constitution. Ed. Jonathan Elliot. 2d ed. Philadelphia: J. B. Lippincott, 1901 (contained in the *American Reference Library* CD-ROM, Western Standard Publishing Company).

Democratic Study Group. 1994. "A Look at the Senate Filibuster." DSG Special Report No. 103–28. June 13.

Diamond, Martin. 1959. "Democracy and *The Federalist:* A Reconstruction of the Framers' Intent." *American Political Science Review* 53 (March): 52–68.

Documentary History of the First Federal Congress of the United States of America, March 4, 1789–March 3, 1791. 1972–. Ed. Linda Grant De Pauw. Baltimore: Johns Hopkins University Press.

The Documentary History of the Ratification of the Constitution. 1976–. Ed. John Kaminski and Gaspare Saladino. Madison: State Historical Society of Wisconsin.

Dole, Bob. 1989. *Historical Almanac of the United States Senate.* Washington, DC: Government Printing Office.

Eaton, Clement. 1952. "Southern States and the Right of Instruction, 1789–1860." *Journal of Southern History* 18 (August): 303–19.

Eidelberg, Paul. 1968. *The Philosophy of the American Constitution.* New York: Free Press.

Elkins, Stanley, and Eric McKitrick. 1993. *The Age of Federalism.* New York: Oxford University Press.

Ellenbogen, Paul D. 1996. "Another Explanation for the Senate: The Anti-Federalists, John Adams, and the Natural Aristocracy." *Polity* 29 (winter): 247–71.

Ellis, Joseph J. 1993. *Passionate Sage: The Character and Legacy of John Adams.* New York: W. W. Norton.

Epstein, David F. 1984. *The Political Theory of the Federalist.* Chicago: University of Chicago Press.

Ernst, Robert. 1968. *Rufus King: American Federalist.* Chapel Hill: University of North Carolina Press.

Eskridge, William N., Jr. 1995. "The One Senator, One Vote Clause." *Constitutional Commentary* 12 (summer): 159–62.

Farrand, Max. 1913. *The Framing of the Constitution of the United States.* New Haven: Yale University Press.

———, ed. 1966. *The Records of the Federal Convention of 1787.* 4 vols. New Haven: Yale University Press.

Fenno, Richard F. 1982. *The United States Senate: A Bicameral Perspective.* Washington, DC: American Enterprise Institute.

Ferling, John. 1974. "The Senate and Federal Judges: The Intent of the Founding Fathers." *Capitol Studies* 2:57–70.

Fink, Zera S. 1945. *The Classical Republicans.* Evanston, IL: Northwestern University.

Fiorina, Morris. 1980. "The Decline of Collective Responsibility in American Politics." *Daedalus* 109: 25–45.

Fisher, Louis. 1991. *Constitutional Conflicts between Congress and the President.* 3d ed. Lawrence: University Press of Kansas.

Frank, Barney. 1993. "Now It's Your Turn, Senator." *Washington Post,* October 12, A19.

Gamm, Gerald, and Kenneth Shepsle. 1989. "Emergence of Legislative Institutions: Standing Committees in the House and Senate, 1810–1825." *Legislative Studies Quarterly* 14 (February): 39–66.

Geoghegan, Tom. 1994. "The Infernal Senate: The Real Source Of Gridlock." *New Republic* 211 (November 21): 17–23.

Gillespie, Michael Allen, and Michael Lienesch, eds. 1989. *Ratifying the Constitution.* Lawrence: University Press of Kansas.

Goldstein, Joel K. 1982. *The Modern Vice Presidency: The Transformation of a Political Institution.* Princeton: Princeton University Press.

Grant, C. L. 1981. "Senator Benjamin Hawkins: Federalist or Republican?" *Journal of the Early Republic* 1 (fall): 233–47.

Grant, Ruth W. 1987. *John Locke's Liberalism.* Chicago: University of Chicago Press.

Grotta, Gerald L. 1971. "Phillip Freneau's Crusade for Open Sessions of the U.S. Senate." *Journalism Quarterly* 48: 667–71.

Hall, Wallace Worthy. 1936. *The History and Effects of the Seventeenth Amendment*, Ph.D. dissertation, University of California, Berkeley.

Hamilton, Alexander, James Madison, and John Jay. 1961. *The Federalist*. Ed. Jacob E. Cooke. Middletown: Wesleyan University Press.

Harrington, James. 1992. *The Commonwealth of Oceana and A System of Politics*. Ed. J. G. A. Pocock. New York: Cambridge University Press.

Harris, Fred R. 1993. *Deadlock or Decision: The U.S. Senate and the Rise of National Politics*. New York: Oxford University Press.

Harrold, Frances. 1970. "The Upper House in Jeffersonian Political Theory." *The Virginia Magazine* 78: 281–94.

Hart, James. 1948. *The American Presidency in Action, 1789: A Study in Constitutional History*. New York: Macmillan.

Hayden, Joseph Ralston. 1920. *The Senate and Treaties, 1789–1817: The Development of the Treaty-Making Functions of the United States Senate during Their Formative Period*. New York: Macmillan.

Haynes, George H. 1906. *The Election of Senators*. New York: Henry Holt and Company.

——. 1938 [1960]. *The Senate of the United States: Its History and Practice*. New York: Russell and Russell.

Hemberger, Suzette. 1996. "A Government Based on Representations." *Studies in American Political Development* 10 (fall): 307–15.

Hibbing, John R., and Elizabeth Theiss-Morse. 1997. "What the Public Dislikes About Congress." In *Congress Reconsidered*. 6th ed. Ed. Lawrence C. Dodd and Bruce I. Oppenheimer. Washington, DC: Congressional Quarterly Press, 61–80.

Hoadley, John F. 1980. "The Emergence of Political Parties in Congress, 1789–1803." *The American Political Science Review* 74 (September): 757–79.

——. 1986. *Origins of American Political Parties, 1789–1803*. Lexington: University Press of Kentucky.

Hobson, Charles F. 1979. "The Negative on State Laws: James Madison, the Constitution, and the Crisis of Republican Government." *William and Mary Quarterly*, 3d ser., 36 (April): 215–35.

Hoebeke, C. H. 1995. *The Road to Mass Democracy: Original Intent and the Seventeenth Amendment*. New Brunswick, NJ: Transaction Publishers.

Hoffer, Peter Charles, and N. E. H. Hull. 1984. *Impeachment in America, 1635–1805*. New Haven: Yale University Press.

Hofstadter, Richard. 1969. *The Idea of a Party System; The Rise of Legitimate Opposition in the United States, 1780–1840*. Berkeley: University of California Press.

Hume, David. 1985. *Essays: Moral, Political, and Literary*. Indianapolis, IN: Liberty Fund.

Hunt, Gaillard. 1896. "Office-Seeking during Washington's Administration." *The American Historical Review* 1 (January): 270–83.

Hunt, Gaillard. 1897. "Office-Seeking during the Administration of John Adams." *The American Historical Review* 2 (January): 241–61.

Huntington, Samuel P. 1965. "Congressional Responses to the Twentieth Century." In *The Congress and America's Future*. Ed. David B. Truman. Englewood Cliffs, NJ: Prentice-Hall, 5–31.

Hutson, James H. 1987a. "Riddles of the Federal Constitution." *William and Mary Quarterly* 44 (July): 411–23.

———, ed. 1987b. *Supplement to Max Farrand's The Records of the Federal Convention of 1787*. New Haven: Yale University Press.

Inter-university Consortium for Political and Social Research and Carroll McKibbin. 1997. *Roster of United States Congressional Officeholders and Biographical Characteristics of Members of the United States Congress, 1789–1996: Merged Data*. [Computer file.] 10th ICPSR ed. Ann Arbor, MI: Inter-university Consortium for Political and Social Research [producer and distributor].

Jefferson, Thomas. 1984. *Writings*. New York: Library of America.

Jensen, Merrill. 1981. *The New Nation: A History of the United States during the Confederation, 1781–1789*. Boston: Northeastern University Press.

Jillson, Calvin C. 1977. "Realignments in the Convention of 1787: The Slave Trade Compromise." *Journal of Politics* 39 (August): 712–29.

———. 1981. "The Representation Question in the Federal Convention of 1787: Madison's Virginia Plan and Its Opponents." *Congressional Studies* 8, no. 2: 21–41.

———. 1988. *Constitution Making: Conflict and Consensus in the Federal Convention of 1787*. New York: Agathon.

Jillson, Calvin C., and Thornton Anderson. 1978. "Voting Bloc Analysis in the Constitutional Convention: Implications for an Interpretation of the Connecticut Compromise." *Western Political Quarterly* 31 (December): 535–47.

Jillson, Calvin C., and Rick K. Wilson. 1994. *Congressional Dynamics: Structure, Coordination, and Choice in the First American Congress, 1774–1789*. Stanford, CA: Stanford University Press.

Kelly, Alfred H., Winfred A. Harbison, and Herman Belz. 1983. *The American Constitution*. New York: Norton.

Kerr, Clara H. 1895. *The Origin and Development of the United States Senate*. Ithaca, NY: Andrus and Church.

King, Anthony S. 1997. *Running Scared: Why America's Politicians Campaign Too Much and Govern Too Little*. New York: Free Press.

King, Ronald F., and Susan Ellis. 1996. "Partisan Advantage and Constitutional Change: The Case of the Seventeenth Amendment." *Studies in American Political Development* 10 (spring): 69–102.

Knupfer, Peter B. 1991. "The Rhetoric of Conciliation: American Civic Culture and the Federalist Defense of Compromise." *Journal of the Early American Republic* 11 (fall): 315–37.

Kramnick, Isaac. 1982. "Republican Revisionism Revisited." *The American Historical Review* 87, no. 3: 629–64.

——. 1987. Introduction to *The Federalist Papers,* by James Madison et al. New York: Penguin: 11–82.

Krasno, Jonathan S. 1994. *Challengers, Competition, and Reelection: Comparing Senate and House Elections.* New Haven: Yale University Press.

Krehbiel, Keith. 1996. "Institutional and Partisan Sources of Gridlock: A Theory of Divided and Unified Government." *Journal of Theoretical Politics* 8:7–40.

——. 1998. *Pivotal Politics: A Theory of U.S. Lawmaking.* Chicago: University of Chicago Press.

Kurland, Phillip B., and Ralph Lerner, eds. 1987. *The Founders' Constitution: Major Themes.* Chicago: University of Chicago Press.

Kurtz, Stephen G. 1968. "The Political Science of John Adams, A Guide to His Statecraft." *William and Mary Quarterly,* 3d ser., 25 (October): 605–13.

Lancaster, Lane W. 1928. "The Initiative of the United States Senate in Legislation, 1789–1809." *The Southwestern Political and Social Science Quarterly* 9 (June): 67–75.

Lazare, Daniel. 1996. *The Frozen Republic: How the Constitution is Paralyzing Democracy.* New York: Harcourt Brace.

Lee, Frances E., and Bruce I. Oppenheimer. 1999. *Sizing Up the Senate: The Unequal Consequences of Equal Representation.* Chicago: University of Chicago Press.

Lerner, Ralph. 1987. *The Thinking Revolutionary.* Ithaca, NY: Cornell University Press.

Levy, Leonard W. 1997. "Foreign Policy and War Powers: The Presidency and the Framers." *The American Scholar* 66, no. 2: 271–76.

Lewis, Anthony. 1994. "The New Bolsheviks." *New York Times,* October 10, A11.

Lijphart, Arend. 1999. *Patterns of Democracy.* New Haven: Yale University Press.

Lind, Michael. 1998. "75 Stars: How To Restore Democracy in the U.S. Senate (And End the Tyranny of Wyoming)." *Mother Jones,* January/February, 44–49.

Locke, John. 1980. *Second Treatise of Government.* Indianapolis, IN: Hackett.

——. 1983. *A Letter Concerning Toleration.* Indianapolis, IN: Hackett.

Lofgren, Charles A. 1972. "War-Making Under the Constitution: The Original Understanding." *Yale Law Journal* 81:672–702.

Longley, Lawrence D., and David M. Olson. 1991. *Two Into One: The Politics and Processes of National Legislative Cameral Change.* Boulder, CO: Westview Press.

Longley, Lawrence D., and Walter J. Oleszek. 1989. *Bicameral Politics: Conference Committees in Congress.* New Haven: Yale University Press.

Lynch, Joseph M. 1999. *Negotiating the Constitution: The Earliest Debates Over Original Intent.* Ithaca, NY: Cornell University Press.

Lynd, Staughton. 1966. "The Compromise of 1787." *Political Science Quarterly* 81 (June): 225–50.

MacPherson, C. B. 1962. *The Political Theory of Possessive Individualism*. New York: Oxford University Press.

Madison, James. 1969–1985. *The Papers of James Madison*. Vols. 1–10. Ed. William T. Hutchinson and William M. E. Rachal. Chicago: University of Chicago Press. Vols. 11–15. Ed. Robert A. Rutland and Charles F. Hobson. Charlottesville: University Press of Virginia.

Main, Jackson Turner. 1967. *The Upper House in Revolutionary America, 1763–1788*. Madison: University of Wisconsin Press.

———. 1974. *The Antifederalists: Critics of the Constitution, 1781–1788*. New York: W. W. Norton.

Malbin, Michael J. 1987. "Congress during the Convention and Ratification." In *The Framing and Ratification of the Constitution*. Ed. Leonard W. Levy and Dennis J. Mahoney. New York: Macmillan, 185–208.

Manent, Pierre. 1995. *An Intellectual History of Liberalism*. Princeton: Princeton University Press.

Mansfield, Harvey C., Jr. 1989. *Taming the Prince: The Ambivalence of Modern Executive Power*. New York: Free Press.

———. 1991. *America's Constitutional Soul*. Baltimore: Johns Hopkins University Press.

Martineau, Harriet. 1838. *Retrospect of Western Travel*. New York: Saunders and Otley.

Martis, Kenneth C. 1988. *The Historical Atlas of Political Parties in the United States Congress 1789–1988*. New York: Macmillan.

Mathias, Charles M. 1994. "Gridlock, Greedlock or Democracy?" *Washington Post*, June 27, A21.

Matthews, Donald R. 1960. *U.S. Senators and Their World*. Chapel Hill: University of North Carolina Press.

Matthews, Richard K. 1995. *If Men Were Angels: James Madison and the Heartless Empire of Reason*. Lawrence: University Press of Kansas.

McCoy, Drew R. 1980. *The Elusive Republic: Political Economy in Jeffersonian America*. Chapel Hill: University of North Carolina Press.

McDonald, Forrest. 1979. *E Pluribus Unum*. Indianapolis, IN: Liberty Press.

———. 1985. *Novus Ordo Seclorum: The Intellectual Origins of the Constitution*. Lawrence: University Press of Kansas.

———. 1994. *The American Presidency: An Intellectual History*. Lawrence: University Press of Kansas.

McGuire, Robert A. 1988. "Constitution Making: A Rational Choice Model of the Federal Convention of 1787." *American Journal of Political Science* 32, no. 2 (May): 483–522.

McPherson, Elizabeth G. 1946. "The Southern States and the Reporting of Senate Debates, 1789–1802." *Journal of Southern History* 12:223–46.

Melton, Buckner F., Jr. 1998. *The First Impeachment: The Constitution's Framers and the Case of Senator William Blount.* Macon, GA: Mercer University Press.

Moffett, S. E. 1895. "Is the Senate Unfairly Constituted?" *Political Science Quarterly* 10 (June): 248–56.

Monroe, James. 1898. *The Writings of James Monroe.* Vols. 1 and 2. Ed. Stanislaus M. Hamilton. New York: G. P. Putnam.

Montesquieu, Baron. 1989. *The Spirit of the Laws.* Cambridge: Cambridge University Press.

Morgan, Edmund S. 1986. "Safety in Numbers: Madison, Hume, and the Tenth *Federalist.*" *Huntington Library Quarterly* 49: 95–112.

Morris, Richard. 1987. *The Forging of the Union, 1781–1789.* New York: Harper and Row.

Nelson, William E. 1987. "Reason and Compromise in the Establishment of the Federal Constitution, 1787–1801." *William and Mary Quarterly* 44, no. 2 (April): 458–84.

Nicgorski, Walter. 1991. "Cicero's Focus: From the Best Regime to the Model Statesman." *Political Theory* 19, no. 2: 230–51.

Nichols, Roy F. 1967. *The Invention of the American Political Parties.* New York: Macmillan.

Onuf, Peter S. 1989. "Reflections on the Founding: Constitutional Historiography in Bicentennial Perspective." *William and Mary Quarterly* 46, no. 2 (April): 341–75.

Paine, Thomas. 1945. *The Complete Writings.* 2 vols. Ed. Philip S. Foner. New York: Citadel Press.

Pangle, Thomas L. 1973. *Montesquieu's Philosophy of Liberalism.* Chicago: University of Chicago Press.

———. 1988. *The Spirit of Modern Republicanism.* Chicago: University of Chicago Press.

Pangle, Thomas L., and Peter J. Ahrensdorf. 1999. *Justice Among Nations: On the Moral Basis of Power and Peace.* Lawrence: University Press of Kansas.

Parsons, Theophilus. 1983. "The Essex Result." In *American Political Writings during the Founding Era: 1760–1805.* 2 vols. Ed. Charles S. Hyneman and Donald S. Lutz. Indianapolis, IN: Liberty Press, 481–522.

Patterson, Samuel C., and Anthony Mughan, eds. 1999. *Senates: Bicameralism in the Contemporary World.* Columbus: University of Ohio Press.

Peters, B. Guy. 1999. *Institutional Theory in Political Science: The "New" Institutionalism.* New York: Pinter.

Peters, William. 1987. *A More Perfect Union.* New York: Crown.

Pierson, Paul. 2000. "The Limits of Design: Explaining Institutional Origins and Change." *Governance* 13 (October): 475–99.

Pocock, J. G. A. 1975. *The Machiavellian Moment.* Princeton: Princeton University Press.

Polsby, Nelson. 1968. "The Institutionalization of the U.S. House of Representatives." *American Political Science Review* 62 (March): 144–68.

Polybius. 1923. *The Histories.* Trans. W. R. Paton. New York: Putnam's.

Rahe, Paul. 1992. *Republics Ancient and Modern: Classical Republicanism and the American Revolution.* Chapel Hill: University of North Carolina Press.

Rakove, Jack. 1984. "Solving a Constitutional Puzzle: The Treatymaking Clause as a Case Study." *Perspectives in American History,* n.s., 1:233–81.

———. 1987a. "The Structure of Politics at the Accession of George Washington." In *Beyond Confederation: Origins of the Constitution and American National Identity.* Ed. Richard Beeman, Stephen Botein, and Edward Carter II. Chapel Hill: University of North Carolina Press, 261–94.

———. 1987b. "The Great Compromise: Ideas, Interests, and the Politics of Constitution Making." *William and Mary Quarterly,* 3d ser., 44 (July): 424–57.

———. 1996. *Original Meanings: Politics and Ideas in the Making of the Constitution.* New York: Knopf.

Reedy, George E. 1986. *The U.S. Senate: Paralysis or a Search for Consensus?* New York: Crown.

Reveley, W. Taylor, III. 1981. *War Powers of the President and Congress: Who Holds the Arrows and Olive Branch?* Charlottesville: University Press of Virginia.

Richard, Carl J. 1999. "The Classical Roots of the U.S. Congress: Mixed Government Theory." In *Inventing Congress: The Origins and Establishment of the First Federal Congress.* Ed. Kenneth R. Bowling and Donald R. Kennon. Athens: Ohio University Press, 3–28.

Riker, William H. 1955. "The Senate and American Federalism." *American Political Science Review* 49 (June): 452–69.

———. 1987. *The Development of American Federalism.* Boston: Kluwer Academic Publishers.

———. 1996. *The Strategy of Rhetoric: Campaigning for the American Constitution.* New Haven: Yale University Press.

Roche, John. 1961. "The Founding Fathers: A Reform Caucus in Action." *American Political Science Review* 55:799–816.

Rogers, Lindsay. 1926. *The American Senate.* New York: A. A. Knopf.

Rossiter, Clinton L. 1953. *Seedtime of the Republic: The Origin of the American Tradition of Political Liberty.* New York: Harcourt Brace.

———. 1966. *1787: The Grand Convention.* New York: Macmillan.

Ryan, Mary P. 1971. "Party Formation in the United States Congress, 1789 to 1796: A Quantitative Analysis." *William and Mary Quarterly,* 3d ser., 28 (October): 523–42.

Saladino, Gaspare J. 1989. "Delaware: Independence and the Concept of a Commercial Republic." In *Ratifying the Constitution,* ed. Michael Allen Gillespie and Michael Lienesch. Lawrence: University Press of Kansas.

Schmitt, Gary J., and Robert H. Webking. 1979. "Revolutionaries, Anti-

Federalists, and Federalists: Comments on Gordon Wood's Understanding of the American Founding." *Political Science Reviewer* 9:195–229.

Senate Executive Journal (*Journal of the Executive Proceedings of the Senate of the United States of America*), at http://memory.loc.gov/ammem/amlaw/lawhome.html.

Senate Journal (*Journal of the Senate the United States of America, 1789–1873*), at http://memory.loc.gov/ammem/amlaw/lawhome.html.

Shalhope, Robert E. 1972. "Toward a Republican Synthesis: The Emergence of an Understanding of Republicanism in American Historiography." *William and Mary Quarterly*, 3d ser., 29, no. 1: 49–80.

Sharp, James Roger. 1993. *American Politics in the Early Republic.* New Haven: Yale University Press.

Shklar, Judith N. 1959. "Ideology Hunting: The Case of James Harrington." *American Political Science Review* 53, no. 3 (September): 662–92.

Sidney, Algernon. 1990. *Discourse Concerning Government.* Ed. Thomas G. West. Indianapolis, IN: Liberty Classics.

Sinclair, Barbara. 1989. *The Transformation of the U.S. Senate.* Baltimore: Johns Hopkins University Press.

Skeen, C. Edward. 1991. "An Uncertain Right: State Legislatures and The Doctrine of Instruction." *Mid-America–An Historical Review* 73 (January): 29–47.

Smith, David G. 1987. *The Convention and the Constitution: The Political Ideas of the Founding Fathers.* Lanham, MD: University Press of America.

Smith, H. F. Russell. 1971. *Harrington and His Oceana: A Study of a 17th Century Utopia and Its Influence in America.* New York: Octagon Books.

Smith, James Morton. 1956. *Freedom's Fetters: The Alien and Sedition Laws and American Civil Liberties.* Ithaca: Cornell University Press.

Smith, Page. 1962. *John Adams (Vol 2: 1784–1826).* Garden City, NY: Doubleday.

Smith, Steven S., and Christopher J. Deering. 1990. *Committees in Congress.* Washington, DC: Congressional Quarterly Press.

Spurlin, Paul Merrill. 1940. *Montesquieu in America: 1760–1801.* Louisiana: Louisiana State University Press.

Stark, Steven. 1995. "Too Representative Government." *Atlantic Monthly* 275, no. 5: 92–106.

Steinmo, Sven, Kathleen Thelen, and Frank Longstreth. 1992. *Structuring Politics: Historical Institutionalism in Comparative Analysis.* New York: Cambridge University Press.

Stewart, Charles, III. 1992. "Responsiveness in the Upper Chamber: The Constitution and the Institutional Development of the Senate." In *The Constitution and American Political Development.* Ed. Peter F. Nardulli. Chicago: University of Illinois Press: 63–96.

Stewart, Donald H. 1969. *The Opposition Press of the Federalist Period.* Albany, NY: State University of New York Press.

Storing, Herbert J., ed. 1981. *The Complete Anti-Federalist.* 7 vols. Chicago: University of Chicago Press.

Stourzh, Gerald. 1970. *Alexander Hamilton and the Idea of Republican Government.* Stanford, CA: Stanford University Press.

Strauss, David A., and Cass R. Sunstein. 1992. "The Senate, the Constitution, and the Confirmation Process." *Yale Law Journal* 101:1491–1524.

Swanstrom, Roy. 1985. *The United States Senate, 1787–1801.* Washington, DC: U.S. Government Printing Office.

Swift, Elaine K. 1993. "The Making of an American House of Lords: The U.S. Senate in the Constitutional Convention of 1787." *Studies in American Political Development* 7 (fall): 177–224.

———. 1996. *The Making of an American Senate.* Ann Arbor: University of Michigan Press.

Swindler, William F. 1974. "High Court of Congress: Impeachment Trials, 1797–1936." *American Bar Association Journal* 60 (April): 420–28.

Tansill, Charles C. 1924. "The Treaty-Making Powers of the Senate." *American Journal of International Law* 18 (July): 459–82.

Thach, Charles C. 1922. *The Creation of the Presidency, 1775–1789: A Study in Constitutional History.* Baltimore: Johns Hopkins University Press.

Thorpe, Francis N., ed. 1909. *The Federal and State Constitutions, Colonial Charters, and Other Organic Laws of the United States.* 7 vols. Washington, DC: Government Printing Office.

Trenchard, John, and Thomas Gordon. 1995. *Cato's Letters.* Ed. Ronald Hamowy. Indianapolis, IN: Liberty Fund.

Tsebelis, George, and Jeannette Money. 1997. *Bicameralism.* New York: Cambridge University Press.

Ulmer, S. Sidney. 1977. "Realignments in the Convention of 1787: The Slave Trade Compromise." *Journal of Politics* 29 (August): 712–29.

Vile, M. J. C. 1998. *Constitutionalism and the Separation of Powers.* Indianapolis, IN: Liberty Fund.

Von Fritz, Kurt. 1954. *The Theory of the Mixed Constitution in Antiquity.* New York: Columbia University Press.

Walbank, F. W. 1972. *Polybius.* Berkeley: University of California Press.

Warmuth, Francis D., and Edwin B. Firmage. 1989. *To Chain the Dog of War: The War Power of Congress in History and Law.* Urbana: University of Illinois Press.

Warren, Charles. 1967. *The Making of the Constitution.* Cambridge: Harvard University Press, 1928. Reprint, New York: Barnes and Noble.

Washington, George. 1989. *The Papers of George Washington: Presidential Series.* Vol. 3. Ed. Dorothy Twohig. Charlottesville: University Press of Virginia.

Werner, John M. 1972. "David Hume in America." *Journal of the History of Ideas* 33 (July–September): 439–56.

Westlye, Mark. 1991. *Senate Elections and Campaign Intensity.* Baltimore: Johns Hopkins University Press.

White, Leonard D. 1961. *The Federalists.* New York: Macmillan.

White, William. 1956. *Citadel: The Story of the United States Senate.* New York: Harper and Brothers.

Wills, Garry. 1981. *Explaining America: The Federalist.* Garden City, NY: Doubleday.

Wilson, Woodrow. 1961. *Constitutional Government in the United States.* New York: Columbia University Press.

Wirls, Daniel. 1998. "The Consequences of Equal Representation: The Bicameral Politics of NAFTA in the 103rd Congress." *Congress and the Presidency* 25 (Autumn): 129–45.

———. 1999. "Regionalism, Rotten Boroughs, Race, and Realignment: The Seventeenth Amendment and the Politics of Representation." *Studies in American Political Development* 13 (spring): 1–30.

Wolfe, Christopher. 1977. "On Understanding the Constitutional Convention of 1787." *Journal of Politics* 39, no. 1 (February): 97–118.

Wood, Gordon S. 1972. *The Creation of the American Republic: 1776–1787.* Chapel Hill: University of North Carolina Press.

———. 1987. "Interest and Disinterestedness in the Making of the Constitution." In *Beyond Confederation: Origins of the Constitution and American National Identity.* Ed. Richard Beeman, Stephan Botein, and Edward C. Carter II. Chapel Hill: University of North Carolina Press: 69–109.

———. 1992. *The Radicalism of the American Revolution.* New York: Knopf.

Wood, Neal. 1988. *Cicero's Social and Political Thought.* Berkeley: University of California Press.

Wooddy, Carroll H. 1926. "Is the Senate Unrepresentative?" *Political Science Quarterly* 41 (June): 219–39.

Young, James Sterling. 1966. *The Washington Community, 1800–1828.* New York: Columbia University Press.

Zagarri, Rosemarie. 1987. *The Politics of Size: Representation in the United States, 1776–1850.* Ithaca, NY: Cornell University Press.

Zuckert, Michael P. 1986. "Federalisms and the Founding: Toward a Reinterpretation of the Constitutional Convention." *Review of Politics* 48:166–210.

———. 1994. *Natural Rights and the New Republicanism.* Princeton: Princeton University Press.

Index

BOOKS IN THE SERIES